WHERI
HOPE

Rev Blenkansh
ROMANS 15:13

WHERE THERE IS DESPAIR

HOPE

Romans 8:28 For Women in Suffering and Those They Love

KALA KRZYCH
& REX BLANKENSHIP

TATE PUBLISHING
AND ENTERPRISES, LLC

Where There is Despair, HOPE
Copyright © 2016 by Kala Krzych & Rex Blankenship. All rights reserved.

No part of this publication may be reproduced, stored in a retrieval system or transmitted in any way by any means, electronic, mechanical, photocopy, recording or otherwise without the prior permission of the author except as provided by USA copyright law.

This book is designed to provide accurate and authoritative information with regard to the subject matter covered. This information is given with the understanding that neither the author nor Tate Publishing, LLC is engaged in rendering legal, professional advice. Since the details of your situation are fact dependent, you should additionally seek the services of a competent professional.

The opinions expressed by the author are not necessarily those of Tate Publishing, LLC.

Published by Tate Publishing & Enterprises, LLC
127 E. Trade Center Terrace | Mustang, Oklahoma 73064 USA
1.888.361.9473 | www.tatepublishing.com

Tate Publishing is committed to excellence in the publishing industry. The company reflects the philosophy established by the founders, based on Psalm 68:11,
"The Lord gave the word and great was the company of those who published it."

Book design copyright © 2016 by Tate Publishing, LLC. All rights reserved.
Cover design by Norlan Balazo
Interior design by Richell Balansag

Published in the United States of America
ISBN: 978-1-68352-083-2
Religion / Christian Life / Women's Issues
16.05.12

To the special women in my life

My Girl Vicki the love of my life and the crown jewel of my heart

My Sweetheart Kala the best and most loved daughter in the world

My Coach's Wife Alexis the gift to our family

My Princess granddaughters Ireland, Channing, and Landry the radiant beams of joy in my eyes

My Mom who wrote her book on the hearts of her sons and students

Acknowledgments

I want to thank Renee Neugart whose heart for this project pushed it to completion. Her counsel, suggestions, and editorial skills were invaluable. Her gifted experience as a lifelong teacher was evident in her encouragement as well as her expectations. She gathered the life stories, shaped the book's structure, and prayed for its message to become a blessing to someone in need of God's help and hope. After working with me on this endeavor, she has enough of her own material to write this book's sequel, *Where There is Despair, Practice Patience.*

Thanks to Kala for the concept and format. It is her heart and hope that pervade the pages. I cherish Vicki for being the God-sent picture of hope in my life. Her patience and prayers helped the words move from my heart to its printed form. I am forever grateful to the ladies who so graciously opened up their hearts to share these chapters in their lives. I pray that the transparency of their faith and hope will benefit many readers and encourage them to share their own story of hope with others. I am deeply thankful for all the women from Springs of Grace. Each one has a story of faith, hope, and love worthy of its own book. I hope they will be inspired to add their story to this work. Their faithfulness to God in the midst of suffering encourages my soul to finish strong in my journey of faith. The passionate pursuit of Christlikeness by the Springs of Grace men of all ages continues to motivate me to pick up the pace.

I am also indebted to the preachers who have faithfully fed my soul with the supremacy and sufficiency of God's Word. They shaped my teaching and my testimony. I have not suffered as much in life as many of the readers of this book nor as greatly as multitudes of other women in need of its message of hope. However, I can acknowledge the practice of this magnificent obsession, *Where There Is Despair, HOPE.*

Lord, make me an instrument of your peace.
Where there is hatred, let me sow love.
Where there is injury, pardon.
Where there is doubt, faith.
Where there is despair, hope.
Where there is darkness, light.
Where there is sadness, joy.

—Attributed to Francis of Assisi

Contents

Preface 13
Introduction 21

Part 1: The Right Understanding

1   The Loss of a Child 31
2   The Dreaded C-Word 51
3   Abandoned but Not Alone 73
4   Loving a Physically Challenged Child 93
5   Mom, Forgetful but Not Forgotten 109
6   When the Worst Happens 125
7   Our Pregnant, Unwed Daughter 141
8   My Sister's ALS Love Outside Your Circle 157
9   My Mom's ALS Love Inside Your Circle 171
10 The Most Unlikely Person to Be Saved 193

Part 2: The Right Questions

11 The Interrogation Interlude 211

Part 3: The Right Application

12 A Rough Road through Childhood	219
13 Death Came Sooner than Expected	235
14 Living in the Darkness of Depression	253
15 Come Home	273
16 Live for Something that Outlasts This Life	283
17 In Sickness and…in Sickness	301
18 A Rock, a Hard Place, and the Hope Between	317
19 Never Good Enough on the Performance Treadmill	333
20 The Childless Mother	349
Application Review: Hope	363
Conclusion	367
Epilogue	373
Write Your Life Story or the Story of a Woman You Admire	375

PREFACE

Kala's Story

Even Here. Even Now. Even This.

At first glance, my story is one of infertility and loss, a story you may or may not identify with, but if you dig a little deeper, you will see a story of anger and bitterness, of envy and hate. But even better? You will see a story of grace and redemption from the emotions that sought to destroy my life and my family.

To set the stage, you have to know that I have always been a good girl. I'm talking about the "I didn't say the word *butt* until I was nineteen years old" kind of good. I blame it on being both the firstborn and a pastor's daughter. Of course, I had my faults, but I don't ever remember intentionally doing something wrong to someone else. I wanted people to be happy with me, so I walked the line. Yet life never quite went the way I wanted it to go. At fourteen, I didn't have the close friends I wanted; at seventeen, I didn't have the money to attend the college I wanted; at twenty, I couldn't get the right guy; and at twenty-two, I had no clue what to do with my life. For most of my life, I felt as though other people always had it better off than I did. Things always worked out for them, and it never worked out for me. And there I was, doing my very best to always do what was right, to follow God in the best way I knew how. I felt gypped. But I was *a good girl*, so of course, I would never actually vocalize those feelings (what was that about God being able to see your heart?)

Fast-forward to me at twenty-nine. It was January, and this mantra—even here, even now, even this—began to flood my mind. For three years, my husband Scott and I had been trying to have a baby. At first, it was a "We'll just see what happens" kind of thing, but it didn't happen. We were young and not quite ready for a baby, so I didn't worry. But then a year passed, and another year, and soon I found myself wondering, "What if I'm one of those women who *can't* have a baby?" The thought shook me to the core of my being. Doctors were visited. Tests were run. Hope was fading. I did what I could to get my body to respond, but it wasn't working. I would take a pregnancy test "just in case." It was always negative. I was lost, dejected, bummed. But I just kept thinking, "It will happen when it's supposed to happen," all the while wondering if that were true and thinking about the possibilities if it weren't.

And then came the phone call that changed my life: my brother- and sister-in-law, Brian and Ali, were pregnant. It is a Friday night I will never forget. I was home alone and tired. My phone rang, and I saw it was my sister-in-law, which was weird because we don't talk on the phone all that much. I think I knew instantly, but I dismissed it because, after all, she told me it would be years before they would have a baby. So I called her back. She and Brian answered on speakerphone and told me the news. My heart sank. I went through every emotion imaginable, well, every emotion except happiness for them: "How is this possible? They haven't even been married a year, and now they're experiencing the joy of a baby? Why is this happening? Scotty and I are good people who have an amazing marriage. Why aren't we the ones being blessed?" I hung up the phone and cried more than I knew was possible. I called my mom and couldn't even get the words out. The worst part is that Scott wasn't home, and I couldn't call him to say I needed him. I felt more alone than I have in a long time. And there was nothing I could do about it. Scott came home a few hours later, and I did my best to act as though nothing was wrong. I told him he needed to call Brian. He did, and I stayed in the other room. I heard the excitement in his voice, and I was so, so angry. They hung up, and I waited for Scott to come in the bedroom. He didn't. I finally walked out into the living room to find him with tears streaming down his face. In my own hurt, I hadn't imagined what this would be like on my husband. I didn't realize how this would affect him. We hugged and cried and just held each other. It was a long night.

It was actually a long couple of months. I don't think I've ever cried that much in my life. I was depressed—I didn't want to see anyone, I didn't want to go to work, and I definitely didn't want to hear about the baby. I was angry. I justified it because, in my eyes, it was *my* place to get pregnant, not Ali's. And I was so, so furious. I began to hate—I hated God for allowing this to happen. I hated Brian and Ali for getting pregnant. I hated Scott's family for being excited about the baby. I hated that I had gotten married because now I had to deal with this. I hated Scott for asking me to try to deal with it. It was the first—and only—time in my life that the word *divorce* began to cross my mind. I loved Scotty so much, but I wanted out of this situation. I didn't know if I could handle being in this family anymore now that a baby (and not *my* baby) was involved. I told him I wasn't going to California for Christmas and that I didn't want to see Brian and Ali or hear one word about the baby. Brian called Scott on occasion to see if we could all get together, but I refused; I told Scott that he could go but that I wanted no part of it. I could not even bear the thought of being around them. I was so sad and so bitter. And I couldn't get past it.

But then God…

God, in His grace, began to move in my heart to show me that I needed to trust Him *even here, even now, even with this.*

But, God, really? Why this? Why me? But God kept pushing. He told me to turn on the music, up loud, and just dance, and I did. I danced around the house, like a fool, with tears streaming down my face, and with a heart crying out to God to help. I *knew* I had to choose happiness, to choose to rejoice, *but I didn't know how*. The next Sunday, I forced myself to attend church, where we sang a song I will never forget. The verse says,

> This is my song in the desert
> When all that within me feels dry
> This is my prayer in my hunger and need
> My God is the God who supplies
> I will sing praise
> I will sing praise
> No weapon formed against me shall remain
> I will rejoice
> I will declare
> "God is my victory, and He is here."

This part resonated with me, but then we got to the bridge:

> All of my life, in every season
> You are still God, and I have a reason to sing
> I have a reason to worship
> All of my life, in every season
> You are still God, and I have a reason to sing
> I have a reason to worship.

As the congregation sang these words, I found myself with head bowed, tears streaming down my face. My heart began crying out to God: *You* are *still God, and I have reason to worship. You are still God!* That was the beginning of change. I was still hurting, but I was able to bow myself at His feet and offer my hurt at His throne. I was reminded of His goodness, a goodness that completely overshadows my hurt—a goodness that exists despite the fact that I wasn't getting what I wanted. This was a season of pain, but it didn't mean that God wasn't good to me or watching out for me. He has blessed me in so many areas; why would I ever not worship Him? Why would I allow hate and bitterness to well up within me? I determined at that moment, sitting on the pew with tears streaming down my face, that I had to let my anger and bitterness go and to place my faith back where it belonged, to lift up my eyes to the hills, where my help comes from (Ps. 121).

It wasn't easy. And it didn't happen overnight—and it is still a process I am working on. However, I can honestly say that God showed me more about Himself during that time than I ever deserved to see. He began to soften my heart toward my brother- and sister-in-law so that I wasn't just able to tolerate them but I was actually able *to rejoice* with them. I could honestly say I was excited for them and happy to think about my future nephew. We invited them over for July 4, and I was genuinely happy to see them. God used this time to open my eyes to how I could be a better sister-in-law, to look for ways that I could love her more and encourage her during this time. I was so grateful, thanking God for helping me let this bitterness go. Little did I know at the time, but God was also doing something else. He was growing a tiny little baby inside of me too!

I find it so funny now—God must have a sense of humor: There I was, finally getting to the place where I needed to be, finally able to rejoice over God's blessings for someone else, finally able to genuinely feel love in my heart and no bitterness, all the while having no idea that God was choosing also to bless me. How in the world did I deserve such a blessing? I didn't. I began to pray that I would not ever forget that time in my life—because it was a time where I learned what it meant to truly depend on God for everything. I was so hurt that I couldn't take my next breath without Him. And, even still, despite my faults and failures as a wife, a sister-in-law, and a daughter-in-law, God chose to look beyond that and show Himself to me. He chose to teach me to truly worship—even here, even now, even this. He chose to show me His goodness, by saving me from myself, even before that goodness was manifested in the tangible form of a baby. He chose to show me love, even when I didn't deserve it.

I am often reminded of a Bible verse I taught my youngest brother when we were little: "Rejoice always. Pray continually. Give thanks in all circumstances." This was all great when we were little, but how do I do this now that I'm grown up, when I've actually experienced some measure of heartache? How do you rejoice *always*? How do you give thanks *in all circumstances*? How do you teach your heart to look upward and not inward? How do you love when you don't feel it? How do you stop the worry when it's eating you up inside? How do you bow your head in submission and just let God be in control—in *real* control? How do you trust that everything God does *really is* wise, right, and good? How do you let go of anger and heartache and pain?

I'll be honest: I don't know. I don't have it figured out, and I'm not there yet. I may never get there. But I'm trying. And so, I have started to anchor my soul with this prayer: even here, even now, even this.

God, I don't know how to rejoice always, but help me to learn to rejoice *even here* where you've placed me, *even now* at this very moment, *even this* very circumstance.

God, I don't know how to thank you for everything, but help me to do so, even here, even now, even with this.

Help me to love even here, even now, even this.

It's not a magic wand or a magic sock or a magic pillow. It doesn't instantaneously make things better nor does it make it all just go away. But it has been slowly chipping away at this selfish, self-centered heart, and my hope is that one day, my prayer of desperation—*even* here, *even* now, *even* this—will turn into a prayer of satisfaction: *always* here, *always* now, *always* this.

And this is my prayer for you, dear reader, as you read through the stories in this book. Some of the women may have experienced suffering far greater than yours, some might seem like less suffering, but all the stories are designed for one purpose: to help lift your eyes to the One who is good, to help remind you that God is working for your good *in all things*. Sometimes this truth is hard to see when you are in the midst of suffering, so let the women in this book be your reminder: God is greater. He is greater than your circumstances. He is greater than your emotions. He is greater than your suffering. He is even greater than your failures. He is greater.

One of my favorite books of all time is the very old book *The Christian's Secret of a Happy Life* by Hannah Whitall Smith. In this book, she does a little exercise to remind herself of who God is, and I challenge you to do something similar as you read through this book. She repeats the same sentence over and over, only each time, she emphasizes a new word in the sentence, to fully work through what God is for her today:

He is greater. *He* is greater. He *is* greater. He is *greater*.

Remind yourself of this as you read through the stories in this book. These women were in desperate need of God. They needed Him to be greater, and they found Him to be greater. We, too, are in desperate need. Come alongside them and drink from the springs of hope in the desert of despair.

Where there is despair, *hope*. Even here. Even now. Even this.

Introduction

Standing outside with binoculars turned toward the sky, my four-year-old grandson, Cooper, stared at the varied cloud formations and made a very important observation. "It sure looks like Jesus is up to something!" As I look back over my life, I see that Jesus has been up to something every day. I stand in amazement as I see how all the dots in my life are connected by those big divine conjunctions: *And God…But God.*

For most of us, our days of childlike wonder and youthful joy have been scarred by suffering, chilled by circumstances, and distorted by spiritually impaired vision. My prayer is that this book might become your spiritual binoculars by which you gain a new perspective into the darkened clouds surrounding your life. I pray you will see the reality of hope in the fog of despair and be encouraged by the clouds of witnesses moving through the pages of this book in their varied shapes and circumstances, sharing the same sky in common with your cloud. Each has a story and an observation about life and hope in the Jesus who is always up to something good in our lives. Sometimes we just do not see the goodness—or feel it.

Real faith struggles with doubts and questions. Like hope, it ebbs and flows through highs and lows, but the source of our faith and hope never wavers, never shakes, never weakens, and never lessens. Our God is unchangeable, immoveable, unconquerable, and unquestionable in His wisdom, rightness, and goodness toward us. Despair is not the end of hope; despair is where hope shines the brightest.

This collection of stories from somewhat ordinary women, providentially members of the same church family, pictures the struggles, sicknesses, sufferings, and sorrows common to us all. Together they share what every woman needs to hear in her time of stress and trouble: "Where there is despair, *hope*."

Each chapter can stand on its own as a beacon of hope. Together they form a chain of lighthouses to help you navigate hope through the dark and dangerous waters of suffering. Each chapter focuses on one form of suffering which may or may not directly affect you or your loved ones, but the truths of hope are just as applicable to your life. In fact, the chapters serve as building blocks of hope which form a sure and solid foundation that can stand strong in any storm of life. Isn't that what we all need and want?

This is a book to honor and encourage your mom, your sister, your daughter, your best friend, women in your business or Bible study group. Share it with fellow sufferers in search of hope and with women whose similar faith, although never written about on this side of heaven, has inspired you. There is a place in the back of the book if you wish to add your story or the life story of a special woman whose example has provided you with encouragement, hope, and perseverance.

This book does not seek to replace those heart-stirring stories of faith birthed in the most difficult challenges by a few women who have been widely and wonderfully used by God to illustrate the great truths of faith lived out in the most trying circumstances. Books have been penned about them, and I recommend them to you from Amy to Elisabeth to Joni and other truth talkers woven into God's magnificent tapestry of grace with threads from the heartaches of humility and colors dyed in the darkened shades of suffering. Some have overcome great physical challenges. Others have endured horrible sorrow or triumphed over unthinkable tragedy. Their names and stories stand the test of time and truth. I pray that their faith will continue to stir and inspire multitudes to find the same faithful God in their own circumstances.

Neither does this book address the immense suffering of the real brutalities of persecution endured in faith by sisters in Christ throughout the world. Many live where it is extremely difficult and even dangerous to follow Jesus. Tears are the same in any language and the truths of God's promises are the same, but I dare not equate our sufferings with those being tortured or murdered for their faith, socially ostracized, imprisoned, raped, forced into marriage or trafficking, or those having their children stolen or killed. Let us all renew our compassion and prayers for our struggling sisters whose faith in the face of persecution will be highlighted in the heavenly stories.

This book has a different setting. It seeks to honor the God of hope through retelling the stories of "ordinary" women and their sufferings of the heart. Despair is a shared commodity among women around the world. Thankfully, hope knows no borders and excludes no nationality. These women have different backgrounds and different baggage, but they share the same tears and the same hope. They struggled through the frenzied chaos of changing circumstances, tired from carrying the weight of the world on their shoulders. These women drank often and freely from the springs of hope while I knew they were still tasting the desert dryness that threatens to overcome any soul, no matter how spiritually well nourished.

This book is for those who have found grace in the wilderness or still desperately need it. In those desperate moments of the darkest nights, when no other human knows how badly the heart aches and how bleak the horizon appears, the soul thirsts for living water that gives new life, bright hope, and fresh joy.

I offer no pat answers or easy recipes. I will not pretend to tell you that what happened to you is good. I do not intend to say you should just shake it off and act as though nothing hurtful has happened; neither do I suggest that I can forecast how your loss and suffering will turn out for good. *Where There Is Despair, Hope* will not answer all your questions, but it will answer the right questions which are necessary for hope in "all things."

In all your hurt and heartache, I am pleading with you to look to the God of comfort and hope. He suffers and cries with you, His dearly loved child. God can fix you, but the process is lifelong. It will take time for you to see and feel differently, but healing can begin this very moment. I am convinced that "God's goodness and mercy follow us all the days of our lives" (Ps. 23:6) and that His goodness will eventually amaze you beyond anything you could have imagined.

Sometimes the preacher can be heard shouting what your heart can only whisper. "Everything the Lord God does is wise, right, and good." You hear that. You believe that. You can even repeat it, but sometimes life just does not feel good. The wasteland winds swirl around your parched lips, blurring your vision and burning your face. The desert of despair bleeds your heart, baits your soul, and blasts your mind with doubtful suggestions that maybe this stuff about God's goodness is just not true for you. Maybe it is just not worth it to go on—unless there really is hope.

There is *hope*. It is not the stuff of wishful thinking or fantasy dreams. Hope is grounded in truth. That truth is revealed in God's Word. It is real and relevant and reliable. It is supremely sufficient for your suffering and circumstances. With the aid of spiritual binoculars of truth, you will see *hope* on the horizon and feel *hope* in your soul.

Hope: the confident expectation of experiencing all the future goodness God has promised you...somehow...someway...sometime.

Because of the future dynamic of hope, we have to learn to fight for that confidence in God during the present sufferings. We all struggle with the external forces of changing circumstances and the internal pressure of emotional stress. Even though God has promised us future good beyond our imaginations, there are times it feels as if God has forgotten us and it looks as if God's love is absent from the scene.

There comes a time in all our lives when we cannot see and do not feel any hope; we need an outside voice to speak to us of truthful things blurred by our tears and numbed by our despair. If we are honest, we have all been there. We have felt the emptiness and heard the tempter's taunt: "Maybe your God does not care or has just forgotten about you. Maybe your God is cruel or just unable to change your circumstances. Maybe your God is punishing you for your past sins. Maybe your God's promises are not true, and living by faith in your God is just not worth it."

What do you do when it seems as though God has failed to come through for you? "Now faith is confidence in what we hope for and assurance about what we do not see" (Heb. 11:1).

In those moments when the sights and sounds of hope become distant memories, a picture of hope can be a useful reminder. These stories of ordinary women living in similar circumstances to yours spotlight women well acquainted with thoughts fragmented by despair. As a companion who has been where you are now, they will serve as a guide who knows where to find the springs of hope in the desert dryness, lending you spiritual binoculars to more clearly see the God of hope who is up to something good in your life.

Life is God centered, so the focus of any life story must be centered on this God of hope. Stories like these can inspire you, but only God's Word can change you and give you *hope* where there is despair. My conviction of this biblical principle is why each chapter uses the life story to lead you to the life-transforming truths from God's Word, truths which give life to hope, like the focus verse of this book. "And we know God causes all things to work together for good to those who love God, to those called according to His purpose" (Rom. 8:28).

Each life story confronts the critical issue, "Does the promise of hope really include *all things* or just *some things*?" To better understand and appreciate this great promise, the book has been divided into three primary sections.

1. "The Right Understanding" (chapters 1–10). To gain a better grasp of the truths that breathe life into hope, each chapter in the first half of this book will highlight one word/phrase of Romans 8:28.

2. "The Interrogation Interlude" (chapter 11). This chapter will introduce you to the right questions, found in Romans 8:31–39, concerning "all things" that do not look or feel good at the time.

3. "The Right Application" (chapters 12–20). The last part of the book will combine illustrations from the book of Ruth to the contemplation of those right questions about suffering and the suggested applications of hope to your situation.

The goal of this book is to state these great unfathomable truths in the simplest words possible, not to trivialize your hurt but to treasure your story, not to dispel your suffering but to propel your hope in God. Read it. Preach it to yourself over and over. Rewrite it with your own life story. Share it with others. Where there is despair, *hope*.

Ye fearful saints, fresh courage take;
The clouds ye so much dread
Are big with mercy and shall break
In blessings on your head
—William Cowper

PART I

The Right Understanding

And we know God causes all things to work together for good to those who love Him and are called according to His purpose. For those God foreknew He also predestined to be conformed to the image of His Son, that He might be the firstborn among many brothers and sisters. And those He predestined, He also called; those He called, He also justified; those He justified, He also glorified.

—Romans 8:28–30

1

The Loss of a Child

Cristy's Story
Understanding the Divine Conjunction *And*

Great hearts are made with great suffering. Although that is not a politically correct statement, it is a true one, verified by divine principle and guaranteed by eternal promises. Its reality was made visible to the whole world by Jesus Christ and has been privately viewed in the lives of countless multitudes of His followers from every generation of human history, but the whole concept still takes a beating in popularity polls. Politicians vow to eradicate suffering; advertisers offer relief from it; organizers petition and protest against it; some religious leaders even enrich themselves teaching how to circumvent it. No one, including me, wants to have more of it.

Greatness out of suffering would never be our plan. We want to avoid any and all suffering. We desire to eliminate all possibilities of the heart being subjected to feelings of hurt, sorrow, and despair. Have you ever considered the possibility that in the skillful hands of our Creator, those same ingredients might be beneficial to the divine design of a great heart?

Now you probably desire to have a great heart, but the process sounds a little intimidating, if not just outright frightening. God never asked us to search for suffering or live in the dread of its shadows. God created our hearts for love, not fear. In demonstration of the infinite greatness of His own love for us, God perfected the process of suffering in Jesus. God created our hearts for infinite love, and He uses the crucible of adversity to mix exactly the right amount of suffering into the main components of faith, hope, and love. The pain burns away all superficiality and creates a stronger, more loving, compassionate, humble, and hopeful heart. The same principle holds true for each one of us. The more suffering, the more God's comfort abounds in us and through us to others—the greater the heart.

There is a divine process for the creation of a great heart and a book full of divine promises designed to showcase it. Hope does not come through calculations, research, or focus groups. Hope comes from God's Word communicating with your mind and heart. The primary focus of this book will spotlight one specific biblical verse intended to counter despair with hope, the wonderful and all-encompassing promise of God found in Romans 8:28: "And we know God causes all things to work together for good to those who love Him and are called according to His purpose."

Is there really hope for good in *all things*? How can anyone dare connect the loss of a precious child to the wonderful goodness of God? That sounds absurd! Yet that is Cristy's story. She knows firsthand there is no heartache like the loss of a child. Perhaps you or someone you dearly love has experienced that same devastation. *All things* work together for good? We will not avoid the tough questions, and we will not offer over-the-counter generic solutions. The lessons do not come without tears, but a great heart learns how to hope even as it weeps.

The pain from the death of a child never ends; it is only tempered by hope. The loss is never lessened, only tilted on the scales of suffering by the greater gain of heaven. The hurt never leaves your heart even when it leaves the conversations with dear friends. The despair is as deep as it gets. And yet, God has promised to cause *all things to work together for good*, even for those carrying the heaviest heartache.

Hope will come, maybe not as quickly as you can turn the pages of this book, but just as surely. This chapter is not a "how to help you cope" manual full of tips and steps to help you through the tragic loss of a child. I am not sure there are any proven methods for living with a heart torn from the child carried in your womb. I trust you might benefit from the love and support of family and friends as well as women who have been down that same path, but that does not necessarily translate into feeling less hurt. The purpose of this book is to point you to hope—real, substantive, heart-encouraging, life-sustaining hope. Hope for you and for your child.

How can you hope when you hurt so badly? Watch the transformation in Cristy as you read about how she learned to cling to this great promise of hope in the heartache of her greatest adversity. I watched her firsthand. In fact, it was the observation of the faith and hope of Cristy and her husband during the loss of their child that generated the first thoughts of this book. In those first moments of their tears intermingled with their hope, there was an awareness of this book's subject (hope), its story (suffering in the lives of ordinary people like Paul and Cristy), and its significant purpose (showcase the glory of God's goodness in a way that offers hope to you, the reader).

During those days, I witnessed a young woman who grew up without many earthly things and absolutely no spiritual teaching display such confident faith, hope, and love in the midst of unspeakable grief from the loss of her child. Did she question God? Certainly. But eventually, she learned to ask the right questions that produced an undeniable, unconquerable hope in her time of hurt. I thought others could be blessed to hear her story. I pray it will not only encourage you in your suffering but also inspire you to tell your story of hope to others.

God's promises do not make life easier. If you think a book about God's promise to work everything together for good means you will have less suffering and fewer difficulties, then you would be mistaken. Faith in the God of that promise will get tested. This book is about the proven answer when the tests come.

Our journey through these life stories of "ordinary women" like Cristy will seek to better understand God's glorious promise of hope in Romans 8:28 by breaking down the verse into individual words and phrases. These definitions and descriptions will serve as spiritual binoculars to aid our awareness that Jesus is really up to something in our lives even when all we see are dark clouds. The goal is to gain a stronger grasp of the magnitude of our hope. The first word, *and*, in Romans 8:28 is a conjunction, connecting what has been previously said with what will follow. This divine conjunction is vitally important to seeing "our loss" through the lens of God's promised "good."

Are all things that happen to you good? *No*. The loss of a child is never good no matter how sick the child. Are suffering, tragedy, evil, and death good? No. Are troubles and tornados good? No. God's promise does not say they are good. This is not fantasy world where everyone just rides off into the sunset and lives happily ever after. The powerful promise in this verse is that the sovereign God of everlasting goodness is at work for your benefit, using His superlative conjunctions (*And God…But God…*) to link your painful story to His promised goodness.

When circumstances in life fall apart like jagged edges of shattered glass cluttering the room, you need a picture of hope, not a lecture about its theological reality. Take a good look at Cristy's story picture. Observe how the combination of all the colors of crisis and the schematics of suffering produce a visible vision of hope. Hope for Cristy. Hope for you. When she appeared cast down the lowest, she was lifted up the highest. In her time of darkest despair, the light of her hope became most visible. In her heart's greatest loss, she gained a greater heart for God and others. This is a picture worthy of your study and admiration of its Artist.

Cristy's Story

It was a year in which God revealed Himself to me in ways I could never have imagined. Our family was thrilled when we found out we were having another baby. We already had a precious son, Keegan, and an adorable daughter, Elissa. Now there would be another blessing to hold, love, and cherish. What unspeakable joy!

That joy soon turned to anxiety. I knew something was wrong from the beginning, something didn't feel right, and there was much spotting. After many ultrasounds, we were told our Sarah Ainsley was very small as was the sac that protected her.

Fear set in over the long weekend as we waited for an appointment with a specialist. Our minds were consumed with thoughts that something could be wrong with our baby.

The worst news never sounds good.

That Monday brought the news that no expecting parent wants to hear. Sarah Ainsley's brain and heart were not developing as they should, and she was extremely small. The amniotic fluid was noticeably low. The specialist told me he was expecting me to miscarry. Then sorrow overwhelmed us. I don't think my husband, Paul, and I have ever cried that hard in our lives. They wanted to do an amniocentesis; we turned it down. We knew she was sick and that was enough. We didn't want to do anything to hurt her. We did let them take my blood; it came back that there was a one-in-four chance she had trisomy 18; her life expectancy would not be good.

Emptied—we just prayed for hope.

The Lord emptied us that day. We didn't know what to pray for. So our prayer was to ask God what we should be praying for. The Lord gave us a total peace that just cannot be explained about Sarah's condition. He let us know from the beginning not to pray for healing because that was not His plan.

We prayed for hope—hope in knowing that whatever happened, God was going to take care of us. I will never say I did not have days of crying; I had many. I can truthfully say that we never dwelled on why us; we never got angry with God. Once again, we had an unexplainable peace. We knew God was with us; we could feel Him holding us up. He was allowing this to happen for a reason that only He may know.

God's word spoke to me from Psalm 27:14: "Wait for the Lord, be strong and let your heart take courage; yes, wait for the Lord." Wow! Isn't that what life is all about? Waiting. What are we waiting for? We are waiting for the Lord. No matter our circumstances, wait for Him. After every doctor visit with news that was the same from the previous one, I clung to this verse. From anxiety, fear, and sorrow, God now moved me to a place of courage and strength to walk in this season where He had placed me.

On July 8, the day came. When I went for my doctor's appointment, they found that my Sarah's heart had stopped beating at twenty-five weeks' gestation—six months. The first words out of my mouth were, "God is good." I cried as I said these words but truly meant them. Our Sarah's soul was with Him. I was checked into the hospital where they began inducing me to deliver Sarah Ainsley. It was two days of the worst pain I have ever been in, but also two days of prayer and rejoicing and crying with so many of our church family.

My family members are not believers. Those two days, they saw the love of Christ demonstrated. They saw His people come together in prayer and faith. They saw His comfort.

Sarah Ainsley was taken from my womb on July 10. The only cries heard in the delivery room were the cries of her mother. After the delivery, I got to hold this precious gift in my arms. *I got to hold her!* Paul and I prayed over her and handed her to the nurse, knowing we will see her again in heaven.

In the most painful moment, God is with you.

The presence of God was felt in that room. Our loving Savior was there, sitting in that hospital bed with me, holding my hand

and not letting me go. My sweet husband opened his bible and read Revelation 21:1–5:

> Then I saw a new heaven and a new earth; for the first heaven and the first earth passed away, and there is no longer any sea. And I saw the holy city, new Jerusalem, coming down out of the heaven from God, made ready as a bride adorned for her husband. And I heard a loud voice from the throne, saying, "Behold I am making all things new," and He said, "Write, for these words are faithful and true."

The moment my husband opened his bible and began to read, we could feel Jesus Christ in that hospital room. He had His arms around me, holding me up, allowing me to comfort my daddy as he wept over the granddaughter he would never see on this earth.

I had spent two days in a labor and delivery room being induced. When it was time to leave the hospital, I thought I was ready. I was ready to be home. I was ready to hold and hug Keegan and Elissa. I was ready for Paul to hold and hug me. I never expected the feelings that would surface as I left the hospital. I was leaving without the fruit of my labor. I was leaving with nothing but a broken heart. I was alone. Paul was making funeral plans, so it was my brother in that elevator with me when it hit. I had no husband at that moment to cry out to. I was surrounded by strangers in an impersonal elevator, and I felt as though I had no one to cry with me.

This was the most hurt I have ever felt in my life. I sat in that wheelchair and dried silent tears as my heart shattered. When I finally made it home, I was able to cry out to God. He knew my heartache, and He gave me the strength to endure this heartache.

In the bigger picture, God is for you.

We had a funeral for her on July 12, and her sweet little grave marker has the first words that came out of my mouth when I learned her heart no longer was beating and she was healed—

"God is good." It was only our God who brought me out of that hospital, sustained me that first night at home with no baby, and sat by Paul and me as we celebrated the short life Sarah had lived inside of me at her funeral.

"Naked I came from my mother's womb, and naked I will leave this life. The Lord gives, and the Lord takes away. Praise the name of the Lord" (Job 1:21).

My Sarah Ainsley made it to the finish line before me. I can only rejoice knowing she has won the race. She never had to cry or hurt or face the ugliness of this world. She has eternity with our Loving Father.

Two years later, the Lord blessed us with Jonah Andrew. After Sarah, I was not sure, to be honest, if I wanted to have any more children. I let fear creep back in. After we celebrated Sarah's one year "heavens day," the Lord took my fear completely away, and we began trying to get pregnant.

The Lord used this pregnancy to help me grieve over things I did not know I needed to grieve over. Feeling Jonah move inside of me was something I needed. Getting big and uncomfortable was absolutely amazing. Hearing a baby's first cry was so bittersweet and leaving the hospital with Jonah in my arms was a feeling I cannot explain.

God knew we needed Jonah. The Lord used Jonah to help with closure. No baby will ever take my Sarah's place, but I know I will see her again and through losing her, I am able to appreciate life and family so much more. Somehow, my heart grew bigger. I am able to love and see so many of the Lord's blessings that I might have missed if not for that one blessing, Sarah.

"And we know God causes all things to work together for good to those who love Him and are called according to His purpose" (Rom. 8:28).

Desert of Despair

The night is so dark, and yet the morning is the darkest part of the day when reality starts to set in. This is not a dream. The questions spiral in your mind. The unknown tramples the peace. Fear fills the room. You have to get up. The clock is not stopping for you to question and mourn. The world moves on expecting you to do the same as if nothing really happened.

Move on as if nothing happened? Is that what the world did after God gave up His Son on the cross? Did the people just go back to their normal lives as if nothing had been lost? Your world with all its hopes and dreams has come crashing down; an irreplaceable part is missing. The world might go back to their familiar turf, but the landscape of your circumstances has dramatically changed. You cannot forget the loss of your child any more than God could forget the death of His child. The story is not over. It means something. But what?

What is your life story? Is it similar to Cristy's or dramatically different? Undoubtedly, you have suffered loss and somewhere in your life questioned God's goodness. Surely there have been times when you did not see, feel, or understand how the circumstances could be called "good."

Most likely, your dark nights and darker mornings, like Cristy's, swarmed with many questions and few answers. Why? Why this? Why me? Why now? Why this child? Why would God ever give this child if He intended to take her right away? What did I do wrong? This is not fair. What should I do now? This hurts too much. This is so overwhelming. I do not know how I can go on.

If you have been there, you know the questions and you have felt the agonizing loss. Like Cristy, you cry until there are no more tears. Then you cry some more, but the new tears never fall down your cheeks because they flow from a dry and thirsty soul lost in the desert wilderness. You do not feel like you are in a good place; it looks more like a good place to just give up and die.

There is no question your life has a story, and like Cristy's story, one chapter does not tell the whole story. The loss of Cristy's child is connected to all the events and experiences which preceded her horrific heartache, and her story cannot be completed without being equally united to all that has followed, even after Jonah's arrival.

For whatever time you carried that precious gift in your womb or held in your arms, he or she knew your love. Certainly you miss her and wish she could still be in your arms, but if you could see Cristy's child and yours playing and singing and dancing in the presence of their Heavenly Father, you would not bring them back here, even as much as you hurt without them. A mother always wants what is best for her child, and so does the Heavenly Father. The only difference is He actually knows what is best.

The absence of those we love brings sadness and suffering, but it also enlarges the heart for an even greater capacity to love. Someday soon God Himself will gladly reunite you. Your child will recognize you, and the joy of that anticipated event will surpass anything known in this life. I pray where there is great despair in your heart, there will be greater hope.

Throughout Cristy's story, she learned to hope in God's promise, *And we know God causes all things to work together for good to those who love Him and are called according to His purpose.* In some circumstances, she could shout it, sing it, and share it. In other moments, the same words came out of her mouth in whispers, sighs, and cries.

Perhaps you are familiar with the words in Romans 8:28. Maybe you have this verse highlighted in your bible or even memorized. You might keep it on a placard attached to the refrigerator or mirror. Even if you are familiar with what it says, do you know what it means? Does it sustain you with hope when you hear the worst news possible?

There are times when circumstances turn out much differently than you dreamed. What happens when what you *know* does not match up to what you *see*? Sometimes you just do not *know* that God is in control for your good because you cannot see anything about the circumstances that look good. The despair is overwhelming, the heartache unbelievably painful. You definitely do not see how your particular situation in life could ever turn out for good even when God's Word promises that assurance.

Cristy's story throws you a lifeline. For this brief moment in your life story, God has connected your storyline to Cristy's. Why? Is it to help you find God's hope in your desert of despair? Could it be for you to help someone else in a similar situation? Whatever the reason, Cristy's story is now forever linked to this present chapter in your story. Maybe God will clearly show you why in these next paragraphs or chapters.

Charles Dickens began his novel, *A Tale of Two Cities*, with the now classic words:

> It was the best of times, it was the worst of times…It was the season of light, it was the season of darkness; it was the spring of hope, it was the winter of despair.

The subsections of each of these chapters were not taken from Dickens' work; but they convey his contrast. The concepts of Despair and Hope are on different ends of the spectrum. However, my experience finds them running on parallel tracks, often arriving at the same place and time.

Despair and Hope are the products of two very different perspectives of the same circumstances where eventually one overrides the other. The writer of Ecclesiastes describes one view of life as "under the sun," a self-centered human perspective that tries to make sense out of life without taking God into account. It will always look like *vanity*, no substance and no significance, just running in circles chasing the wind. The proven futility of that perspective always ends up with nothing but despair. However, *Ecclesiastes* also depicts a better view of life "under heaven" where God's Word becomes spiritual binoculars into the darkened clouds of adversity. Where there is despair, hope breaks through as you begin to understand that Jesus is up to something good in your life. You just have to learn where to look.

There truly are never-failing, never-ending springs of hope which can be found in Romans 8:28. This life-giving water flows in the midst of the desert wilderness. That is where the refreshing water tastes the sweetest and the light of hope shines the brightest. Find that oasis of hope and camp out there. Then share the good news with another woman thirsting to find a life-sustaining gulp of hope for her suffering soul. She might not know that where there is despair, *hope* abounds in its midst.

Springs of Hope

And we know God…

In her loss, Cristy had to decide whether she would wallow in grief or wade through truth. That is the choice you face. Consolation or transformation? Both have tears. One has hope. God understands there is no greater heartache than the loss of a child. He gave up His own Son Jesus so that the greatest good would be given to us. This is foundational truth for your hope.

It is vital for the sanity of your soul that you learn to navigate life by truth and not by feelings.

These next paragraphs are dedicated to that purpose. It might take some time and attention to wade through them, especially with a heavy heart. This stuff is not fluff to ease your feelings; it is not a quick read for a short attention span. The style intentionally stays simple but thorough so that it might show you truth-based reasons you can have real, substantive, lasting hope in your grief.

God's truth builds and sustains hope. Not sad stories. Not vented feelings. If you will choose to wade and not wallow, truth will not just shine a glimmer of hope into your suffering, it will build you a lighthouse.

God does not have problems, only plans.

God has plans for your welfare so that you might have hope. Those plans are revealed in God's Word like the hope-sustaining promise of Romans 8:28, which begins with a conjunction that connects the specific truth to a larger context which provides the undeniable evidence for your assurance of future good. These next paragraphs highlight the biblical truth that became spiritual binoculars for Cristy and her husband to see the reality of hope in the midst of their tears and despair. There is an ocean of truth deep enough for us to swim, but let's just hold hands and wade through it.

Conjunction

This verse of hope begins with an important conjunction that connects the dots of your life to the truths of God's Word. It lays the groundwork to build a solid foundation for your faith's confident hope in the goodness of God. This *and* connects the promise to something else which precedes it. Do not just overlook the *ands* of your story. Each circumstance of your life has meaning beyond its own time.

Now some English lesson concerning conjunctions will not lessen the pain in your heart, but it does have relevance to your loss. I am not suggesting it will make you forget the devastating hurt you feel, but it can help you understand its significance from an eternal perspective. Too often we evaluate our life stories by our present circumstances. Especially in hard times, we tend to overlook previous blessings and minimize the past's significance. In the midst of difficulty, our tendency is to be fearful of the future and oblivious to the prospect of better days. In reality, this moment in your life is intrinsically connected to all the forgotten past and to all the unknown future events.

The story of your life cannot be told without conjunctions. Everyone's journey through life is filled with the roadside conjunctions *and God* (points to connections) and *but God* (points to contrasts). This happened *and* this just happened *and* this just happened...*But God* did this *and* this *and* this. Your story is God's story told to the world and the heavenly hosts through the chapters of your life. All connected with divine conjunctions.

Your life becomes a composite of all your yesterdays *and* today *and* all your tomorrows. Your life even began with an *and*. Ultimately your life story is connected to all of God's longer and bigger and more glorious stories told in God's Word from before the beginning of time *and* throughout an endless eternity. The Creator God had loving thoughts of you before the beginning of this world, *and* He will continue those acts of surpassing kindness throughout the ages to come.

And your life's story is connected to the lives of those who were here before, *and* your earthly life will end with an *and* that connects your story with those who follow. Every moment counts forever. Every circumstance in your life connects to innumerable events in the lives of others past, present, and still to come. That is one reason to hope.

And now God has connected Cristy's story to yours to point your thoughts back to what you know. *And we know*...It matters what you actually know. Why? It can be the difference between hope and despair. The conjunction points us to the context. Let's wade out a little farther.

Context

There are some basic guidelines for gleaning truth from the reading or study of the Bible that can be beneficial to every one of us in need of help and hope. God has spoken to us through His Word. All of God's Word is true. The truth and beauty of God's Word can never be exhausted even by the most technical and trained theological scholars, but its message is so simple and straightforward that a child or grieving mom can understand. Each sentence means exactly what it says within its larger context (paragraph, chapter, book). If you will always seek to understand that context and any specific application to your life, it will lead you to bedrock truths that form the building blocks of hope presented in every chapter of this book.

Just as your heartache and anguish come from the context of your grief and loss, your future hope springs from the context of the reality of truth. The conjunction *and* calls for consideration of the great truths which precede it. A quick summary of the first seven chapters of Romans reveals good news which is full of hope. God sent His Son to die on the cross in our place for our sins and then resurrected Jesus as our Lord in demonstration of God's power to give us sinners a new life. God did all of that to showcase His righteousness (His life and love) and our need of that same life and love. In the greatest transaction of human history, the deserved condemnation for our sinful self-centeredness was charged to Jesus while the life and love of Jesus was undeservedly credited and transferred to our account. Jesus took death on the cross, and we received eternal life.

This first half of *Romans* reveals a divine plan and purpose linking our grief to our hope. When God poured His love into our hearts, we became united to Jesus Christ for one purpose that we would no longer live for ourselves but live for Him at all times. This new life comes with assurances of hope throughout the whole spectrum of life, from peaceful simplicity to painful suffering. Following Jesus becomes more about direction than perfection, Him holding on to us than us holding on to Him.

I understand that you feel as if you have lost everything, your heart is full of grief, and your mind struggles to focus on these words but keep wading; the water gets clearer and the view more breathtakingly beautiful as we arrive at Romans chapter 8. Two lighthouse towers of truth emerge on the horizon regarding God's miraculous plan for your hope: *No condemnation. No separation.* God uses the conjunction and its context to communicate to you His vow of no condemnation for your sins and no separation from His love. In fact, the entire context before and after the promise of hope concerns pain and suffering. The present sufferings are not worthy to be compared to the glory to come (Rom. 8:18), and that glory cannot be lost in tribulation, distress, persecution, famine, nakedness, peril, or even death in the future (Rom. 8:36). Hope is real, even when you do not see it or feel it. "Hope that is seen is no hope at all. Who hopes for what they already have? But if we hope for what we do not yet have, we wait for it patiently" (Rom. 8:24-25).

Now what does all that conjunction and context have to do with the loss of a child or any other suffering situation? Everything. It does not change what has happened; it does not lessen the heart's pain, but it assures you that this was not an act of punishment or a neglect of love. The loss of your child must have a purpose in God's plan; there must be hope. The certainty of this truth cannot be overemphasized. You will never stop loving that child, and God will never stop loving you.

If you could just get the right spiritual binoculars, you would see that God is up to something good in your life. Start looking here. There is now no condemnation to those who are in Christ Jesus, and there is no possibility of separation from His love. As a follower of Jesus, you are finally and forever accepted by God without being judged on how you measure up to some performance treadmill test—*and* you will never be separated from God's love no matter what happens. *Never!* Not today, not tomorrow, not when you fail and fall. Not when your heart suffers from the loss of a child. *Never!*

God weeps as He wipes away your tears. He stares directly into the eyes of your soul and confidently, compassionately whispers, "Your present sufferings are not worth comparing with the glory that will be revealed in you" (Rom. 8:18).

Who else but God could dare say that to you? At some point in each season of loss and suffering, like Cristy, you have to decide between your present feelings and God's promised reality. God never tells you not to hurt; He just assures you that the more you suffer, the more His comfort abounds in you and through you to others. The Gospel of Jesus Christ has always been a transforming power, and it always will be. As the Lord ordains, orders, and orchestrates everything in your life to do you the greatest good, He is creating a great heart in you.

How could Cristy *know* that is really true? Perhaps more importantly, how can you know with certainty God's promise is true in the midst of your chapter of loss, heartache, and crushed dreams? It starts with focus. Just like a pilot trusting his instrument panel when atmospheric circumstances hinder his vision, you have to focus on the truth instead of staring at your darkened skies and disappointing circumstances.

Your feelings are real, but they do not determine what is real.

The bold magnitude of God's promises unveils a reality of goodness far beyond your present feelings. We will use the next chapters of this book to sharpen your focus, strengthen your spirit, and spotlight your story with the life-changing truths from God's Word. As we continue to wade through the never-ending waves of truth, I want you to *know* why there is hope for you in any life crisis. I want you to *know* why there is hope in your loss and grief. We might even dive in and swim in this vast ocean of goodness.

Whether you choose to wallow, wade, or swim, this one secure life jacket of truth safely surrounds your heart: The greatness of your suffering will never eclipse the horizon of God's hope. God is greater. Even here. Even now. Even this.

The next chapters will connect some life stories of *ordinary* women to the truths of Romans 8:28 in a way that places the hard questions from the desert of despair up against answers found at the springs of hope. We will explore what the Bible says regarding what *we can know about God causing all things to work together for our good.* We will not shy away from the vital issue at stake in this assurance of hope. Does the promise really include *all things? Most things? Some things?* Or *no things?*

What you see and feel might not change, but what you know can change you.

Everything God does is wise, right, and good even when you cannot see it that way and do not feel it could ever be that way.

Take this truth to the bank. Give it a prominent and permanent place in your mind. Write it on your heart. There are times of heartbreak where all you can see is darkness. *But God* is there with you. There will be more moments when all you can feel is pain and loss. *But God* is good. There will be days you cannot see anything good in your circumstances or feel any hope for the future. *But God* is greater even here...even now...even this.

Believing in the greatness and goodness of our God assures us He will cross every *t*, dot every *i*, and connect every circumstance of our life in accordance with His will. This is a promise we build our lives around. Knowing our God has endless power to accomplish this and endless love and mercy for His children, we remain faithful even when we do not see all the ands and buts of our life connecting. If not now, then surely someday, you will be able to share your story about whenever it felt like a helpless dead end, there was *and God*, and every time it looked as if there was no hope, there was *but God*.

There were days Cristy felt pretty downcast, but her story was being lived out in the reality of tears and truths, not fearful feelings or insane thoughts or spiritual blindness. Your story is different, but the reality is the same. Where there is despair, *hope*.

This is where the healing begins. Your present hurt is connected to your future good. The hurt never lessens; the hope just grows bigger—and so does your heart!

"To all who mourn, the Lord will give a crown of beauty for ashes, a joyous blessing instead of mourning, a garment of praise instead of despair, they will be like great oaks that the Lord has planted for His own glory" (Isa. 61:3).

May the Lord share your tears while you embrace His truth of promised hope.

The Right Understanding of Hope

God would never have allowed the suffering if He did not have a wise plan to work it out for your greater good.

"May the God of *hope* fill you with all joy and peace as you trust in Him, so that you may overflow with *hope* by the power of the Holy Spirit" (Rom. 15:13; emphasis added).

Standing on this mountain top
Looking just how far we've come
Knowing that for every step
You were with us
Kneeling on this battleground
Seeing just how much
You've done
Knowing every victory
Was Your power in us
Scars and struggles on the way
But with joy our hearts can say
Yes, our hearts can say
Never once did we ever walk alone
Never once did
You leave us on our own
You are faithful, God,
You are faithful
You are faithful, God,
You are faithful.

—"Never Once," Matt Redman

2

The Dreaded C-Word

Pat's Story
Understanding *We Know God*

Cancer does not just weaken the body; it can suck the hope right out of you. Just the prospect of a diagnosis can overwhelm your mind and heart with anxiety. Waiting on CT scan results or a biopsy can be nerve-racking. Fear can run unabated as the rest of your life grinds to a halt.

Then if the dreaded news comes, the heart sinks and an ongoing battle against despair ensues. Immediately, the mind goes numb and the eyes become blurred by the fog of the fight. Our feeble senses get overwhelmed as everything starts to shut down. It all feels so negative. If you are blessed with tears, you use them up. You do not remember much of what the doctor said, you do not understand God's ways, and you definitely do not see any good in having cancer.

Cancer is not good. The news of cancer immediately thrusts you into a crash course in theology. It is no longer about theoretical discussions but real tests. Does the phrase *all things* really mean all things? What you feel at that critical moment will not be how you feel as time passes. Faith steadies itself. Hope returns, even stronger, if not for this life, then for the next one. Love grows like a well-watered garden. Cancer cannot prevail against God. It cannot take away from you the things that matter most, love for God and love for your family. Nothing else matters.

Hope in God is absolutely essential to living. We need it as much as we need air to breathe. Without it, the soul suffocates. People who lose hope struggle to live; they lose energy to confront life's challenges. They have great difficulty getting out of bed in the morning and even greater problems putting the anxious mind to rest at bedtime.

Hopelessness makes the heart grow empty, the mind darkens with despair, and the steps falter along the journey. Going through the motions of life with no hope has been the downfall of many marriages, parent/child relationships, school and work endeavors, and most importantly, spiritual journeys. Whatever problem is causing you to feel anxious, you can be certain your anxiety will not lessen the problem. It will only make you more miserable. All of us need hope or else we cave in, fall apart, and give up.

God did not design our lives to crash and burn. There is hope available on the horizon. In Romans 8, Paul wrote, "We know." He was not talking about awareness of some facts; he used the word for coming to a resolved, fixed conclusion. Through years of suffering and affliction, he became convinced of God's great faithfulness. That is the same confident hope Pat exhibited in her struggle with cancer.

Hope in God can be described as the confident expectation of experiencing all the future good God has promised. Those divine promises will become the soul's safety, security, and satisfaction. Hope in God fills the heart, enlightens the mind, and enlarges our steps. It will shape us, motivate us, and comfort us. Hope in God will breed encouragement that is not only life-sustaining but also life invigorating.

If we find that hope, how does it coexist with the heartache that has come into our life? In the logic of faith, this coexistence makes perfect sense. Cancer, like all suffering, is never meaningless. It helps produce a glory for you that will last forever. Cancer may or may not be terminal, but either way, it becomes an opportunity to showcase hope in God, a hope which values God's love as worth more than life itself (Ps. 63:3). Pat's life radiated with the presence of the Lord Jesus Christ. In the worst chapter of her life, she had hope, a living hope in God. She was chosen by God to display that hope with grace and peace to the fullest measure (1 Pt. 1:2–3).

This chapter will follow Pat's journey of hope through her battle with cancer. Where there was despair, *hope* flourished. That same hope can fill your heart and mind in a way that cancer can never touch or diminish. Many cancer sufferers perish without this hope. God has strategically placed you in this world of suffering in order to display the living hope inside you, a hope with confident expectation of experiencing all the future goodness God has promised those who follow Jesus Christ. Perhaps your story could rescue one woman. It just takes one divine connection for that to happen. Help someone else find the living hope; Pat did.

Pat's Story

My wife Pat was the most moral person I ever knew. Though a church member, she was not a Christian. We were building a house for our family—two small children—at the same time a church was being built near our house. God was drawing us there for a purpose, and we did not even know it. Pat realized that morality and good works do not save a person; it takes the grace of God. Admitting she was a sinner in need of a Savior, Pat became a follower of Jesus. She loved Him more than anyone else I knew. The hand of God continued to work in our lives as our hearts were filled with thanksgiving for how God was blessing us!

Then we heard the dreaded c-word.

Pat shared with our church family, "I have been diagnosed with breast cancer. I do not know what will happen, but either way, I cannot lose."

For about twelve years, the battle with cancer raged. The pain was intense, but I never heard Pat complain. Her pain was physical; mine was heartache and grief over not being able to do more for her. She continued strong in her love for God, his Word, and his church. She wrote words of encouragement to many other women. She kept a smile on her face and continued to attend church where she joined her voice to every song of praise and intently listened to every sermon. She asked the pastor to help prepare her to leave this earthly place. She wanted to remain steadfast in her faith as she crossed the finish line.

Toward the end, she told me she was asking every night for God to take her. I remember the night she said, "Get me to the emergency room." We came to a red light, and she said, "Run it." The pain was bad! My heart ached. In the emergency room when I noticed her lips quivering, I screamed for help; the doctor got there in time to open her passageway. He saved her life. They took her on to ICU. Later, they explained they had done all they could. The next morning, I was faced with the decision to put her on life support or not. Even though we had both decided to never be placed on life support, this was a living nightmare. I told my pastor, "If it was within my power, I would be in there and she would be out here talking with you."

We experienced the wonderful presence of God as we walked through the valley of the shadow of death.

But God, who promises us He is a very present help in time of need, came to my rescue. Pat had rallied, and I did not have to make that decision. Isn't God good? We brought her home and set her up in a hospital bed. God gave the family seventy-seven more days to prepare ourselves for the inevitable. But Pat was already prepared. She knew her Heavenly Father was preparing a place for her and He would come and take her home. She told us if she could go back to the time before she had cancer and know then what she knew now with the choice to choose cancer or not to have cancer, she would choose to have it because she had never felt the presence of God in her life as she had during this illness.

June 15, the family gathered. I had gone to lie down awhile, and my son was with his mother. At 1:00 a.m. on June 16, my son woke me. When I reached her bed and saw that same quiver of her lips, she took her last little breath. There was no need to scream for a doctor's help; she was in the arms of the Great Physician. There would be no more suffering or pain. "The Lord gives and the Lord takes away. Blessed be the name of the Lord." There had been a cloudy look in her eyes those last days, but right at the end of her struggle, those big beautiful green eyes were as clear as a bell. We all believe God gave her a glimpse of heaven. God is so good in life and in death.

Pat's testimony lives on. I shared it recently with someone spiritually searching for help and hope. I told him about Pat's courageous bout with cancer, her walk with God through that valley of the shadow of death, and her steadfast faith to the end. I took him a bible and gave his son, a high school football player, a sports devotional book our pastor had written. I am praying God will rain down His grace and mercy on that man and his household. I pray you will find hope in God through your sickness and sorrow. God cares for you.

In living and in dying, Pat expressed her confident hope. *And we know God causes all things to work together for good, for those who love Him and are called according to His purpose.*

Desert of Despair

Cancer. Just the word is scary. Stories of the dreaded disease are told in books marked with triumphs and tragedies, successes and setbacks. Fear and anxiety roll off the pages. Any honest testimony cannot leave out the pain and the tears. Neither should it exclude the special caregivers who become the wind beneath the wings.

Perhaps the worst part of cancer is not just what it does to weaken the body but what it does to the emotions and spirit. It breeds despair as quickly as it kills good blood cells. It disrupts emotional equilibrium. Hope struggles to survive. Cancer survivors should be lovingly acknowledged with pink accessories to mark the celebrations as well as the needed research to conquer the disease. Just as importantly is the remembrance of those courageous women who survived in hope even when the physical battle was lost.

There are many things in life that cannot be called good. Cancer is not good. I would never say it was good for Pat to suffer from cancer; she might disagree. She told everyone she would have chosen cancer if she had known how near and dear the presence of God would become. That sounds very strange and maybe downright insane. Usually cancer is more of a shocking intruder than a welcomed guest, staying longer than wanted and never cleaning up its mess.

It is amazing that when suffering comes it surprises us. The Lord has told us again and again, we will all suffer; do not be surprised when it happens. No matter how many spiritual lessons we hear about suffering, we are still surprised, if not shocked, when some unwanted circumstance, like cancer, happens to us.

We are in disbelief when any of those critical c-words show up without prior notice at the door of our lives. Cancer, coronary disease, car accident, calamity, crisis, or your child's problems. Or the dreaded d-words appear as surprise guests. Discouragement, debt, divorce, drug usage, difficulties, or depression.

There are no garage sales to get rid of cancer, no garbage dumps to unload the pain, no discount shopping centers to purchase a healthier body. It cannot be wished away. No one can trade you places, not even a loved one who would. Whenever suffering comes, it disrupts life much like throwing a big rock into a smooth, peaceful lake. The shocking disturbance creates big waves with a continuous ripple effect. Suffering messes up your normal routine; it lingers and affects other things in life.

Cancer is not the result of bad luck nor is it cause for a pity party. Suffering with cancer can help you stop caring about all the wrong things. The appeal of the toys, trinkets, and trivia of this world fade away and pale in comparison when you are fighting to live.

There are medical centers and wonderfully trained personnel to help you or a loved one cope with this horrible disease relentlessly attacking your body. The goal of this chapter is to remind you to revisit God's sure and steadfast hope which is not dependent upon any physician's prognosis or your fluctuating feelings. Be prepared, not surprised. People who hope in God get cancer just like those who do not believe in God's existence. Atheist, agnostic, apathetic, admirer, they all get cancer. Each copes in her own way; each hopes in her own way. Some hope in doctors, or treatments, or experimental drugs, or natural herbs, or miracles. Some have no more substantive hope than the kind that comes from making wishes or rolling the dice.

Hope in God is different. It strengthens and sustains the cancer patient and the caregiver with a confident expectation of experiencing all the future good God has promised, whether in sickness, remission, recovery, or death. Oh, wait, I just wrote the most dreaded d-word. With cancer, preparation for death needs to be addressed for life to be paramount and precious.

Hope in God has the last word, even over death. For all those who believe and follow Jesus Christ, death is gain (Phil. 1:21). Death is no longer to be feared (Heb. 2:14–15). It becomes the departure port to set sail into the heavenly hope God placed before us where we gain our heavenly inheritance in all its glory while not losing anything of eternal value from this earthly life. However, the certainty of death calls for preparation in life, not with traumatic fear or foreboding reticence but with personal knowledge of the God of hope and His purpose for your life.

Cancer raises many questions about God's goodness at work in *all things* when cancer is definitely not a good thing. Those same questions which can be asked about all kinds of suffering will be addressed in subsequent chapters. In fact, we will highlight the right questions to ask. For now, it is a mistake to equate the goodness of God to the rightness of your circumstances.

You are going to suffer in this world, but there is no reason to live in fear or anxiety. Cancer is not cause to live with a negative attitude or pessimistic outlook. You will feel the swirling dust and dry thirst from your trek through cancer's desert of despair, but there are springs of hope sufficient for the entire journey. In fact, the Scriptures remind you to enjoy the life that God has given, even when you have to carry the extra baggage from various forms of suffering.

Somehow Pat found her chapter of cancer to be a better life. How can anyone enjoy life with cancer? It starts with perspective and purpose, essential building blocks of hope.

Springs of Hope

And we know God...

Any life chapter on cancer cannot be written without divine conjunctions. In the worst moment...But God. In the best of times...And God. Everything in between...And we know God. Our purpose in life is to *know God*. In this verse, the Greek word *know* indicates intuitive knowledge, not learning acquired from theological studies.

This understanding is built into the spiritual DNA of every believer, characterized by confident assurance in the truth about God. Knowing God is a matter of the heart as well as the mind. The attraction of God's love makes you want to know His person. "He is altogether lovely" (Song of Solomon 5:16). God's superlative beauty and intrinsic excellence are to be adored and loved. The heart and mind have to be captivated by clear teachings from the

Word of God, not theological flights of fancy. Those who *know God* will reflect His life and reveal His character in their own life stories. How did Pat know God so well and how can you know God that way?

Divine conjunctions connect us to knowledge of God. Suffering makes that knowledge personal. These conjunctions signal that God is still with us and for us all through life's journey. Standing like tall road signs along the highway, these divine conjunctions alert us to mile markers, construction zones, and future sites worthy of notice. They all point to hope and its final destination, reminders that the road is not a dead end even when it looks as if it is headed nowhere.

When things in life are as bad as they can be, when the pain is as unbearable as it can get, when you feel as far away as possible, look to God's promises like the one in Romans 8:28. God's promises serve as billboards pointing to hope on the horizon. Place your hope in God's goodness, not doctors' reports or medical research. This is the time to *set your hope fully* on the grace that will be brought to you at the revelation of Jesus Christ (1 Pt. 1:13). Literally "hope fully." This is an imperative command to feel confident in the final outcome.

What is the foundation for such confident expectation? Wherever you are on the cancer journey, God is with you.

God is with you every step of your journey. Perspective and purpose are road signs to hope. God is with you in this chapter of cancer. There are places between the road signs where your spiritual cell phone reception might seem to drop service, places like the oncologist's office or a late-night trip to the emergency room. The divine conjunctions in God's promises help you stay connected to the powerful cell towers of hope, which have the strongest and widest coverage available to anyone traveling down new paths. There is even a personal APP available to know God better.

Perspective

God is bigger than your cancer. *Bigger.* God is so big He does whatever He wants and so good He wants to love you the very best way possible. God was right there with you when the diagnosis was delivered. God will be right there with you every step of this journey, in surgery, in treatment, in remission. God will be there to get you safely home.

Psalm 139 is an important hope road sign marking God's perpetual presence with you. You actually live in the presence of God, whether you are aware of it or not or whether you want to or not. *Where can you go from God's Spirit? Where can you flee from God's presence? Nowhere.* Wherever you go, God is there. From the highest place to the lowest place, God is there. As far as the east is from the west, God is there. If you go to where the sun dawns, God is there. If you go to the remotest part of the sea where the sun sets, God is there. God is everywhere all the time, and all of God is there at one time.

Hope for a cancer patient or caregiver is all about perspective. All of God is with you as you go through this battle with cancer. When you sink into the depths of despair, you are not farther away from God. You might feel as though *the darkness overwhelms you, but your darkness is like light to God.* He is present as if you were the only one He had to think about. What an amazing and comforting thought! God is with you, and yet He is with your loved ones wherever they might be, because God is not limited by time or space like you. Whatever causes you to be anxious or fearful is completely controlled, limited, and used for good by the God who is everywhere, all the time, all at once.

If you take the wings of the dawn and go to the remotest part of the sea, God is with you. The wings of the dawn is a phrase for the speed of light. When the sun comes up over the horizon, and the first rays shoot across the sky toward the west at the speed of light (approximately 186,000 miles per second or six trillion miles in one light-year), God is already there waiting on their arrival. God was there with you the moment the first cancer cell began to extend its influence over your body. No matter how fast the cancer might spread, it will never approach the speed of light, so God will be there waiting for any and all future challenges.

When you fall down in the desert of despair, drink from the springs of hope. When your life comes to an end, God is still going to be there with you to do you good. *How precious to me are Thy thoughts, O God! How vast is the sum of them! If I could count them, they are more than the stars in the sky; they are more than sands in the sea. When I am awake, I am still with you.*

That is a lot of thoughts! The grains of sand are countless. Get some perspective. The next time you are at a beach or playground, pick up two handfuls of sand and begin to count. If you were able to somehow load up into your counting machine every single, solitary grain of sand from every beach and desert on the face of this earth, it would not come close to equaling the vast numbers of stars in the countless galaxies of the universe scattered over light years of miles beyond human comprehension. The God who never forgets named every one of those stars (Ps. 147:4). The next verse is almost an understatement, *Great is our Lord, and abundant in power; His understanding is beyond measure.*

When you are hurting from the cancer and dreading the process, just go to the beach and run your fingers and toes through the sand or go outside at night and look up at the stars. God put them there as a reminder that He is thinking about you. God's thoughts of you are vast, *exceedingly great, beyond that which can be numbered.* Nothing exceeds the number of God's thoughts of you. Nothing!

It would be wonderful if the infinitely great God would think of you even once, but the Bible says God thinks about you all the time. Every care, every trial, every step, every day, every detail, from the most trivial to the most vital, are part of God's continual thoughts about you. Every test, every biopsy, every diagnosis, every chemotherapy, every surgery, every pain, every problem, every day, God is there with you and for you.

Somehow, every thought of God is connected to how He will love you and intertwine His life with your life for your good. God has thought of everything you need in life and in eternity. There is no better way to do you good than what He has already planned, and since God has thought of everything you need for the future, you have no need to worry or fear. The dreaded c-word can sound terrifying but when the dust from its windstorm settles and the eyes clear, God is there. Even here…even now…even this.

Perspective requires understanding. Cancer can do a lot of things to the body, but it cannot take away hope. The reason God preserved you through the night is so you might honor God today and God might fill your day with genuine happiness in your hurting heart. How did Pat exalt God with her cancer-stricken life? She learned to rejoice in the beauty of God, who He is and what He does.

You can learn to do that as well. It is not as difficult as it sounds. Just rejoice as you would when you see your children and grandchildren. Whenever you think about the ones you love, your eyes light up, your smile grows wider, and your heart wants to burst out of its place. Love drives your heart to things greater than the pain inside you. Hope draws your thoughts to things far beyond yourself.

With or without the burden of cancer, God is beautiful. Seen amidst the backdrop of cancer's ugliness, God appears even more gloriously beautiful, as welcomed as a loved one's embrace. The breathtaking glory of God's greatness and goodness is infinite. Your cancer will never add or take away from that. However, your happiness in honoring God through your cancer can magnify God's greatness and goodness the way a telescope enlarges objects in the sky.

A telescope opens up our eyes and mind to the massive enormity and grandeur of what is already there but often hidden from our sight and thoughts. If you look at God through the wrong end of the "suffering" telescope, God will seem very far away, maybe too distant to see or care. However, the right perspective of cancer can magnify your awe and admiration of God's immense, immeasurable, incalculable goodness to you.

How does a woman like Pat show value for something in her life? Is it not by the depth of delight it produces in her heart? There is a divine call waiting for all cancer sufferers, cancer survivors, and cancer caregivers. "Oh, magnify the Lord with me, and let us exalt His name together" (Ps. 34:3). When in despair, see hope through the telescopic lens of God's Word to gaze on the handiwork of God's goodness sung about in the heavens.

Cancer has to be seen in perspective. You were not created to be an empty shell. You are a container of something that cannot be contained, the glory of God's goodness. You were not born for cancer to drag you down into despair; you were born to soar in hope unchained by the bonds of earthly sufferings. The trained medical staff will do what they can to help you cope, but God gives mercy to cancer patients so you have hope. "I received mercy so that Jesus Christ might display His perfect patience in me as an example to those who would believe in Him for eternal life. To the King of ages, immortal, invisible, the only God, be honor and glory forever and ever. Amen" (1 Tim. 1:16–17).

Your body might feel as though it is wasting away, but that never means you have to waste your life.

There are essentially two spiritual responses to the dreaded c-word. Your life can be driven by *fear* of its destructive cells, or it can be drawn by *fascination* into a greater knowledge of the God who promised to work together all things, including cancer, for your ultimate good. Cancer might cross a few things off your bucket list, but do not lose your sense of awe, amazement, and wonder of God's goodness to you, most of which still lies in the future.

Cancer might affect your appetite and weaken your body, but you can still taste the sweetness of God's goodness and hear the symphony of His love. In heaven, the greater knowledge of God leads to greater praise of God. The adoration in heaven moves out from the throne of God in ever-widening circles like the ripple effect of moving water (Rev. 4). The same is true in this earthly life. Cancer becomes an advanced introductory course in the knowledge of our great and glorious God. One day in its classroom could have a snowball effect that leads to an avalanche of praise. Make this chapter of cancer count! See your life from an eternal perspective! Live it for an eternal purpose! Your life story could create a ripple effect through generations of family and friends.

Hope in God changes your perspective in the midst of suffering. Every day is a gift from God whether it is the first day of a long life or the last day of a shortened life. Each new day becomes more precious—and purposeful.

Purpose

What is that purpose? God created you so He might communicate the happiness of His immeasurable and everlasting love to you for you to share that same love with others.

What do you do when cancer darkens the skies of your heart and hides all happiness in life? Borrow some spiritual binoculars from the life stories in the Bible or in this book. Jesus is up to something! He is restoring the important things in your life to their divinely designed position and purpose.

First and foremost, above everything else, *love God with all your heart and with all your soul and with all your mind and with all your strength.* There is no greater assignment regarding your life's purpose. You were created to be a lover of God in *all things.*

Next, *love other people more.* Loving others is just as primary and significant as the first commandment in life. Love for God is expressed by love for others. Cancer tries to throw cold water on your love, but God just pulls you closer to His heart to feel the warmth and passion of His love. Nothing can separate you from God's love. Not cancer. Not death. Nothing. This is such an important anchor of truth for hope that I have devoted several upcoming chapters to the subject.

If great hearts are made with great suffering, then there is little wonder why Pat loved others so much. It was just a product of the irony of her hope. The more Pat suffered from the cancer, the more love poured out in her words and prayers and smiles. The greater miracle was not a physical healing; it was the growth of love and hope in the face of intense suffering.

God will help you love others while you suffer. God is there with you, side by side, loving you and enabling you to love others better than ever before. Make these days count! Your time spent as a cancer sufferer or a caregiver in suffering can be the most impactful days of your life.

There is always an ultimate divine purpose to suffering. Many of life's great spiritual lessons are learned in the arena of adversity. Without the boiling process, a teabag is useless. Sometimes God places your life into the hot water of affliction to prepare you for greater usefulness.

Getting a firm grip on your ultimate purpose in life will transform how you think and feel and love and pray and live and die. Pat never let inquiries into her well-being stop with a health update. She used every well-wisher's visit as an opportunity to talk about the God she loved. She preferred to focus on the hope and not the suffering. Oh, the suffering was very real, but so was her hope! The former would soon disappear; the latter would become a lasting reality. Pat could tell you better than I that cancer is not good, but anything (like cancer) or *all things* that cause you to turn loose of everything but your love for God and love for others should definitely be counted as good.

God designed your life for maximum love and happiness that can grow in delight and duration throughout endless ages.

Cancer becomes the hot water for your tea bag's purpose. Do not be surprised when things heat up; you will have to struggle with thoughts of unfairness and regret, anger and anguish, fear and despair. That is the battleground on which hope wins its most precious victories! Do not give in; do not give up. Hope in God, if not for a physical miracle then for the greater miracle of happiness in honoring God now and forever.

God can heal, so pray for healing, but double down on God's will to be done. Sometimes God miraculously heals; sometimes God providentially delivers; sometimes God waits because of something "better" than deliverance from the problems (Heb. 11: 29–40). All those sufferers had faith. Some were rescued from their suffering while others were strengthened to endure their suffering. Put your faith in God, not your agenda for how God should help you. God is always better than what life can give you and far better than what death could ever take away from you.

If God chooses not to heal, it does not shortchange your life or its significance. Your suffering is part of a larger drama. The anger, doubts, and confusion are normal reactions, but not healthy ones. None of us know what the future holds regardless of the diagnosis. Because our God is bigger than cancer, then our hope in God is bigger than the despair that can come from cancer. Since God is bigger than your cancer problem, then so is His purpose for you as you live with cancer.

We are fragile people living in a flawed and futile world. A miraculous healing is always purposeful but so is continued sickness. One seems more praiseworthy than the other, but both will only be temporary. Live for what will outlast the miracle or the sickness. Live to love God and to love others with the love of God. Pray that God would take your love to a higher level where miracles do not add to its intensity and sickness can never diminish its wonder.

Pat was soft-spoken, but her life's testimony continues to ring loud and clear. Living with cancer became another opportunity to demonstrate her faith and hope in God. Not faith in a miracle but faith in God. Not hope in controlled circumstances but hope in God. "Now faith is confidence in what we hope for and assurance about what we do not see" (Heb. 11:1). The faith of hope "believes that God is really God and He is a rewarder of those who love Him" (Heb. 11:6).

God's staggering pledge of Romans 8:28 is that *all things*—not just the good but also the bad things—work for your good. Life's worst pains are for your eternal joy. *All things* is an all-inclusive phrase with massive implications. There are no exceptions. It does not take much to believe that the best things in life work for our good, but what makes *Romans 8:28* such a life-transforming promise is that the worst things are included in the *all things*.

Synchronize your soul in harmony with God's design. Get on the same page with God. Get well-acquainted with God's perspective and purpose for your life.

God is bigger than your suffering. Cancer does not change that perspective. You were created to love and enjoy God. Cancer does not change that purpose. Your God-given purpose and pleasure are independent of the gain or loss of physical comfort and security, health and wealth, achievement or gratification. They cannot be found in self-centeredness or worldly things, only in God. "God made known to me the path of life; in His presence is fullness of joy" (Ps. 16:11).

Despair and hope are both connected to perspective and purpose. Your perspective is formed by knowledge of God's character, which has not changed since your cancer diagnosis. Your life still has the same purpose as before; only now it goes more public as the news spreads faster than the cancer. Put God's glory on public display by your gladness in Him, not gladness in the rightness of your circumstances. Where there is despair, *hope*.

Jim Elliot, martyred missionary, once wrote, "I pray that my life will be a testimony to the value of knowing Christ." Make that your purpose. That was Pat's purpose in life and in her sickness.

Knowing Jesus Christ is the greatest treasure and the greatest pleasure in life. The same is true in the face of death. If your life includes cancer, then that is where your testimony of the value of knowing Jesus Christ will shine the brightest.

Some of you readers are battling cancer or caring for a loved one who is. Some are in the middle of very difficult times. It is vital for you to keep remembering that this struggle is not primarily about you, but about God and the spiritual welfare of others. God will take care of you. Your life is here to be an encouragement to others that God is great in faithfulness. Hold their hand; weep with them and in those moments where there is despair, *hope*. Hope for them. Be the presence of hope with them. Show them the love that outlasts any suffering.

You are never anywhere by accident. Divine conjunctions have connected you to this place and its people. Everything is by divine appointment, even the people around you at the doctor's office, chemo treatment, or the hospital. Give them love. Show them hope. Some will want to tell you their life story. Listen. Care. Pray for them. They do not need a long sermon or a theological lesson. Share a Bible verse that has encouraged you.

> *When I am afraid, I will trust in God. The Lord is my Shepherd. God will never leave us or forsake us. Cast all your anxiety upon the Lord because He cares for you. Why so downcast, O my soul; put your hope in God.*

Where there is despair, *hope*. We have a hope so extravagant that it seems impossible. *When I walk through the valley of the shadow of death, the Lord is with me.* Cancer does not win if you or your loved one dies. You do not beat cancer by surviving its devastating effects. Cancer is overcome with love and hope. If God chooses to use cancer to get you closer to Him and then ultimately face to face with Him, then embrace it. Do not waste any of your days. "Teach us to number our days that we may get a heart of wisdom" (Ps. 90:12). Spend your time loving God and others. That is a day, a life, well spent!

Most likely you have had many questions related to the cancer, perhaps this chapter raised some new ones. There are "Why?" questions and "How?" ones. "What if?" questions and "What did he (the doctor or your God) say?" wonderings. The coming chapters will address as many of them as possible by arranging them under the heading of the "Right Questions" found in the "Interrogation Interlude" (chapter 11).

Setbacks? Sure, expect them and take them in stride. You are ascending heights of hope never before seen in your lifetime. The happiness of heaven is irresistible. The enablement of God's grace is inexhaustible. The extravagance of God's love is immeasurable. Each new day of your journey is more precious than the last. You are blessed to have been placed into a situation where that awareness is inescapable.

Right now counts forever.

> We know that the one who raised the Lord Jesus from the dead will also raise us with Jesus and present us with you to Himself. All this is for your benefit, so that the grace that is reaching more and more people may cause thanksgiving to overflow to the glory of God. *So we do not lose heart.* Though our outer self is wasting away, our inner self is being renewed day by day. For this light momentary affliction is preparing for us an eternal weight of glory beyond all comparison, as we look not to the things that are seen but to the things that are unseen. For the things that are seen are transient, but the things that are unseen are eternal. (2 Cor. 4:14–18; emphasis included)

In the lowest depths of human despair, *we know God is there*. In the highest heights beyond all human hope, *we know God is there*.

Much like a post-doctor's visit, it takes some time to process what was said with what went through your mind like a blur. It might benefit you to give some time to think through the Great Physician's words concerning your purpose and perspective in life. I am just a nurse reminding you that you can call the doctor if you have further questions. For now, here is your prescription and treatment plan—and do not forget to read the Doctor's personal note to you at the end.

Every day, take a biblical dose of perspective and purpose. Where there is despair, *hope*.

The Great Physician who is there with you 24-7 of every year has written you a personal note to pull out and read during those times of suffering that threaten to hide His presence with feelings of despair.

"I have engraved you on the palms of my hands" (Isa. 49:16).

God has engraved *you* on the palms of His hands. Not your name or next appointment. *You.* God will never forget to be there with you and for you. Take that *hope* with you to the next chapter.

The Right Understanding of Hope

Hope blossoms upon the awareness of God's goodness; therefore, the better you know God, the greater your hope.

"We have this *hope* as an anchor for the soul, firm and secure" (Heb. 6:19; emphasis added).

Weak and wounded sinner
Lost and left to die
O, raise your head for love is passing by
Come to Jesus, Come to Jesus
Come to Jesus and live
Now your burden's lifted
And carried far away
And precious blood has washed away the stain
So sing to Jesus, Sing to Jesus
Sing to Jesus and live
And like a new born baby
Don't be afraid to crawl
And remember when you walk sometimes we fall
So fall on Jesus, Fall on Jesus
Fall on Jesus and live
Sometimes the way is lonely
And steep and filled with pain
So if your sky is dark and pours the rain
Then cry to Jesus, Cry to Jesus
Cry to Jesus and live
Oh, and when the love spills over
And music fills the night
And when you can't contain your joy inside
Then dance for Jesus, Dance for Jesus
Dance for Jesus and live
And with your final heartbeat
Kiss the world goodbye
Then go in peace, and laugh on glory's side
And fly to Jesus, Fly to Jesus
Fly to Jesus and live

—"Untitled Hymn (Come to Jesus),"
Christopher Rice

3

Abandoned but Not Alone

Joy's Story
Understanding *God Causes*

Abandoned. Take a moment and just look at that word. Abandoned. It makes me want to cry.

Abandonment rips out your heart and stomps on it on the way out the door. It leaves you devastated. Life feels like the aftermath of a hurricane disaster zone. Everything is shattered, changed—gone.

Perhaps you have experienced those feelings of loneliness and felt the emptiness in your heart when your trust has been betrayed. Standing in the shock of abandonment, all you can see are dark nights, gray skies, and foggy mornings. Fear surrounds you; the unknown future haunts your every thought.

Life never goes according to our plans. Never. Other people do not do what we want, when we want, and in the way we want. Duh? Circumstances change without consulting our permission or preferences. We cannot control the circumstances and we cannot fix them, just as we cannot control or fix all the people interacting with our lives. How many times are we confronted with that, whether it be a spouse, a child, a parent, a friend, or an enemy?

Our lack of sovereign control over the people and circumstances in our lives can be frustrating at best. In the lowest moments, it can be devastating. It hurts. It crushes. It angers. It embitters. When things have not worked out as we expected or dreamed, we can feel lost as to direction in life and significance in this vast universe. Perplexed and confused, we are not sure what is happening or what to do in life. In those difficult times, we can become cynical and hopeless.

Sometimes life can become like a taste of sand in your mouth as you travel through the desert of despair. It grinds away as a constant irritant, and you seem to never be able to spit all of it out. The swirling sandstorm blinds your sight, blows you off course, and distorts your sense of direction. There is no clairvoyant of the clouds or sage of the skies who can discern what lies ahead. However, there is hope and there is a way to survive the harshest storms.

The Scriptures provide spiritual binoculars to enlarge your perspective into the hidden mercies of God. With the most used admonition in the Bible, God tells you not to fear the future. The Scriptures pinpoint the emotion, fear of the unknown, that makes us doubt and question God's goodness. Satan's first act in the Bible was to question the goodness of God's sovereignty. The same issue the evil one raised to Adam and Eve in their perfect circumstances was presented to Job in his pit of despair. In those moments of fear and doubts, help comes from the ability to consider biblical truth.

"My soul is downcast within me. Yet this I call to mind and therefore I have hope" (Lam. 3:20–21).

In our darkness, we can lose sight of God. We can feel abandoned. Life can become so hard and feel so hopeless, we want to give up. That is Joy's story. She was abandoned, but she was not left alone. In her abandonment, Joy discovered her purpose in life and her reason to go on into the unknown future.

Truth in the mind gives life to hope in the heart.

Joy would rebuild her shattered life on the rock of truth. The circumstances surrounding our lives are no accident. Neither is the hope. *And we know God causes...*

Joy's Story

My world was close to ideal. I was raised in a Christian home with parents who made sure our family was involved in our church. I attended a Christian university, where I met Rick, who was planning to become a pastor. However, after one semester of questionable biblical teachings, he became disillusioned with some of his professors, so he chose the Air Force for his career. We kept in touch, started dating, and married two years later.

God is sovereign and in control of all things.

Rick studied God's Word every day and introduced me to the concept of God's sovereignty, a biblical teaching I had never understood before. I grew to realize that my God was truly ruler over everything.

My ideal situation just kept getting better; our first son was born, and I was blessed to be able to stay home and care for him.

Rick made the decision to leave the Air Force because he did not feel it was a good environment for a family. We eventually moved back to our home state. We chose a church with good Bible teaching. Some events with our church staff left us devastated, and we stopped going to church; Rick reenlisted in the Air Force, and we moved to another city. We attended a church where we went faithfully until he got his orders to move to Panama. During that time, we met some wonderful brothers and sisters in Christ.

Then your world falls apart.

By this time, I had a second son and was pregnant with our third son. A dear family in our church offered us a home with them the year Rick would be away, but we followed him to Panama where our third son was born. We could not find a church there we liked, so we did not attend for three years.

Drifting away is a dangerous thing, especially spiritually. I was not attending church; I did not stay in God's Word. Little did I know my safe world, as I knew it, was about to fall apart. God was going to show me what was most precious in life, Him.

Rick sat me down one afternoon and said, "Don't take it personal, but I don't love you anymore."

I was stunned! I thought, "Are you kidding me? Don't take it personal after sixteen years of marriage and three sons."

My first thought was to run through the concrete wall of the house. I could not turn to Rick; he was abandoning us. I was obviously not in control mentally, physically, or emotionally. I went to our bedroom, closed the door, fell on my face and cried out to God, "Please show me you really are sovereign and that you are in control of all this mess." That prayer was the beginning of an incredible journey of faith. Circumstances did not change overnight, but I started changing.

No detail of your life escapes God.

I opened God's Word, and the Holy Spirit brought life to my soul. I took the boys to the one church we had not attended the following Sunday, and the pastor boldly preached on the sovereignty of God. Our gracious God gifted me with two precious ladies to mentor me in His Word. Bev taught a weekly Bible study and shared sermon tapes with me. God's Word blessed my heart as I began to memorize it and God began to teach me more and more of who He is.

Some friends from church invited the boys and me to go with some other families to the beach for spring break—another gift from God. I had packed John MacArthur's book *Anxiety Attacked* to read again. I sat on the balcony and watched the boys playing while I read. At the top of page 35, it said, "*No* detail escapes Him" (Ps. 147:5; emphasis added). *Wow!* All the weight on my shoulders was gone.

I did not have to fix everything.

I did not have to fix Rick or our marriage. The Great God who built this universe and dearly loved me has everything under control because He is sovereign. And no detail escapes Him.

That night, I turned in my bible to that verse, and God made its meaning crystal clear for me. "Great is our God and mighty in power, His understanding is infinite" (Ps. 147:5). Thank you, Father.

The time had come to leave Panama. Where do I go, Lord? Do I go to my parents? I fell on my face and cried out to my provider, my Heavenly Father for direction. I saw the image of the family who had invited us to live with them before we left for Panama, so I called to explain our situation and asked them to pray about it. They opened their hearts and home to us immediately.

Just before we left to return to the States, our church held a special prayer time for the boys and me. The church had asked me to share my spiritual journey of the past few months; it was an awesome chance to glorify my God. No detail had escaped Him. Bonnie prayed that God would find us a three-bedroom home with a fenced backyard and a dog for the boys. The church sent us away with a $1,500 love offering. God helped me find a car and six months of insurance with that money; there was even enough left for Happy Meals from McDonald's.

Then God provided a job. The first place where I interviewed needed computer experience; I had none. However, the man led me to a job at a gift shop run by the sister of our associate pastor. Now I had a car and a job. Then God's guiding hand found me an apartment two blocks from my best friend. The church up the street had a day care where I would leave my son in the capable hands of a dear college friend.

The pieces of my abandoned life were being put back together by the Creator of the universe. Life was not easy, but there was hope. Perhaps my greatest hardship was handling the exhaustion. I worked six days a week and did the best I could to care for the well-being of my three boys. Without the help of their father, some days, it was all I could do to put one foot in front of the other.

The love and goodness of our Heavenly Father never left me alone.

How does the story end? Do you remember that the church prayed for a home for the boys and me? After five years of apartment living, I spoke with a realtor. She called me the next day and told me there was a family who wanted to make the down payment and pay closing costs on a house for us. I went to see it—yes, a lovely three-bedroom house with a fireplace and fenced backyard with a tree swing.

No detail had escaped my Heavenly Father as He helped my boys and me put our lives back together. What a love He lavishes on us! And thank you, Lord, for Rick who taught me You are Sovereign.

Desert of Despair

Consider William Shakespeare's characterization of Macbeth. His indifferent view to the tragedies and victories in his life left him disillusioned and depressed.

> Tomorrow, and tomorrow, and tomorrow,
> Creeps in this petty pace from day to day,
> To the last syllable of recorded time;
> all our yesterdays have lighted fools
> The way to dusty death. Out, out, brief candle!
>
> Life's but a walking shadow, a poor player,
> That struts and frets his hour upon the stage
> And then is heard no more. It is a tale
> Told by an idiot, full of sound and fury, Signifying nothing.

To Macbeth, all the world is a stage. Life just moves from scene to scene in some rhythmic beat of tomorrows laid end to end until that "crack of doom." Death seems more like the last act of a very bad play told by an idiot. There might appear to be much melodrama, but it all happens without any meaningful purpose. It all becomes more of an illusion of mere shadows and brief flickers of light.

In some ways, all the world is a stage, and we are actors. We are front stage busy performing the play entitled *life*. Certainly there are days when we feel Macbeth's emptiness. However, this life is not an illusion and not without significance. God is unseen back stage in real control of all that happens.

Every scene has eternal purpose. Every player has infinite worth. Every *today* and every *tomorrow* are divinely choreographed to do you the greatest good. Everything has to do with everything, each scene interlocked by divine conjunctions until God reveals the final chapter met with thunderous applause of countless heavenly observers. You are not some poor performer fretting away your moment in the spotlight of recorded time. You have not been abandoned; you are not alone. My dear lady, you are God's star, scripted to shine in hope until the glorious Lover of your soul makes His appearance.

However, without the defining panorama of biblical truth, we do not perceive reality from God's perspective. Our feelings are often formed by our perspective of reality as we know it. We look at our lives from the stage of this ungodly culture seeking health and happiness in fleeting pleasures. Relationships are tenuous, goals are selfish, solutions constantly evolving. The source of comfort today might be jettisoned tomorrow. A promise is only as certain as the weather's changing winds, a truth only as bedrock as the culture's shifting sands. One day, together forever; the next day, "See ya"—abandoned.

Abandonment can produce feelings of disillusionment and depression, but the realization we are not alone can awaken hope. We desperately need to know God. Not caricatures or platitudes. Not cultural christianity or pop theology. Not "Seven Steps to Happiness" or a roadmap to bypass suffering. Our strutting and fretting on stage occur when we forget who is backstage working all things together for good. We need to see the reality of our lives from God's perspective. To do so, we need to know God and that is precisely where the great promise of hope begins. *God*.

But God...was there with Joy. *And God*...worked out every detail in her life.

Abandoned by a husband to sink in despair, Joy got to know God better. Looking at her life from God's perspective, she saw hope, not in financial or physical security but hope in the God who was there. The God who was in control. The God who did not need her help to fix things. Joy held on to that promise of hope. She had been abandoned, but she was not alone.

Springs of Hope

> I will never, never, never, never, never
> leave you or abandon you.
>
> —Hebrews 13:5

God vows in the strongest, most emphatic manner in any language that no matter what happens to you, He will always be there with you. There is absolutely nothing that can change that. Not abandonment by spouse or parents, not divorce, not widowhood, not medical confinement, not mental treatment, not loss of work or home, not the most isolated uninhabited circumstance ever. Others might abandon you, but God will never leave you alone to fend for yourself. Never.

You will never come out of your emotional prison until you understand God's steadfast love never wavers with your changing circumstances. The journey to healing and recovery from abandonment by a spouse begins with awareness and acknowledgment of who is still with you. This chapter presents a very important foundational truth regarding God and His goodness to you, the source of your help and hope.

And we know God causes...This great promise of hope begins with a divine conjunction followed by a declaration of absolute confidence. *We know God.* The goal is not to feel better; it is to think rightly. Feelings do not determine truth. Feelings fluctuate; truth never vacillates. Right thinking precedes right feelings. Right thinking begins with personal knowledge of God and His incomparable love for you. Truth in the mind really does produce hope in the heart.

The ultimate purpose in life is to know God as your personal God. *We know God* is a language learned by heart. Who is this God we know?

1. We know God is real.
2. We know God rules.
3. We know God is relational.
4. We know God is relevant to hope.

1. *We know God is real.* Do you know the real God? There is an enormous difference between just knowing about God and actually knowing God personally. It is the difference between abandonment and not being alone. Joy had been abandoned by Rick, but she was not alone.

God is eternal and has always been there. God had no beginning and He has no end. *In the beginning God* (who was already there) *created...*(Gen. 1:1). God exists and has always been there from the everlasting past to the everlasting future. God is self-existent; "I am who I am" (Exod. 3:14). The eternal God was there with Joy; she was not alone. Wherever you are, God is there with you.

We do not know what to do when our world falls apart, so the Spirit of God intercedes on our behalf. We do not know where to go when we are abandoned and left to ourselves, but when we do not know what or where or how or when, God is still there with us, at work to do us good.

We know God is real *until* the dark nights, gray skies, and foggy mornings interrupt our normal days. Then confusion and doubt reign over our present surroundings or prospective future. We often act unsure about God's control, confused regarding His sovereignty, and fearful trusting His goodness.

These are the times you need to know the God who causes all things to work together for your good, not while you are reading a book or listening to music. These are the times that try our souls, and somehow these are the times when we learn God still loves us and has plans for our future welfare. Knowing God is not mind over matter or positive confession. It is not wishful dreaming or expressions of will power. It is real, substantive hope joined to personal knowledge of the real God.

The fog of change might hide our ability to see the hope, but it is there, as sure as the sun rules the sky above those dark clouds. Even when we cannot feel its warmth, we know the sun is there. It is as real as a mother's love even when distance prevents the feeling of her strong yet tender hug. That same truth concerning God's reality generates real genuine hope in our hearts.

There is spiritual DNA inside every child of God that knows God is faithful, and His hope is real. The question is resolved. The proof is conclusive. The truth is personally embraced.

2. *We know God rules.* You need a God bigger than your problems. If you are to think right about the current chapter in your life, then you need to know God rules. Circumstances get out of control and problems get too big for you to fix everything. Coping with the mess and stress of life can overwhelm the best of intentions.

The good news for you and Joy is that God is not only bigger than your problems but He also controls them for your good. Think about it. The God who rules is at work on your behalf to control every problem for your good. This becomes the foundational basis for your hope in the face of loss, abandonment, and all forms of suffering. These next paragraphs intend to shore up the foundations of your thinking with simple but solid truth that can survive the storms of life.

Romans 8:28 reveals a very important aspect of God's character, God's sovereignty. Whenever you read the word *sovereignty* in this book, think "God is in control for my good."

God is in control of all things, all the time, in a way that is permanently and irrevocably connected to His goodness.

I believe this simple but life-governing principle is the key truth which glues all the pieces of life's puzzle into their proper places.

Sovereignty is not just some theological doctrine embraced by a few and misapplied by many. It is simply a word that means God has the right, the authority, and the power to do whatever He pleases. The wonderful news is that it pleases God to do you good. God truly is unseen backstage in complete control of everything that happens. This is not book clutter or a page filler; it is vital to your hope in abandonment, accidents, agony, anguish, etc. "God in control" ensures you the greatest good in whatever circumstance and chapter in your life from *A* to *Z*.

God's sovereignty is always connected to His goodness to you.

Throughout the Bible, God testifies, describes, and demonstrates His self-existent sovereignty by means of the revelation of His name, Lord. "No one is like you. O Lord; you are great, and your name is mighty in power" (Jer. 10:6). He is Lord of lords, a position higher than any and all other claims of authority and power.

The Lord God's unique position in the universe is embedded in the name, the Most High God, "the highest one." Whoever is the highest is the Most High God in control of all things, all the time, from start (Creator, Gen. 1:1) to finish (Eternal Judge, Rev. 4:2) and everything in between (Almighty King, Ps. 24:10). "Let them know that You, whose name is the Lord—that You alone are the Most High over all the earth" (Ps. 83:18).

God's absolute control is not really up for debate philosophically or theologically. That truth has been decided by the Most High God, and it is not subject to human ratification or recall. Likewise, God's promise of good in Romans 8:28 stands on His ability to oversee *all things*. So whether you have been taught about God's sovereignty for your good or whether this is your first foretaste of this glorious thought, it is a fundamental nonnegotiable truth. Whoever is God is sovereign.

You might not agree with this reality or even like it, but you cannot change it. Now God's sovereignty raises many questions, some of which we will seek to address in other chapters. Why do bad things happen under the control of a good God? How does God use bad things to make *all things* good? You might not understand how this truth of God's absolute rule guarantees that God is working all things out for your good, but you can *know* God is in control of all your life, all the time. God's sovereignty is unquestionable. No detail escapes Him.

If you are still interested in how this sovereignty stuff relates to the pain and suffering of your abandonment, then, at some point, you will be confronted with another question. How do God's sovereignty and our free will coexist? That remains a mystery. I am not smart enough to understand much less explain what brilliant theologians and philosophers have failed to reconcile in libraries full of books written in every generation. Neither am I as dumb as I write.

God in control and human free will can be illustrated as two parallel rails of a railroad track. Both tracks are part of the train's journey, inseparable and necessary for the design to work. If the train of my life travels through rough spots or dark places, I can know it is for my good because God never leaves my side. I am not a puppet on a string. I can choose preferences and direction. However, when I mess up and make the wrong decision about my direction in life, the "God in control" never lets my life train jump the tracks and wreck beyond repair. His track runs alongside my track, but His rails are always sure and secure. How that works together remains a mystery to me (and every human), but I am convinced it is not a mystery to God. He rules and somehow overrules to do us the greatest good. I can accept that intellectually and spiritually.

Divine sovereignty and your choices can also be illustrated (not explained) as two sides of the same coin, inseparable and necessary; God in control is heads and your freedom of choice is tails. Now if you ever get to make the call at any point in your life, always call heads! Heads, you win! I am extremely thankful that in spite of my best and worst decisions, no detail of my life escapes the God in control of my life for my own good.

God in control is the key to hope.

For now, you probably question what this has to do with your dilemma and despair, your abandonment and anguish. Everything. The promise begins with *"and we know God…"* The Most High God chose to link His control to working *all things together for your good.* That truth promises goodness can come out of all the bad stuff that happens in this world. Even in things like abandonment, the God in control never leaves you alone or without the hope of future good. So "God in control" becomes something wonderful to embrace, not something fearful to fight. When in despair, hope in God.

3. *We know God is relational.* We were created and saved for relational nearness to the God of infinite greatness and unending goodness. The God in control of everything introduced Himself and His relationship to us in the same way He did to Adam and Eve in the Bible book of Genesis. The Creator God revealed Himself as our personal (1) Life Giver (Gen. 2:7, 22), (2) Loving Partner (Gen. 2:8–15), and (3) Eternal Lord (Gen. 2:16–18).

God wired us to know there is a powerful and personal God who relates to us this way. Every person knows that. Not every person admits or likes it, but it is in their spiritual DNA. How can I say that? God said He created us with the awareness of

His existence and that the only ones in denial have to willfully and knowingly lie to themselves in a futile effort to ignore reality. Sadly, some grow up in that kind of environment because of man-made parental or cultural influences created to suppress that God-centered knowledge.

> Since the creation of the world, the invisible qualities of God's eternal power and divine nature have been clearly seen. They are understood from what has been made so that people are without excuse. Every person was created by God to instinctively and intuitively know there is a God. When they choose not to honor or give thanks to God, their thinking becomes futile and their foolish hearts go dark. (Rom. 1:20–21)

Get to know God better for your own good. God alone is supreme and sovereign, first and foremost, before everything else and above everything else. His incomparable grace undeservedly rescues us from our futile thinking and His relentless love wins over our darkened, unwilling hearts. This results in an ever-increasing awareness of our unbreakable relationship with our God, not with religious formalities but relational intimacy. God encourages you to call Him your Dad (*Abba, Father*, Rom. 8:15). The Most High Creator God just happens to be your Daddy who promised you future good. Let Him decide when and how to fix things.

Learn to focus on the character of God, not your circumstances.

When your world is caving in on you and your circumstances seem to be going from bad to worse, it is a beautiful opportunity to get to know God better. Whatever the path and whatever the cost, it will be worth it. That sounds good until the cost of waiting is more than just a missed meal or the twenty-four-hour flu. What about when you are abandoned by your promised provider? Or your dreams of the future are crushed on his way out the door?

Focus on who God is—and wait. God's Word exhorts you to *wait on the Lord and He will renew your hope.* The Hebrew word for *wait* used in Psalms and Isaiah means "to be stretched tight" like a rope. It conveys the idea of confident expectation, not dreary delay.

There are different ways to wait for someone you intend to meet at the mall or stadium or airport. You can just passively sit back behind the crowd, texting a friend or Googling a recipe until your loved one interrupts your concentration with an announcement of arrival; or in the biblical concept of waiting, you stand on your tiptoes in eager anticipation, stretched upward in hope of catching that first glimpse.

Waiting is never meant to be passive paralysis or wasted time. Waiting is relational, time set aside to know your God better. Whether you are waiting on a new baby or waiting on lab tests, there is a certain amount of uncertainty and unknown that comes with the waiting. Our ways and plans and thoughts are not on the same page as God's. Our hurried clock is not set to the same time zone. God's ways are better and so is His perfect timing. God knows how to take on our fixer-upper project. The work starts inside us and no detail escapes Him.

The very best place to "wait" is in God's Word. You can benefit from contemplating God's greatness and goodness in the skies and within the secret places of your heart, but the most effective and efficient place to "wait" is in the Scriptures. Spend time in God's Word expecting your Constant Companion to speak to you. You will learn more about God's character and God's ways in relationship to you and your circumstances. It will renew your hope.

4. *We know God is relevant.* The sooner you embrace God's sovereignty, the better you will appreciate God's goodness in your life. The "God in control" is totally for you. You should want the one who is totally for you to be sovereign so that nothing can stop Him. Right?

God's love will outlast your suffering. That is pretty relevant to you and your situation. When it feels as though your life is falling apart and the pieces of your puzzle are scattered on the ground, your Heavenly Father promises to fix every detail messed up by human decisions. "God in control" becomes the sweet and sure hope for your soul. Wait in hope of God's goodness. Look for the divine conjunctions of God's providence. They seem to appear in the worst of times.

Joy discovered the reality of her God in the agony of her abandonment. Stop staring at that door where your man departed and start looking for hope. The clouds of change are moving. You are not alone. Your God is real; He rules. God relates to you and your suffering. He is relevant to your future good. God can fix this…even here…even now…even this.

And *we know God causes* all things to *work together*. How do bad things and God's goodness *work together*? That is the focus of our next chapter, but it builds on your getting to know God better. How do you get to know God? Through the Scriptures and through suffering.

Instead of reading the divorce papers or the "I don't love you anymore" note, read the Bible stories which *were written for your encouragement and hope* (Rom. 15:4). In some stories, abandonment from family and friends intensified the suffering, but God was always there in the shadows of each life. With each divine conjunction, hope would spring up in their desert of despair. "We are hard pressed on every side, but not crushed; perplexed, but not in despair; persecuted, but not abandoned" (2 Cor. 4:8–9).

Suffering is designed to help you know the God of comfort and show that same comfort to others in need of help and hope (2 Cor. 1:3–4). In suffering, wait on God who is real, ruling, relational, and relevant. From abandonment to anguish, God is there. Wait on Him to show His goodness. Get on your spiritual tiptoes and anticipate the arrival of hope, the confident expectation of enjoying all the future goodness God has promised you.

And we know God causes... The stage is set; the spotlight has turned onto you. Nothing is more relevant to hope than knowing your God is behind the curtain, in control of everything in order to do you the greatest good. God has devoted His whole heart to doing you good, and He promised to never stop. "I will never stop doing them good...I will rejoice in doing them good with all my heart and soul, this is what the Lord says" (Jer. 32:40–41).

God will never abandon you; you will never be alone. Where there is despair, *hope.*

The Right Understanding of Hope

Absolutely nothing can stop God from doing you good; God is in total control of everything, all the time. God never wastes your time or your experiences. God knows where you are, where you need to be, and how to get you there.

"For you have been my hope, Sovereign Lord" (Ps. 71:5).

In Genesis, He's the breath of life
In Exodus, the Passover Lamb
In Leviticus, He's our High Priest
Numbers, The fire by night
Deuteronomy, He's Moses' voice
In Joshua, He is salvation's choice
Judges, the law giver
In Ruth, the kinsmen-redeemer
First and second Samuel, our trusted prophet
In Kings and Chronicles, He's sovereign
Ezra, true and faithful scribe
Nehemiah, He's the rebuilder of broken walls and lives
In Esther, He's Mordecai's courage
In Job, the timeless redeemer
In Psalms, He is our morning song
In Proverbs, wisdom's cry
Ecclesiastes, the time and season
In the Song of Solomon, He is the lover's dream
He is, He is, He is!
In Isaiah, He's Prince of Peace
Jeremiah, the weeping prophet
In Lamentations, the cry for Israel
Ezekiel, He's the call from sin
In Daniel, the stranger in the fire
In Hosea, He is forever faithful
In Joel, He's the Spirit's power
In Amos, the arms that carry us
In Obadiah, He's the Lord our Savior
In Jonah, He's the great missionary
In Micah, the promise of peace
In Nahum, He is our strength and our shield
In Habakkuk and Zephaniah, He's pleading for revival
In Haggai, He restores a lost heritage

In Zechariah, our fountain
In Malachi, He is the son of righteousness
rising with healing in His wings

In Matthew, Mark, Luke and John,
He is God, Man, Messiah
In the book of Acts, He is fire from heaven
In Romans, He's the grace of God
In Corinthians, the power of love
In Galatians, He is freedom from the curse of sin
Ephesians, our glorious treasure
Philippians, the servant's heart
In Colossians, He's the Godhead Trinity
Thessalonians, our coming King
In Timothy, Titus, Philemon, He's our
mediator and our faithful Pastor
In Hebrews, the everlasting covenant
In James, the one who heals the sick.
In First and Second Peter, he is our Shepherd
In John and in Jude, He is the lover coming for His bride
In the Revelation, *He is King of kings and Lord of lords*
He is, He is, He is!
The prince of peace
The Son of man
The Lamb of God
The great I AM
He's the alpha and omega
Our God and our Savior
He is Jesus Christ the Lord
and when time is no more
He is, He Is!

—"He Is," Jeoffrey Benward and Jeff Silvey

4

Loving a Physically Challenged Child

Cherie's Story
Understanding *Work Together*

Hope paints its most beautiful portraits on the faces of adversity. Sometimes it takes a second look through those spiritual binoculars to see how God uses the clouds of adversity to do you even greater good. God masterfully works together hope and adversity to develop you into all He designed you to become. Physical and emotional challenges might describe the difficulties and hardships in your life, but they should never define or destroy your identity. They might alter your dreams but not your destiny or your view of God.

David Powlinson reminds us of the dangers of obsessing over the magnitude of our problem in a way that diminishes our consideration of God's character and care for us.

> Honesty is able to feel the weight of things that arouse fear and dismay. The problem is not that we feel troubled by trouble and pained by pain. Something hurtful should hurt. The problem is that God slides away into irrelevance when we obsess over suffering or compulsively avoid it. God inhabits a vague afterthought—weightless and distant in comparison to something immediately pressing. Or, if God-words fill our minds and pour forth from our lips, it's easy to make the "god" we cry out to someone who

will magically make everything better if we can only catch his ear.

Whenever our dreams get crushed, it hurts. It really hurts! Most likely you wanted the perfect husband or the perfect family or the perfect life, or at least a "normal" one. When your idea of normal life changes without your consent, it can be quite frustrating if not downright depressing. In your private talks with yourself, God can become irrelevant and a vague afterthought. Talk to God. Be honest. It will be beneficial to air out your feelings to His listening ear.

Do you know that it is all right to be honest with God about your feelings? Several years ago, I stood in a hospital room beside the bed of my cousin, a young mother of two children now battling terminal cancer. As we talked about how she was feeling, she blurted out, "I am just so angry with God."

I replied, "Why don't you just tell God instead of me? I do not think it will surprise Him since He already knows what you are feeling."

My remark shocked her but later took her to a special place and time where she had a new dialogue with God, an honest talk. No church sounding words or theological terms, just authentic feelings of the heart expressed in tears and fumbled sentences. Despair can leave you murmuring and muttering about God and your feelings as if God is not part of the conversation, but God is always listening with love and without condemnation. My cousin said that talk with God changed her perspective. It replaced her fears and anger with hope and peace.

Expressing how you feel never changes God, but it can begin to change you.

Read the Psalms. They are full of feelings from despair to hope, sorrow to rejoicing, questions to confidence. Feelings are part of who we are. They are meant to be expressed through words, music, and art, but few expressions can convey more depth of love than a mother rocking her child.

Raising a child is a challenge; it is joyful, but it will tax the best of mothers. Caring for a physically challenged child takes the joyful journey through additional stress levels invoking need for both greater compassion and stronger courage. Maybe you have been there. God is there with you too.

Together. There is something special about the word *together*. You are not alone. It conveys the idea of "two or more as one." The Lord chose to place you and your special child together so that the two of you might have the best view of how He works things in concert for your good. No one has a better seat for appreciation of God's love for His spiritually challenged children than the mother of a physically challenged child.

Cherie's story will help you better welcome all the wonders of togetherness. She compassionately describes the challenges of working with disabilities and the unexpected blessings which unfold. Whether you parent in a similar situation or work with physically challenged children, God's promise *to work together* is a sure sign of hope. Hope for you and hope for any and every child in your life. I pray Cherie's story will encourage you to have an open honest conversation with God about your feelings in the face of hope and adversity. You will never be the same.

Cherie's Story

Our story started twenty-five years ago. Though nothing unusual was detected on ultrasounds, and I had a normal pregnancy, our son was born with what the OB-GYN said was a "cyst" on the back of his head, actually measuring the same diameter as his head—22 cm. He was taken immediately for tests to determine what the bulge consisted of. It was brain tissue that had been forced through a crack in his skull and was removed the day of his birth. While waiting for him to come through surgery, my husband, unknown to me, had decided to call him Joshua because our son would be taking us into a different land, one we did not know anything about, full of unexpected trials, heartaches, as well as victories.

Someone special is there.

Joshua had what was called an encephalomeningocele and various bilateral birth defects—eyes crossed, corpus callosum thin, cross-fused kidneys, hernias, and underdevelopment of his frontal lobes, to name a few. During the early years of his life, Joshua had nine surgeries, seven doctors, and various therapists. He was hearing impaired at birth and lost the remaining hearing with spinal meningitis at age one. At birth, we were told he probably would never walk nor be able to pass things from one hand to the other. Developmentally delayed, it took him much longer on his milestones—walking at three years very unstable.

As an infant, Joshua didn't seem "to see me," and the eye surgeon assured us his eyesight was fine. Joshua's countenance was somewhat flat and appeared to be unresponsive to me, except when I held him in a particular chair in the corner of our living room. That was the place, for months, where he would look up past me and smile, coo, and try to talk.

I believed he saw Someone very special there. I realized my little boy had a spirit just like ours, but it was trapped in a body that did not work like ours.

Josh struggled and I struggled.

Having a brain-injured child, I had no idea how much that would truly encompass. He was tight and balled, not opening his hands or touching anything. His brain actually could not interpret the world and sensations around him properly. This started months, years, and even continuing today, training and educating his brain concerning external and internal sensations.

Before he could even crawl, we had to get his body to open his hands to weight bear. That process happened through sitting and scrubbing his hands and body with surgical scrub brushes, then putting him into a huge rice box, then later ice packs, heat packs, slapping, and light touch sequences every day Monday through Friday.

His facial muscles needed work as well as his throat muscles. He had to be trained how to swallow without choking. Our home consisted of standing frames to put weight on his feet in order to grow, benches for balance, chair forms, leg braces—just about anything and everything to help Joshua improve.

Not only struggling with fine motor, gross motor, oral motor, tactile processing, motor planning, tone and strength, balance, sensory issues, Joshua didn't sleep. We remember watching much of the Mid East War while up with Joshua all hours of the night. There were allergies and breathing complications, which required treatments throughout many nights. I would sleep on the floor next to his bed and continue the treatments when he did sleep to stay on schedule.

Not only did Joshua struggle, I struggled. I stayed exhausted. I felt the heavy weight of carrying the sole responsibility when my husband was working. Who is prepared for this? Where is the training manual for all the thousands of decisions that must be made without time to call someone for advice?

I had no outside life of my own; I could not go with friends to lunch, shop with the girls, or even feel comfortable taking a nap. Silence did not mean everything was okay. I had to watch Joshua to know he was crying for help.

I was completely tied to Joshua. I am not complaining, just explaining that life with a physically challenged child was filled with challenges I never anticipated. I would never trade this life for anything else, but it can be lonely. So lonely that your only comfort is to know God is there with you to help you, strengthen you, cry with you, and share those brief incredible joyous moments when your child, like Josh with me, astounds you with his brilliance and humor.

God calls us to be faithful, not successful.

Throughout this journey, God has reminded me of His presence and providence as He would bring alongside the right people to help me at just the right time. God knew I needed Josh; somehow I had been created to be the mother he would need. The lessons learned are precious and priceless, just like Josh. This journey was never just about Josh learning how to live; it was a constant reminder to trust God.

Over the years, I have surprised several moms of handicapped children when I say there are no "birth defects." I believe from the very beginning what my God says, *"We are fearfully and wonderfully made,"* and He has *"known us from the foundation of the world."*

So I take comfort in that and depend totally on God to move Joshua along at His pace and what He has planned for Joshua's life. Even with all the things that went wrong in his body, there is so much that was right. Something my mother told me at the beginning was that God calls us to be faithful, not successful. There would be times after months of doing therapy that I did not see any improvement, but I would continue. That is what we are called to do in every arena of our lives—to be faithful.

God planned and prepared this journey.

Reflecting back, we can see there were no "coincidences." God has been so faithful along the way in our journey with Joshua. First, I recognize my parents whom God blessed me with and their tireless self-sacrifice, love, devotion, and support of our family. My dad had already been involved with the deaf since I was in high school and understood some of the challenges that population and their families face.

There were also therapists who crossed paths with us at just the right time. There was a neurological pediatric physical therapist from Fort Worth, when Joshua was three months old, whose work started the foundation of his moving, crawling, and eventually walking. Joshua would scream as Donna, the PT, would work on him, while other therapists had stopped because "they couldn't do it to him." She was only in our home city for a year, returned to Fort Worth, but we continued to drive and spend weekends with her and her parents, so the work she had started could be completed.

Also, there was an occupational therapist, who trained us on the mouth and facial muscles that enabled Joshua to begin chewing and swallowing appropriately, thus avoiding a feeding tube, which the doctors had mentioned he would need. God directed me to many doctors all over the country who worked with us via phone conversations.

A specific and *huge* piece to Joshua's puzzle was getting to know and working with Dr. Rimland, the founder of The Autism Research Institute and The Autism Society of America. The vitamin mix he developed enabled Joshua to sleep for the first time in his life at three years old. We could hardly believe it! The vitamins calm the neurological system and if Joshua does not get them, he does not sleep—even today.

Dr. Sperry, a pediatric neurologist in Dallas, was the only one willing to take Joshua off Phenobarbital he had been on for possible seizures. Not only professionals, but special people in our church like Paula and Susie have patiently and faithfully interpreted for Joshua at church for many years.

You never stop grieving the loss; however, you gain a better view of the wonder.

These are just a few of the many people God connected us with at critical times. Some of the experiences we had also helped other families with children who just needed one more piece to solve a problem. In reflecting on having a child like Joshua, parents really never stop grieving the loss.

The loss is always there in everyday situations like exclusion from playdates, birthday parties, skating parties, sleepovers, clubs, and sports. As a mom, I cannot wait to get to heaven and see the son I love whole and hear his voice. It keeps me looking, not at this world but at the life to come and continually focusing on God's promises to us.

I often wonder what Joshua really understands. One day, as I was driving home from horse therapy, which Joshua loves, he was making sweet humming sounds and signed to himself, "God is in control." Isn't that what it's really all about? God is in control working all things together for our good.

Desert of Despair

Life will always be full of challenges. Raising children has its own set of tests and trials. If there are additional physical or emotional needs, the endeavor calls for even greater patience and perseverance. As the pressure intensifies, the progress seems slow and the routine never ends. The effort drains you physically, emotionally, and spiritually. There are days where you want to quit. It takes endurance to survive and succeed.

God's Word has a lot to say about the importance of endurance in suffering. The book of Hebrews connects the theme of endurance to the life of faith in God. It describes *endurance* as "the ability to hyper-stand, to keep standing or staying." Word pictures for endurance would include being able to stand immoveable in the midst of rushing water or strong winds or an intense fight.

You feel the pressure of the outside forces, but you remain standing. The pressure does not lessen; you just learn to live with it. Public exclusions, private misunderstandings, and group dynamics all present new pressures. You feel the waves of trouble, but you stay in the middle of the rushing currents in order to accomplish a specific purpose. In a world where society moves down the easiest path driven by the shifting winds of cultural preferences, the faithful mother remains standing in hope, holding to God's promise of future good. "I have set the Lord always before me. Because He is at my right hand, I will not be shaken" (Ps. 16:8).

The worth of any child is precious and priceless. The value of a physically challenged or special needs child is never of any less worth. Not to God. Not to the mother. Not to any of us.

Every child also has a personal promise of divine help and hope. Nurturing that hope requires endurance for both the mother and her child.

There are some core beliefs associated with endurance in hope.

1. God is in control.
2. God will work all things together for good.
3. Willingness to suffer is worth it so that your child can have hope.

Your hope is based on who God is (previous chapters) and what God does (following chapters) and asking the right questions (interlude). The God who promises to work all things together for the good of your child is the One who is in control of all things. The God who put you together with your child is the One who promises that it will be worth it. In the days, months, and years of suffering with your child's sufferings, you can stand immoveable against the hurts because of your hope.

How do we know God's promise of endurance is really true when life takes an unexpected turn? There is no greater example of this than Jesus on the cross where the very worst thing that could ever happen became the greatest good for us. God demonstrated to everyone in heaven, on earth, and in hell that He alone is sovereign, merciful, and good, causing all the imperfect people and bad things to *work together* for His perfect purpose.

> God moves in a mysterious way
> His wonders to perform;
> He plants His footsteps in the sea
> And rides upon the storm.

> Deep in unfathomable mines
> Of never failing skill
> He treasures up His bright designs
> And works His sovereign will.
>
> —"God Moves in a Mysterious Way,"
> William Cowper

God always has your best interests at heart. Life can become confusing and frightening. There will always be much that you do not understand. You do not have to dread the process. It is all designed to teach you that God is in control, just like Joshua signed to his mother. God is in control of everything. In control of everything for your good.

Springs of Hope

And we know God *causes* all *things to work together* for good...

When things happen differently than we dreamed, we all want to ask, "Why?" It would be more beneficial for us to ask, "What now?" God designed us to live by promises, not explanations. The "why" questions turn us to an inward focus on the past; the "what now, Lord" question saves us from the moment and directs our attention to the future. That is where you become part of God's work that is exciting, but in need of endurance. That is where Cherie turned in her new circumstances.

The need for endurance always raises a new set of questions. How hard? How long? God never becomes upset at hearing your questions, but God will also let you listen to how foolish it is to complain to God, question God, or try to correct God.

The Bible gives us examples like Job and Jonah to teach that none of us have the right or the wisdom to question God's motives and purpose regardless of how we feel at the moment. Not Job or Jonah. Not Cherie. Not you.

Expressing how we feel never changes God, but it can begin to change us. God does not think we always need an explanation.

He just wants to help us get to the springs of hope where we can taste their goodness and gaze at their wonder. If God did choose to explain Himself to us, (1) we would not understand it, (2) we would not agree with it, and (3) we would ask Him to change it.

God has a flawless plan for you and your child. Everything God does is wise, right, and good for both of you. God never stops loving and caring for you. God is always with you and always for you. When life does not feel that way, there is something you can and should do. It is precisely what Cherie learned to do.

Look for grace, not an explanation.

God never promised you a life without difficulty and challenges. There will be struggles, suffering, sickness, and sorrow. However, God did promise you waves upon waves of grace and goodness, more numerous than the ocean waves which crash in never-ending repetition upon the beach.

You have a choice to make, just as Cherie faced when her life changed to include loving a physically challenged child. You can sink into your blame-game pit of despair, or you can surf the ocean's endless waves of grace. It is your choice. Learn to look for grace and not an explanation.

Some things that happen in life are bad, even evil. Some things are unplanned, even unwanted. Some things are just different than expected. They all *work together*. In the language of the original New Testament letter to the Romans, the Greek term is literally *fellow worker* or *helper*. Later it developed into the English word *synergy*, when two or more things combine to become something different in order to produce something better. The things in our life which are so difficult and seem to make no sense *work together* in divine synergy to produce something wonderfully good.

Just as God revealed Himself to the first man, Adam, God introduces His sovereign, supreme self to you as your *"fellow worker."* God is Cherie's "fellow worker" in parenting a physically challenged child. In truth, it was God who picked Cherie as the best choice to work with Him in loving Josh. There was no other way for this to work except by divine synergy.

The first and foremost God loves to help you. Each one of us is *fearfully and wonderfully made*. The Creator God wrote the Designer's instructions. He knows how to perfectly connect and interlock all the things in your life in order to cause you the greatest good. If the circumstances call for struggles, suffering, or sorrow, He is right there alongside, working all those things together for good.

#alwayswithyou   *#alwaysforyou*

Go to the Scriptures. See the life stories where God connected all the dots. It is better than any blockbuster movie. God leads His children into crisis and despair. He strips them of all their trinkets, toys, and trivial pursuits. He takes away their spiritual dolls and play clothes. This is grown-up stuff. These stories show you how the world really works. God is in control, causing things to work together for your good. Everything that occurs in your life has a divine design to help you know God more intimately as your caring Heavenly Father.

The better you understand God's love for you, the fewer explanations you will need about your life. God loves you and He knows this circumstance in your life is going to work together for your good…somehow…someway…sometime. The real disability in life is the loss of hope. God is leading you into hope. You can resent God's process like a little child throwing a temper tantrum or you can take your Father's hand and start dancing.

In the Old Testament, the good guy Job suffered without any explanation given to him, yet the Bible tells us why Job suffered as he did (Job 1). God's goodness was on display in the spiritual realm where both God's motives and Job's worship were questioned and accused of being self-serving. God orchestrated the events in Job's life so Job could better know and show God's love. The result was a resounding story of triumph still being told today. God's unselfish goodness cannot be stopped (Job 42:12–17). Job's worship was genuinely heartfelt: "The Lord gives and the Lord takes away. Blessed be the name of the Lord" (Job 1:21).

God designed the circumstances in your life for the purpose of knowing and showing God's love better.

All this suffering was not just about Job. God used Job's life story to teach Job's friends something about God that had become distorted in their view of life and suffering. In times of suffering, they lowered their view of God down to their explanations instead of raising their faith up to what was true about God; His grace is full of sufficiently overabundant goodness. God is using Cherie's story to correct some of our views of God which might have become diminished or distorted by life's circumstances.

God will write the last chapters of your life just as He did for Job, just as He will do for Cherie and Josh. God has all the people, events, and circumstances in your life intertwined into a beautiful tapestry. God connects all the dots. Similar to a child playing with Legos, God puts all the pieces of your life's puzzle together. It is not random or by chance. In fact, it is perfect.

If you met Cherie, her husband, and their beautiful daughter you would think they looked like the perfect family. Attractive, successful, in love with Jesus. Then you see Josh who cannot hear or speak. You shake his hand. You watch the family's sign language, the teaching, the love. In that moment, you see them from God's perspective. Josh makes Cherie's family "perfect."

It reminds me of God's family to which I belong. When you see Jesus, you gaze upon perfection in all its glory. Then God introduces you to the rest of His family which includes you and me. We are all spiritually challenged children born into a world which cannot hear or speak truth, uncomfortable with heavenly things.

With the sign language of love, God positions each one of us for His family portrait and then says to the watching world,

"Perfect." God's love perfects us. This book is my attempt to communicate with you what every spiritually challenged child of God understands but sometimes struggle to convey. I think I will just sign it to myself. "God is in control."

Adversity might threaten to define, defeat, and destroy you, *but God* will use it to develop you. God will highlight your portrait in living colors of faith, hope, and love. God's plan has a purpose, ultimately to do you good by conforming you to the image of His Beloved Son Jesus. God's consequential goal is for your life to become a blessing to those most in need of help and hope. So what does God's plan entail? *All* things. All things? *All* things.

Does God's perfect plan include the imperfect things? Does the promise of *all* things working together for good include the loss of a child? The abandonment by a spouse? The loss of physical abilities? Is it *all-inclusive* in your life's story? The next chapters will test the limits of "all things."

Before you go to the next chapter, thank the Lord for the children in your life. Every child is challenged in some way. Take time to tell them of your love. If possible, go hug them right now. If not, then call, text, e-mail, tweet, Facebook, Skype, write a letter (what is that?), or just go outside and scream at the top of your voice, "I love you! God is in control! Where there is despair, hope! Oh, my soul, *hope!*"

God challenges you, just as He did Cherie, to raise your faith and your hope to where God is, high and lifted up. When you adjust your life to God, you will find what Cherie, Josh, Job, and multitudes of others including our next story have found:

(1) God is bigger and better than you ever imagined. God is always at work coordinating every detail for your greatest good.

(2) Where there is despair, *hope*. You are God's personal project. God will use your life story to help other people find the life-changing springs of hope in the desert of despair.

That is a good plan. That is a great God!

The Right Understanding of Hope

God is always with you and always for you and always working with you to do you the greatest good. Always.

"'For I know the plans I have for you,' declares the Lord, 'plans to prosper you and not to harm you, plans to give you *hope* and a future'" (Jer. 29:11).

Your grace abounds in deepest waters
Your sovereign hand
Will be my guide
Where feet may fail and fear surrounds me
You've never failed and You won't start now
Spirit lead me where my faith is without borders
So I will call upon Your name
And keep my eyes above the waves
When oceans rise
My soul will rest in Your embrace
For I am Yours and You are mine

—"Oceans: Where Feet May Fail," Joel Houston, Matt Crocker, and Salomon Lighthelm

O Lord my God, when I in awesome wonder,
Consider all the worlds Thy hands have made;
I see the stars, I hear the rolling thunder,
Thy power throughout the universe displayed.

Then sings my soul, my Savior God, to Thee,
How great Thou art! How great Thou art!
Then sings my soul, My Savior God, to Thee,
How great Thou art! How great Thou art!

And when I think, that God, His Son not sparing;
Sent Him to die, I scarce can take it in;
That on the cross, my burden gladly bearing,
He bled and died to take away my sin.

When Christ shall come, with shout of acclamation,
And take me home, what joy shall fill my heart.
Then I shall bow, in humble adoration,
And then proclaim, "My God, how great Thou art!"

—"How Great Thou Art," Carl Boberg

5

Mom, Forgetful but Not Forgotten

Amber's Story
Understanding *For Good*

Memory loss is not good, is it? No. Many things that happen in our lives are not good. Some experiences in life are bad, terrible, painful, and downright evil. Some unwanted circumstances are disrupting and disconcerting. We wish we could forget some parts of our lives and other parts we cannot forget even when we try. Then we forget things we want to remember.

Forgetfulness can result from just being distracted, absentminded, or too many things on your mind. You might forget where you placed your cell phone or get rattled searching for your keys. Some days you could not find them if they were attached. Recently I went back into the post office to ask if anyone had turned in some prescription sunglasses. I was slightly embarrassed when the postal worker asked if they might be the ones I was wearing.

At some point in life, forgetfulness creeps in slowly and modifies our memory capability to varying degrees. We might struggle to remember an appointment or fail to buy an item at the grocery store. Other times, forgetfulness storms in suddenly and with great force. It shocks our systems; it troubles our souls. We might begin to forget important things such as directions back to the house or how many pills to take or the names of loved ones. That kind of forgetfulness is feared, not welcomed as good.

Poor memory can affect us neurologically, emotionally, or spiritually. God's Word prepares us for those challenges. Like an effective teacher, it repeats over and over the truths we must engrave on our minds in preparation for the tests in life. The Bible also assures us we will not be forgotten by God even if we do become more forgetful (Isa. 49:15). God also promises He will never forget to *cause all things to work together for good.*

How could dementia turn out good for any person or their loved ones? How could anyone ever believe a brain tumor could turn out for their good? Can God connect the bad things that trigger our forgetfulness to our greater good?

The story of Amber's mom confronts those issues head-on. A sudden diagnosis of a brain tumor played out for her family much like the experiences of families living with a loved one suffering with Alzheimer's or other forms of dementia. Their world changes; little things taken for granted become gigantic obstacles to overcome. Safe places become scary. Routine practices become neglected. Independence becomes impossible. Your loved one might become forgetful or unable to recall who you are or what you have done, but she will never be forgotten by God.

Maybe it is the family that suffers the most in those unwanted circumstances as their hearts ache for their loved one. Dealing with various degrees of dementia can feel like being lost in a desert wilderness for both the patient and the caregivers. Despair is never forgotten. Like any other thought, it has to be replaced with hope. That is Amber's touching story about her mom, now forgetful but never forgotten.

Amber's Story

I want to introduce you to my mom, Chris. She was born and raised in a Christian home by loving parents. She was in Sunday school and church every Sunday morning; that early exposure to Christ resulted in her baptism at the age of eight. At seventeen, she married the love of her life, Randy, when they eloped with the approval of their families.

Their picture-perfect life just got flipped upside down.

At thirty-five, Chris was living what seemed a picture-perfect life. She and Randy had two children, Casey, twelve, and Amber, ten. She was an amazing artist, worked as a sales rep, and ran three miles a day. She was quick-witted, loved to laugh, and enjoyed being surrounded by friends and family. Little did she know her life was about to be flipped upside down.

On a Monday in late summer, she began having severe headaches. After a few miserable days and nights, she broke down and went to her family doctor on Thursday. She assumed he would give her a prescription and send her on her way. The doctor looked into her eyes with that cold sterile instrument and suggested having a CAT scan done. The pressure buildup behind her left eye made him nervous.

The results from the CAT scan showed an abnormality in the center portion of her brain; she was taken immediately to the hospital. The neurosurgeon told her she would need surgery because there was a tumor the size of an orange in her head. He performed the surgery two days later on August 3. A host of family members and nearly fifty church members filled the waiting room; they prayed throughout the six-hour surgery.

My mom spent five days in ICU before she was moved to her own room. For ten days, she was paralyzed on her left side; the doctors were not sure she would ever walk again. She had no memory of anything that was happening. One day, while she was lying in bed, her left thumb moved slightly. Her mother saw the movement; there was a ray of hope that she might not be paralyzed.

Fear can cause you to lose all confidence in yourself.

Chris went into intensive physical therapy. For the first time, she realized she had gone from a capable sales representative with no mental or physical disabilities to a person who had lost all confidence in herself. She had trouble walking a straight line on the floor. Also, as a result of the tumor, she suffered short-term memory loss. She could still remember things that happened years ago, but remembering what she had for lunch was impossible.

Chris was shocked the first time she looked into the mirror after her surgery. She went from having medium-length beautiful brown hair, to having no hair. She burst into tears because she wasn't ready for the "bald lady" look. She felt as if she were an embarrassment to her family. Her amazing husband remained by her side. He would walk through the halls of the hospital with her draped on his arm with a smile so big, people would stare and wonder.

Family, friends, and church members remained faithful throughout the ordeal. When she cried wanting to give up, they urged her on. Their love was a constant encouragement during the ordeal. Finally, good news came; she was released to go home. Then came the bad news. The pathologist's report indicated that the tumor was the kind that could grow back; that meant Chris would have to begin radiation treatments. The hair on her head, now two inches long, was going to fall out! The radiation treatments left her with absolutely no energy. She went from running three miles a day to barely able to walk to bed after treatments.

Love is stronger than fear.

God uses our trials and tribulations as an opportunity to know Him better. After the radiation treatments were completed, Chris went through a series of ups and downs. Her mountaintop experience took place almost one year after her surgery when Chris opened her heart to her Lord and Savior Jesus Christ. God spoke with her as never before. She realized she had not made Him the Lord of her life at age eight. That night, she was baptized at church to demonstrate her new identity and new walk with Jesus for the rest of her days.

Why had God allowed this illness to happen to her? The answer was clear to her family and loved ones. The Lord had given her a second chance to know Him. God often uses adversity in our lives so that we, and those around us, can learn more about Him, His love, and His grace. He uses our trials and tribulations for us to become examples and witnesses for Him.

Adversity is an opportunity to share God's love with others.

Growing up with a mom with short-term memory loss was difficult during my teenage years. I was often jealous of my friends who were so close with their moms. If I shared my heart with her, she would forget what I said. My dad filled in where she couldn't. He was my go-to parent. I went to him for advice, to share good news or bad, or just to talk about the day's events. Anyone would tell you he had the world's biggest heart; I could depend on him for anything.

I grew up watching my dad love my mom unconditionally. He constantly put her needs above his own. He would do things for her expecting absolutely nothing in return. Because he was self-employed and worked from home, he would get up early and work extremely hard to provide for his family, so he could help her throughout the day. When I would get frustrated with her memory, or her physical weaknesses, he would remind me of how blessed we were to have her. No matter what crazy thing came out of her mouth or what accusations she made, he loved her!

After eighteen years of never forgetting to love the woman who could forget almost everything but her love for God and him, my dad passed away of cancer. I lost a part of me that day. Not only did I lose a parent, my brother and I became responsible for our fifty-three-year-old mother who was now disabled and not able to live alone. We moved her into an assisted living center for a short time and later into a nursing home.

As her physical and mental condition has grown worse the past few years, I have fallen more in love with my mom! I may not be able to tell her my deepest secrets or even spend a day shopping together, but I truly treasure her for who she is. I value spending time with her because I know how precious that time is. I have had to learn how to trust in God through the darkest times of my life; it has been a constant struggle.

When Mom had her operation, the surgeons said that most patients in Chris's condition usually live about seven years. Twenty-six year later, God is still using my mom to teach me countless lessons on patience, forgiveness, faithfulness, trust, and hope. I truly believe that God uses our adversity in our lives so that we, and those around us, can learn more about Him, His love, and His grace, so we will show that same compassion and comfort to others.

And we know God causes all things to work together for good for those who love God and are called according to His purpose.

Desert of Despair

What in the world could be "good" about a brain tumor? Chris was vibrant, funny, and artistically talented. She ran on high octane. As my family pulled out of the parking lot following our first visit to the church as their new pastor, she was the last person to tell us good-bye. She came running toward us waving and shouting. I rolled down the car window as she stuck her smiling face inside just to tell us how excited she was about our moving here. Before the week was over, she would be in life-threatening surgery, which turned out to be life changing for her and the family she dearly loved.

Amber is my daughter's best friend. Her mom's life and that of her precious family were flipped upside down that week. Chris's husband, Randy, was one of the kindest and most caring persons I have ever known. The girl he loved and married was much different now, not of her own doing. Her independent, carefree, fun-loving life was suddenly and dramatically altered. She used to plan everything and do everything so her husband's life was made easier by her love. Now Chris was dependent and forgetful. The fact that she did not feel that way made caring for her even more challenging.

Randy taught me much about learning how to love without expecting anything in return. We, husbands, have a tendency to expect payback. We want our acts of love to count, to be stored up in reserve for those days when our wives might not be able to think of one reason to keep us around. I think women often go into marriage with similar thoughts of love being shared on a fifty-fifty basis, and then as time rolls by, their expectations might settle for a ninety-ten exchange. Just give me something in return. Anything. Well, Randy became the role model for every woman's husband wish list.

The opposite of love is not hate; it is selfishness.

The fact that we are all naturally selfish only adds to the desert dryness. The biblical book of James teaches us that every conflict in marriage and other relationships originates from unmet and unrealistic expectations (James 4:1–2). One spouse expects the other to be or do something, often carrying those expectations internally without ever having expressed them to the other person. Eventually the self-interest cannot be suppressed any longer and verbal conflict explodes into the relationship.

Randy learned that it would take unselfishness to truly love Chris. It would take the love of Jesus inside of him being poured out in countless acts of unselfish love for his "forgetful" wife. No one really understood the "challenges" or the "sacrifices" made behind closed doors because Randy never considered his love to be a sacrifice of anything except his selfishness.

"Do nothing out of selfishness, but with humility consider others more important than yourself, and develop the same attitude which Jesus has" (Phil. 2:3–5). An unselfish attitude has to be developed. Learn to give yourself away in love for God and the other person. It takes practice.

God positioned Randy's unselfish love in the center stage spotlight for his buddies to see and emulate. He inspired us all to take our love to a higher level. Any act of loving care for Chris was done solely for love's own reason. That is the way God loves us. Always giving, never demanding returned love.

When Randy did the laundry or cleaned the house, Chris would never remember. She would buy him gifts, hide them, and then not be able to find them. Chris could laugh at her forgetfulness. She did her best to keep up a normal routine, not realizing it was Randy who made that possible by changing his schedule and planning for her care and safety. Chris could remember the story of how they fell in love and the plans they made, but she was unable to remember her husband was dying of cancer. Perhaps that was a blessing!

Springs of Hope

For good...

The preposition *for* introduces a purpose clause. The reason God comes alongside you as your "fellow worker" in life is to make sure your life turns out good. That is the goal guaranteed in His promise.

What do you think about when you hear the word *good*? Happiness? Comfort? Ease? Prosperity? Security? Maybe your idea of *good* would be the life you want, when you want, and the way you want. Those are some of our culturally shaped and molded expectations of the good life. That is certainly the perception presented in the advertising and entertainment media targeted to influence our decision making.

No pains, no problems, no pitfalls. That sounds like the good life most of us want. Anything good should just make life easier and happier. Any product or politician who could back up that promise would be welcomed into our lives, but would God consider it as good?

Throughout the Bible, God's explanation of goodness is *benefit*. That is the meaning of the word used in this promise. Benefit. Eternal benefit, that which is best for your spiritual welfare. Our general use of the word *good* undervalues the enormity of its eternal worth. When God calls something *good*, there is nothing better.

Ultimately, God's "good" is for your conformity to Christ. (Do not miss this.)

God works together all things to enable you to live and love like Jesus. That will be beneficially *good* for you and for those around you. What is the most beneficial thing that could happen to your life? More money, bigger house, better health, longer life? Or living for God's purpose and glory in the way that benefits everyone else? Happiness in life is not about how many things we have, but rather how much of life we enjoy. Chris still enjoyed life.

Chris visited me one day with a letter in her hand. She asked if she could read it to her extended church family. She had written her story, which would have appeared in this chapter had the copies not been lost in the moves and transition. I used to have it posted on my bulletin board. However, her message is still burned into the memories of all who heard her that day.

Chris knew her surgery made life more difficult for her husband and children she wholeheartedly loved. She expressed her gratitude for their love and patience. Typically, Chris had the audience smiling with some in outright laughter as she told of her forgetfully humorous exploits, mostly at Randy's expense. The amusement quickly turned to tears as Chris shared the purpose of her reading the letter she would not have remembered writing. We cried as she wiped away the tears filling her eyes. She knew her life had changed. She recalled the shocking news of her problem, the anxiety of the surgery, and the fear of the life that might follow.

Then Chris shared how thankful she was to God for allowing this to happen in her life.

God had become more real to her. He was bigger and better than she had ever imagined. She was happy, not for the difficulty she was becoming to her family, but for life. Life is precious. This earthly life is fleeting, and we all need to make the most of it while we have time, while we have our health, while we live with or without brain tumors.

Chris said she would continue to forget most things related to short-term memory, but she was so thankful that God remembered forever. God had not forgotten her, and He would not forsake her. She truly believed that however her life would play out, God would cause it to work together for good. Wow! How often do I forget to thank the Lord for His continued goodness to my life? How many of us seem to suffer from our own short-term memory loss of gratitude when some tough circumstances alter our plans? How many of our actions are truly unselfish? And how many times do we question if *all things* really work together for our good and for the good of those around us?

Chris's surgery and survival were miraculous. The follow-up years were joyful and challenging, even more so with Randy's homeward journey to heaven. Randy's life involved showing love to others and conquering his own selfishness. From my perspective, he was at his greatest time of usefulness to the kingdom of God when the Lord finished his life's last earthly chapter. On the other hand, it appeared Chris's life was becoming less active and more dependent on the care of others. Surely, the thought of God taking the wrong one crossed more minds than mine.

Why did Chris stay here with us? She would be so much better off in heaven where her mind and body and heart would be fully and perfectly restored. That would be true for each one of us, yet the Lord has all our days numbered so as to maximize our opportunities to learn unselfish love.

I propose that Chris is here with us for similar reasons as all dementia sufferers or other invalid or partially disabled persons. Her story connects with our story. Their stories connect with your story. This is all about our learning to show and share unselfish love. This is all for our benefit.

Chris and all those like her become target practice where we can refine love just for its own sake. If we are to become more like Jesus Christ during our time spent on earth, then doesn't it reasonably follow that the sovereign God of the universe would orchestrate and allow circumstances to come into our lives where we are provided the opportunity to actually look like Christ, opportunities where we practice denying self in order to demonstrate God's love to others? Those actions might not be returned, appreciated, or even noticed by the person loved, but God notices and nourishes you at His springs of grace, flowing with hope. There in your desert wasteland, love is returned and refreshed, multiplied and overflowing.

Every piece of your life's puzzle is connected to God's purpose for your life. In every circumstance, Jesus lives in you to lead you to others He intends to love through you. What greater good/benefit could there be for you than for your life to turn out to be the greatest good/benefit you could do for others? Every circumstance in your life has the potential to be eternally beneficial to others. Doesn't that sound "good" to you? In all suffering, there is good for you and for those you love. "For I consider that these present sufferings are not worth comparing with the glory (God's goodness) that will be revealed in us" (Rom. 8:17).

The story of Amber's mom is not just about her family suffering with grace and hope; it is actually about the sovereign God of goodness. Brain tumors and forgetfulness do not mean you are forgotten by God or going to miss out on some of His goodness. On the contrary, those "not so good" things from our perspective have been divinely designed and delivered into our lives to maximize the benefit to you and those your life touches. These *all things* are connected and work together for your good.

God considers the circumstances in your life to be eternally beneficial so God calls the end result "good." God causes that present and eternal benefit to happen no matter what the particular piece of the puzzle looks and feels like to you at the time.

Life is hard. Sometimes faith can make it seem harder because it goes against the cultural mind-set. You persevere when you could try to escape; you wait for eternal benefit when you could jettison some of the present suffering; you choose to love when you could just avoid the difficult person altogether.

Trials and troubles are coming. Christians and non-Christians both get cancer, ALS, coronary disease, brain tumors, and dementia. The difference is how they and their caregivers respond to the suffering. It should be a noticeably distinct difference than those without hope. There is hope in God. Some people never see that hope; some forget and some, like Chris, remember to hope in God even when they forget everything else.

The application for each reader is to persevere in hope through the various trials of life. Continue to believe in God's goodness; do not give up; keep going. Walk in faith with God through every circumstance. There is unselfishness to conquer, love to show, and gratitude to give. God truly is bigger and better than we have imagined. Like Chris, let's be thankful in "all things" even when forgetfulness makes life more difficult. Forget the despair; cling to the hope. Good is on its way.

There are reasons to hope even when your picture-perfect life gets flipped upside down. Let me mention three.

1. *God is still in control.* "Why are you in despair, O my soul? Why so downcast? Put your hope in God and praise Him for the help of His Presence" (Ps. 42:5). Who else could or would move heaven and earth on your behalf? Persevere in hope because your God is in sovereign control of all things, causing them to work together for your good.

Chris is still grateful for God's goodness. Perhaps those of us who cannot think of reasons to be thankful are the ones suffering from short- and long-term memory loss.

2. *There are no what-ifs in God's story.* God's plan is perfect. He has taken into account every possibility, every circumstance, every human act, and every act of nature. Your sufferings never happen by accident. In suffering there is no such thing as random chance or bad luck. There is no purposeless misery or heartache.

There are no what-ifs in God's plan. If you try to live in the what-ifs, you are going to end up back in worry and despair, worry over things that you cannot control and despair from placing your hope in temporal things.

The enemy of your soul wants you to play the never-ending what-if game. Learn to play the "what's true" game in order to gain a right perspective. Your emotions will never be right until you fix your mind on the truths of God's Word. Your fear will never be conquered without embracing God's promises of hope.

Learn to embrace as *good* what God embraces as *good*. Eternal benefit is of far greater worth than temporary fleeting benefit. Even the difficult people and the darker circumstances happen in your life as part of the best plan to gain the greatest eternal benefit for you and for those your life touches. There are no what-ifs in the purposes of God. There are no mistakes. There is just a sovereign God who is good to you. Everything He does is wise and right and good.

3. *You will still see good in the future.* Consider the deathbed declaration Joseph made to his brothers whose betrayal led to his abandonment, separation from his family, slavery, and imprisonment in a foreign land where he was misunderstood, misjudged, and mistreated. "You meant it for evil, but God meant it for good" (Gen. 50:20). God

caused everything to work together for Joseph to become the most powerfully influential ruler in the world. God would use him to save his countrymen, the world, as well as his estranged family from starvation. That was good for everyone.

Eternal benefit outweighs any temporal suffering whether it is Joseph's story or Amber's story of her mom. God absolutely guarantees you will see all the good He has promised you. It will take ages and ages of eternity for God to show you the surpassing greatness of His goodness to you (Eph. 2:7), and that will just be the beginning.

There is still future good for Amber and her mother. They wait in hope. Randy already sees how all these things related to the brain tumor worked together; he smiles at what awaits those he loves. God's plan is perfect and His purpose is beneficial, now and in the future. There is nothing to fear except bouts of spiritual dementia which cause lapses in thanksgiving. Hopefully, Amber's story will remind you to thank God for life, even with the parts you seem not to be able to forget.

What about your life? You might still have questions and doubts. Perhaps you are not quite ready to write your story with words of thanksgiving. Do not give up. Focus on who God is, what He has done for you, and all the good He will continue to do for eternity.

Suggestion: There are untold thousands of reasons for you to have gratitude, joy, and hope in the midst of your trials. Write yourself some notes of thanksgiving to be filed away for times of forgetfulness. When and where there is despair, *hope*. The God of hope has not forgotten you. His goodness and mercy will pursue you all the days of your life.

The Right Understanding of Hope

God's greatest "good" is to conform you to express and enjoy the same love Jesus Christ enjoys. That glory comes only through suffering.

"Put your *hope* in the Lord both now and forevermore" (Ps. 131:3; emphasis added).

Bless the Lord O my soul
O my soul, Worship His holy name
Sing like never before
O my soul, I'll worship Your holy name
The sun comes up
It's a new day dawning
It's time to sing Your song again
Whatever may pass and whatever lies before me
Let me be singing when the evening comes
Bless the Lord O my soul
O my soul, Worship His holy name
Sing like never before
O my soul, I'll worship Your holy name
You're rich in love and You're slow to anger
Your name is great and Your heart is kind
For all Your goodness I will keep on singing
Ten thousand reasons for my heart to find
Bless the Lord O my soul
O my soul, Worship his holy name
Sing like never before
O my soul, I'll worship Your holy name
And on that day when my strength is failing
The end draws near and my time has come
Still my soul will sing Your praise unending
Ten thousand years and then forever more
Bless the Lord O my soul
O my soul, Worship His holy name
Sing like never before
O my soul, Worship His holy name

—"Ten Thousand Reasons," Matt Redman

6

When the Worst Happens

Mona's Story
Understanding *All Things or No Things?*

All of life is a stewardship of God's purpose. That includes the gift of pain. Pain packages will arrive in different sizes, shapes, and colors. Hurt and heartache become the common characteristics delivered to the heart's doorstep.

Sometimes the pain is physical, sometimes emotional. It can be sickness, stress, or sorrow. It can come suddenly or slowly; its duration might be short or lengthy, its explanation simple or complicated. One thing is consistently certain; it was not what you ordered.

The context of Romans 8:28 includes the subject of suffering, especially present time suffering. It mentions some of those painful categories like troubles, dangers, distress, despair, trials, and tribulations. I do not believe the verse specifically mentions suffering from flesh-eating bacteria, but like all suffering, it can arrive packaged in sickness, sadness, separation, sorrow, or sleepless nights. The pain of suffering can take you from sadness to the far side of despair.

In the preface of his book, *Faith's Checkbook*, the nineteenth century preacher and author, Charles Haddon Spurgeon, wrote:

> God has given no pledge (promise) which He will not redeem, and encouraged no hope which He will not

> fulfill...I commenced these daily portions when I was wading in the surf of controversy. Since then I have been cast into "waters to swim in," which, but for God's upholding hand, would have proved waters to drown in. I have endured tribulation from many hails. Sharp bodily pain succeeded mental depression, and this was accompanied both by bereavement and affliction in the person of one dear as life. The waters rolled in continually, wave upon wave. I do not mention this to exact sympathy, but simply to let the reader see that I am no dry-land sailor. I have traversed full many a time those oceans which are not Pacific: I know the roll of the billows, and the rush of the winds. Never were the promises of Jehovah so precious to me as at this hour. Some of them I never understood till now; I had not reached the date at which they matured, for I was not myself mature enough to perceive their meaning.

Mona and her family could have written about their familiarity with "the roll of billows and the rush of winds" in the storms of life. For them the tempest came suddenly with sustained force "which, but for God's upholding hand, would have proved waters to drown in." They faced the rough seas and discovered promises of God which had not been fully understood until this season of suffering.

Some suffering is felt from the pain inside us brought on by self-inflicted misery. Some involves pain imposed on us from the outside by others who mess up our lives. Some suffering like in Mona's story seems to sum it all up at its worst.

I cannot explain why bad things happen to good people like Mona. God does not need me to protect Him or to defend His ways. God's plan is far too complex and way too connected to so many lives throughout so many generations that our earthly minds could not comprehend it if it were explained to us.

However, God has given us the simple version of something more glorious than any human mind has ever imagined. The suffering in *all things* will make you live and love like Jesus. God's fulfillment of that promise will benefit you and those around you throughout your eternal enjoyment of God's goodness.

No matter how pain comes and how long it lasts, *all* of it is a stewardship issue. Why? Because all pain, no matter what size, shape, or color, comes with instructions about God's purpose. The crucible of adversity is always for our ultimate good. Some days it does not feel that way; some days it does not look that way. This story is about one of those days.

Mona's Story

It was a scorching-hot August day on the interstate highway as Mona, her son, Adam, and her sister, Linda, made their way home from visiting relatives. When the rear tire blew out, Mona lost control of the vehicle; it left the road and rolled several times before landing upright into a fence.

A paramedic called me, her husband, to report the accident. I drove as fast as I could to the scene where I was informed two ambulances had already left for the hospital trauma center. I called Kim, our daughter, and Mary, Mona's twin sister, to tell them about the accident as I drove to the hospital. It was the hardest drive I have ever made; I could hardly breathe and drive at the same time.

My daughter and I arrived at the emergency room within seconds of each other. When we found out Mona was in critical condition, Kim broke down in the hallway. One of the staff members, who happened to be the chaplain, gathered us around to have prayer as we continued to hold Kim up. We were told Adam had minor injuries, so we were able to see him. He was lying in a neck brace asking, "How is Momma? Is she okay?" He shed tears of love and concern that a child feels for his mother. No one had reported anything to him about her condition. We could only respond that the doctors were still working on her.

We were told at some point she had a laceration close to the right eye that extended to the back of her head. She had suffered several fractured vertebrae and at least six broken ribs. Later, we learned she had bleeding in the brain from the trauma. She was in critical condition but was able to answer questions. Her concern was for the welfare of her son and sister. When Adam was released, we were able to see her. She recognized us and seemed to have her wits about her. Relieved to see her son was okay, she began to smile again in that soft sweet manner descriptive of her life.

From the ER, they moved her to the burn unit ICU because the ICU was full. Kim wanted to spend the night with her and hold her hand, but because of her critical condition, we had to stay in the waiting room that night.

The news got worse.

Mona's condition seemed to improve over the next few days until she had an acute respiratory distress syndrome, and they had to drain fluid out of the chest cavity. On our way to see her after the procedure, she coded, her heart stopped, and we were turned back at the door as the doctors rushed in to resuscitate.

It was at that moment that I said to my children, "Stop, we are not going to be mad at God. We are going to trust Him as your mother would want us to do." We pulled together to pray for Mona's healing, her doctors, and our acceptance of God's will. The nurses brought her back to the ICU, put her on a respirator, and let us go in and see her.

Her decline began to spiral when necrotizing fasciitis, a flesh-eating disease, set in. Her forehead was solid black; they removed 60 percent of her scalp. They continued to remove more and more over the next few days. The decisions got progressively harder to make. They removed her right eye, then the facial skin down to the middle of her cheek; it was a race against the bacteria headed to the brain.

At this point, we decided as a family that we loved her enough to let her go home. We met with the hospital ethical board, and they agreed with our decision. They moved her to a more private room, and we started the process with the entire family gathered around. Our pastor and associate pastor were with us during this heart-rending time. Our God had given us strength; we had heard His "echoes of mercy and His whispers of love" throughout the fourteen days in the hospital. Our church family had been a source of comfort to us.

Kim woke up on August 25, knowing this was the day she would lose her Momma. Our sorrows like sea billows were rolling, but we knew all was well with Mona's soul. We were confident she would go to her eternal home on this day where there would be no more suffering because Mona had given her heart and life to follow Jesus Christ on this earth.

Kim held her mother's hand as she eased from this world to heaven. We all trusted God through the process as we prayed for healing with the assurance God had not failed us because we did not get the answer we wanted. Instead, Mona stepped through the door of death and met her savior Jesus Christ and was made completely whole. The same promise awaits every Christian who has been born of the spirit and washed in His blood. Our family has the blessed assurance we will see her again when it is time for us to go home. Until then, we will live in that hope.

Desert of Despair

All things to work together for good...

There are four lines of thought or belief systems connected to this principle. Either (1) *all* things work together for good or (2) *most* things or (3) *some* things or (4) *no* things. It's all, most, some, or nothing. Those are the only options for Mona's family and for you.

You can pretty much throw out "some things" as any kind of trustworthy philosophy because that leaves everything to a God who controls nothing, not even chance. You can also eliminate "most things" as a viable option because that would mean that God's power can be stopped and His goodness can be diverted by something more powerful. What kind of God is that?

So reality boils down to two options on polar opposites of the spectrum. One choice, "nothing" works together for good because life is just chance, chaos, and confusion. If that is true, then nothing has value or purpose in this world. Suffering has no value or purpose. Pain has no value or purpose. Life has no value or purpose. The future has no value or purpose. Nothing has value.

The other view is for *all things* to work together for good because God is sovereign and has gladly chosen to do you good with all His wisdom and power, even in and through suffering. If that is true, then goodness is guaranteed. Nothing can stop or even hinder God. Which one is it? Nothing or everything?

Now here is the kicker. What you think does not change reality, but reality can change you. It did Mona, Paul, Kim, and Adam. Their collective testimony is unchallengeable. They lived through the worst and still said the correct answer is *all things*.

What would Jesus say? Jesus voluntarily left his home in glory to come down to our fallen world, humbled himself as a man to love, teach, and help us. Yet He was hated, rejected, humiliated, shamed, mocked, beaten, whipped, and killed. What did He experience? All suffering things. All painful things. All bad things by bad people.

However, when mankind, representing and including each of us, made absolutely the worst decision ever in history by rejecting Jesus and crucifying God's Son, God turned that into our greatest good. Now we are forgiven and accepted by God and adopted as His very own children as the result of that suffering.

When everything was on the line and we made the wrong choices and did the wrong things, God still caused it *all* to work together for our greatest good. In the very worst-case scenario, God brought about the very best thing that could ever happen to us. So that is our hope!

All things. God wants you to know this is true at all times in every circumstance. The reality is not most things or some things or no things; it is all things including the most painful struggles and suffering. God connects all the dots and brings together all the plots of your life story. He wraps up the loose ends. God is so big and His loving arms are so wide that He can wrap His goodness around all things including difficult people and despairing circumstances. God's love not only survives in the desert of despair, it thrives there.

There are many things we do not know. We do not know why babies die or families fall apart or children are deaf or loved ones have brain tumors or a mother suffers from flesh-eating bacteria. But we do know God has not forgotten us or stopped loving us nor will He ever be hindered from working all those things together for our greatest eternal benefit.

The worst thing God will ever do to you is drive you to Himself to do you greater good.

Do you believe that reality? Mona's family thought they believed Romans 8:28 until the big test came. Now their hope would have to overcome the deteriorating circumstances. It's one thing to have this wonderful promise marked in your bible with the ability to recite it in the emergency waiting room, but it does not become real without your heart being placed in a humanly helpless and hopeless situation.

"Hope itself is like a star—not to be seen in the sunshine of prosperity, and only to be discovered in the night of adversity. How can you know you have faith unless that faith is exercised?" That is the way the preacher and prolific writer from the past, Charles Spurgeon, described the process.

Could you exercise faith if you received the news that your spouse had been in a car accident? What about learning she is in critical condition? Would hope become a shining star in your night of adversity if her heart stopped? Would you still believe in God's goodness if she began to show evidences of pain and disfigurement from flesh-eating bacteria? Would your confidence in God's faithfulness grow stronger while her skin color turned increasingly darker as more skin died and decayed? My stomach gets sick even thinking about the nightmare that became part of Mona's life and her family's struggle with her last earthly days, days no one could ever have foreseen.

Mona's faith was probably the strongest. Her only concern was for her family. She believed in God's care for her, a belief shared by her husband and two children. Mona prayed for them as they prayed for her. When Mona had to be sedated to live with the pain of the ugly bacteria, her family worked through the horrific tragedy to find their faith firmly anchored to the God of hope.

Was it easy? No. Do not assume this brief summary implies that. They are human and the human heart reacts traumatically to pain, even more so when it is your loved one's pain. Silent screams of protest rage in the heart. Questions abound. Answers are few if any. Why? No one knows. How did this happen? A tire blowout, car wreck, ambulance ride, surgery, ICU? Those things happen. No one wants to get that kind of news, but how does that end up as a story about flesh-eating bacteria? Contamination somewhere, certainly, but what are the odds? And why Mona?

Mona could surely be included in the top echelon of the sweetest, kindest, most soft-spoken godly women who have journeyed through this worldly wilderness. She was the helpmate to her husband as she nurtured her family and cared for others. So why was her life taken so early and why so horrifically? There are no answers for that, so faith looks for grace and not explanations.

Please do not think that this story of faith in trying circumstances was as simple as a prayer away. That would be a mistake. In my many years as a pastor, I have witnessed too many traumatic tragedies. I have cried and prayed with numerous families engulfed in crisis, sat in countless emergency waiting rooms, wept uncontrollably in the hospital chapel, and offered physical, emotional, and spiritual comfort to hurting hearts devastated by sudden events which would redirect the course of their lives.

However, I have never been as overwhelmed with anything in someone else's family as with Mona's sudden suffering. It hurt to watch a husband mourn the loss of his wife, to observe children grieve at the loss of their mother, and see siblings weep for the loss of their sister. But the greater sorrow was watching Mona in her loss of earthly life as it moved from the loss of her abilities to the loss of her identity. It was traumatic beyond words.

Springs of Hope

"The Lord's mercy often rides to the door of our heart upon the black horse of affliction" (another Spurgeon quote). *And we know God causes* all things (or no things?) *to work together for good to those who love Him and are called according to His purpose.*

This was a fearful nightmare coming to life, and yet, I have never seen the presence of God's peace and hope more real than in the midst of Mona's family during those trying days of unspeakable sorrow. I saw the brightness of the Star of Hope shining in the blackness of adversity. Even though this desert wilderness was unchartered, the springs of grace were in full view. Hope was everywhere.

Again, do not misunderstand what I want to convey; I have witnessed God's power and love with many families over the years. This does not take away from their stories or its significance. I, too, have personally experienced God's sustaining grace and future hope when there was no human help, explanation, or prospect of anything good on the horizon. Certainly those times are more significantly precious to my life's story as I embrace the apostle Paul's dying testimony in 2 Timothy 4 as my own: *Surely, the Lord has stood with me in all the trying times both past and present, and I am confident He will guide me safely home in the future.*

However, because of the flesh-eating bacteria, Mona's story became far different from anything I had known. I know how Jesus touched lepers whose skin was rotting away and their limbs falling off. I am certainly not Jesus, but I know Jesus lives in me and leads me to others like Mona and her family for the purpose of reminding them of His presence and love in the midst of their journey through the desert wilderness. This was not a spiritual fairy tale or a Guidepost devotional; this was real-life drama.

So it was not the horror or even the fear of touching her that dominated my feelings in this particular family crisis. Although feared by the masses, contamination with flesh-eating bacteria is only experienced by an extremely small percentage of people, but Mona was one of those people. The prospects are usually terminal. I saw the anguish on the faces of the family, felt the pain in their hearts, and listened to the doubts, questions, fears, anger, and the what-if discussions shared back and forth.

I cared about Mona, but I also shuddered to think about the possibility of my wife being in this frightening scenario. I cringed inside as outwardly my head slowly nodded in disbelief. The physicians' reports would just get worse and then much worse. The decisions went from difficult to impossible, how much skin to cut away to save her versus how much surgery would result in more disfigurement than with what she would want to live.

But Mona's house was built on solid rock and not sinking sand. When this terrible storm came, her household of faith stood strong. And oh, how strong they did stand! Through it all came a demonstration of family confidence in the God of the Romans 8:28 promise which defied the devastating circumstances. The confident faith did not come easily, but it was genuine and it was powerful.

The transforming power of God's promise was on full display. The worse the news, the greater the faith in acceptance of God's will. More tears meant more prayers. More anxiety would suddenly feel like more peace. Paul battled in private so he could be a rock for the family in public. Young Adam would transform from a momma's boy to his mother's warrior.

Kim probably demonstrated the most radical change. I really did not know all that was going on in her life during those years, but it seemed as though she was just going through the spiritual motions, if not actually questioning her family's faith and childhood training. The news of her mother's critical condition from the car wreck sent her into an uncontrollable, if not hysterical, sobbing tailspin. She questioned everything, including the reality of what happened, the doctors' decisions, and why God would allow it. Her understandable questions were spoken without anyone's understandable answers.

Seemingly out of nowhere but heaven, Kim became the solid and sure foundation of the entire family. Her mother had demonstrated how to build a life with Jesus as the cornerstone. Suddenly, Kim had the blueprint fully memorized and beautifully constructed. Her heart was strengthened, her face radiant, her words encouraging. Her love grew, her faith soared, her hope leaped past the medical discussions and family questions. She knew what to ask, what to say, what to do, and what to believe when everything else looked so horribly bad.

I sat in awe of God. I held Kim's hand that once trembled, now firm and assuring. I heard her prayers, earlier full of anguish, now overflowing with gratitude. I saw her face, previously obliviously isolated from everything going on around her but now engaged in the comfort and encouragement of others in need. I saw Hope, right there in the midst of despair.

The hardest times became times of true worship, more so than any church-going experience. What can I say? You would have had to have been there, but then I would not wish that or anything like it on anyone. But God did. Why? I do not know why except for what God has already told us.

God knows what He is doing. He is the God who causes all things to work together for good. All things! Car wreck? All things! Surgery? All things! Code blue? All things! Flesh-eating bacteria? All things! Death? All things! How do you find hope in all things, especially the surprise packages of pain?

I do not have answers for all your questions, but I do have a biblical principle sufficient for all the chapters in your life's story.

You find God's will for your life in God's Word.

I was taught this principle by my parents, and it guided me from childhood through my college years until I was blessed to sit under the preaching of Tom Elliff who shared his life message through this statement passed on to him by Preacher Hallock and others.

The will of God is revealed by the Spirit of God through the Word of God.

God's will is for you to have hope—the confident expectation that you will experience all the goodness God has promised… somehow…someway…sometime. Even here. Even now. Even this. And where do you find that hope? You find it in God's Word.

Mona faced death with that hope. Her family continues to live in that hope. *All things* turn out for our good. That will be true for you. I do not have an explanation or a road map, just a promise. God cannot and will not lie. He rejoices to do you good (Jer. 32:41).

You will find the hope you need in the Word of God. Read it. Cling to it. Saturate your life with it, and when your personal pain package arrives marked all things, God's Word will guard you through the wilderness desert of despair and guide you to the springs of grace flowing with fresh hope.

Your pain package will most likely be unwanted; it will most certainly be unexpected. It will become part of your life's story, probably the best chapter. What are you going to do with it?

Open it with God's Word. Embrace it. Be a good steward of it. Where there is despair, *hope*. Your story might not be told to thousands here on earth, but it will touch somebody's life while Mona and countless multitudes set heaven ablaze with rejoicing at the faithfulness of God's goodness to you.

All of life is a stewardship. There is only one way to learn good stewardship of *all things*. It starts with a pain package. When handled properly, it opens up into a beautiful gift beyond imagination.

The Right Understanding of Hope

God's promise of hope covers "all things."

The death and resurrection of Jesus Christ proved that when everything was on the line and we made the wrong choices and did the wrong things, God still caused *all things* to work together for our greatest good.

"For everything that was written in the past was written to teach us, so that through the endurance taught in the Scriptures and the encouragement they provide, we might have *hope*" (Rom. 15:4; emphasis added).

When peace, like a river, attendeth my way,
When sorrows like sea billows roll;
Whatever my lot, Thou hast taught me to say,
It is well, it is well with my soul.

It is well with my soul,
It is well, it is well with my soul.

My sin—oh, the bliss of this glorious thought!
My sin, not in part but the whole,
Is nailed to the cross, and I bear it no more,
Praise the Lord, praise the Lord, O my soul!

And Lord, haste the day when my faith shall be sight,
The clouds be rolled back as a scroll;
The trump shall resound, and the Lord shall descend,
Even so, it is well with my soul.

—"It Is Well with My Soul,"
Horatio Spafford

Our God, You reign forever
Our hope, our strong deliverer

You are the everlasting God
The everlasting God
You do not faint
You won't grow weary

You're the defender of the weak
You comfort those in need
You lift us up on wings like eagles

Strength will rise as we wait upon the Lord
Wait upon the Lord, we will wait upon the Lord
Strength will rise as we wait upon the Lord
Wait upon the Lord, we will wait upon the Lord

The Lord is the everlasting God
The Creator of all the earth
He never grows weak or weary
No one can imagine the depths of His understanding

He gives power to the weak and strength to the powerless
Even youths will become weak and tired
And young men will fall in exhaustion
But those who trust in the Lord will find new strength

They'll soar high on wings like eagles
They'll run and not grow weary
They'll walk and not faint

—"Everlasting God,"
Brenton Brown and Ken Riley

7

Our Pregnant, Unwed Daughter

Carol Ann's Story
Understanding *All Things or Some Things?*

How big is your hope? Is it as big as your God who promises to cause all things to work together for good? All things? Does that include unwed pregnancies? Does the phrase *all things* encompass the consequences of our sinful acts, or are we left alone to fend for ourselves when we mess up? The opposite of hope is despair. If we are to have any hope at all, much less a real lasting hope, then we must believe the extreme span of God's far-reaching goodness.

God has wrapped His goodness around all our suffering and all our sins, all our choices and all our circumstances.

There is hope even in the midst of despair. When God says, "*All things,*" He means *all things*. Not all things are good. God never said they were. Some things are bad. Some bad things we bring on ourselves by stupid or sinful choices. Some bad things are inflicted upon us by others while some bad things are experienced because we live in a bad world messed up by mankind's sinful self-centered ways. Even then, bad things are inclusive in *all things*. God's umbrella of protection, love, and mercy completely covers us no matter what happens to us or inside us.

A love that continues through *all things* is an awesome love. God's steadfast, long-suffering love never lessens when we make senseless mistakes. It never wavers in the face of our intentional sinfulness. It never takes a leave of absence when it encounters problematic people or circumstances. Carol Ann's story will remind you of the greatness and perseverance of God's love when the *all things* in life move beyond your control. She opens up the window of her heart so you can see hope for you and yours.

The caravan of despair can show up at your heart's door unannounced. It might arrive in a note, a phone call, or a knock on the door. Discouragement and even desperation can move in quickly. The anguish pierces down into your bones; fear shakes every fiber of your being. It becomes harder to hope than to drift into despair. What happens when you hear news that changes your life and more importantly, the life of your loved ones? How do you reconcile hope in God with the harsh realities of life?

It is difficult to feel any hope when your soul sits in the shadows of a joyless night. It is almost impossible to see any signs of hope while staring into the emptiness of a gaping abyss. Then someone hands you a book entitled *Where There Is Despair, Hope*. Really? Are you kidding?

Carol Ann's story is full of hope. There were moments when she did not feel any touch of hope sitting beside her or see some vehicle of hope pulling into the driveway. She sat and read a note that would change her life. Many of you readers have read or written or said those same words, "Mom, I am pregnant."

For some period of time, maybe a brief moment or maybe a long nine months, you sat in shock at the change coming into your life. You needed to gather yourself emotionally and spiritually. You did not know what to say or what to do. Most likely, the concept of hope probably did not cross your mind. At least not at first.

This is a chapter about how God really does include *all things* into His promise of good. When do you really need hope? Isn't it in the very moment you feel most hopeless? That is why Carol Ann's story is so appropriate; God planned to share her hope with others in need of that same hope. Today He did; she left you a note.

Carol Ann's Story

When I was twenty-five years old, God gloriously saved me. He filled me with Himself so that I was turned upside down and inside out. Soon after, I began to desire and pray for a baby. When I was twenty-seven years old, my husband and I had a beautiful daughter. When I say "beautiful," I mean *beautiful*! Her physical beauty was the first thing people would comment about when they saw her. From day one, my prayer for her has been, "Lord, make her as beautiful on the inside as she is on the outside." The Lord has graciously "above and beyond" answered that prayer, but there were some difficult roads to travel first.

There was news no parent is ready to hear. "Dear Mom and Dad, I am pregnant, and I don't know what I am going to do. I do know that I want to keep my baby." That's what the note that we found on our stairs said. And thus began a desert place in our lives. This is not the way I had dreamed I would hear about the coming of my first grandchild. My main goal in rearing my children was always to lead them to the Lord. Both our daughter and our son had sweet spirits and seemed determined to follow God.

As our daughter entered high school, however, she was determined to follow her own ways. The only way to describe the result of this rebellion is that "all hell broke loose" in our home. My husband, our son, and I were brokenhearted and cried out from the depths of our souls to God for help. Surely there were a million tears shed as this war only accelerated through the following four years. Lord, how could this be happening in a home that was devoted to You? Are You listening? Don't You care? Where are You in all of this?

God gave new hope to a suffering heart. Each day was difficult and terrifying. Only grasping for the Lord in prayer, resting in the love and encouragement of Christian friends, and abiding in God's Word saw us through.

"For I know the plans I have for you, declares the Lord, plans to prosper you and not to harm you, plans to give you hope and a future" (Jer. 29:11).

> And we rejoice in the glory of God. Not only so, but we also rejoice in our sufferings, because we know that suffering produces perseverance (endurance), perseverance, character; and character, hope. And hope does not disappoint us, because God has poured out His love into our hearts by the Holy Spirit, whom He has given us. (Rom. 5:4–5)

"For our light and momentary troubles are achieving for us an eternal glory that far outweighs them all. So we fix our eyes not on what is seen, but on what is unseen. For what is seen is temporary, but what is unseen is eternal" (2 Cor. 4:17–18).

These are only a few scriptures that were life to our suffering hearts. Nine months later, our grandson was born. How could we love this child so much? How could our hearts be so wrapped around this precious boy? What a wonder You have performed, oh God! The joy our grandson has brought into our lives has been unspeakable!

Our beautiful daughter now has a beautiful heart and soul to go with her lovely face. She has been a devoted mother for over twenty years now. She is happily married, teaches Christian education, has two more children, and is a Christ-admirer herself.

Have our paths been easy and smooth? No. They have been grueling and rough. We only wish we had gone through this with more joy.

God, I learned where You were in all of this. You were right with us, ruling, reigning, and overruling. We only wish we had trusted You more with our futures as we walked this journey. Thank You for putting us on our faces before Your throne. Thank You for tearing away layers and layers of pride. Only Your springs of grace enabled us to put one step in front of another. Only Your deep well brought us peace. You showed us that Your plans are not ours; that Your plans are lofty, far-reaching, and everlasting while ours are often shortsighted.

You taught us *all things* work together for good because of You.

Desert of Despair

The news of any grandchild is precious and priceless. For Carol Ann, the arrival and subsequent years have been nothing short of special. Her grandson and his mother are loved beyond measure. However, the start of the journey was not easy.

The daughter's note was devastating. Shocked she was carrying a child, she was too scared to tell anyone and horrified by the likely reactions. She did not know what to do or where to go for help. Her parents would be upset and hurt; she suspected they would all face the humiliation of others' judgment. She could not face their disappointment, so she decided to leave her message on the stairs and wait for its reply.

Embarrassed. Ashamed. Guilty. Disbelief. This pregnancy changed her dreams about the future and shattered her parents' visions for her happiness. She had looked for love and acceptance where many have gone before. She made wrong choices and would now have to live with the consequences. Abortion was not an option for her, and neither was hiding the news from her unsuspecting parents.

Her eyes were filled with tears; her heart pounded like thunder; her hands trembled as she wrote the note. She was alone except for this little speck of life growing in her body. Adrift in a sea of unchartered waters yet grounded with the belief that all life is sacred, this teenage girl was determined to take on the shame and the struggle to bring an unexpected child into the world. He would be held and nurtured by a mother who loved him. This was not his fault, and this was not his shame.

Unwed pregnancies are not rare. This is not an isolated story far beyond our concept. Almost every family has been touched by its effects and many more only exempt because the sexual expressions outside of marriage did not result in the conception of a child. No one has the right to judge her any more than the religious leaders had the right to judge the woman brought to Jesus because she had been caught in adultery.

Unwed pregnancy still carries a social stigma, at least in some religious circles. Carol Ann's daughter would face condemnation by some who should have been first to forgive, rejection by some with platforms built on acceptance, and alienation from many who called themselves friends. Ironically, her plight would be whispered by those with the biggest mouths.

Stunned. Shunned. Sensitive. Those are words I would use to characterize my first encounter with the two parents I would soon grow to cherish as dear friends. They put on a good face, smiling and cordial as we were introduced. I did not know of their present struggles, but the hurt was too much to hide.

Stunned by the message revealed in their daughter's note, they felt shunned by some they trusted the most. They were sensitive, very sensitive not just to the imagined whispers of disapproval but sensitive to God and their need for His mercy and wisdom.

Carol Ann and her husband possess two of the more tender hearts I have ever known. They seem always ready to help and serve. They care about others and would do almost anything to ease someone's burden but their own burden broke them.

Doing the right and loving thing does not make life easier; sometimes it becomes harder. Carol Ann wrote about the crushed dreams and seemingly unanswered prayers. Her daughter had been raised right. She was greatly loved and patiently guided. She had been taught and encouraged to appreciate the beauty of godliness.

This situation was not the parents' fault, but it certainly felt that way. They were not only hurt by their daughter; they would hurt even more for her. The more they hurt, the more their love for their daughter grew. Together they would get through this. They would get down on their knees together before God and stand upright together before the rest of the world.

God forgives and so do godly parents. It might take parents longer to get there, but when their mind clears from the shock and grief, the heart will see to it. The words will change from hurt to hope. They did for Carol Ann and her husband. Love overlooks a multitude of sins. That guiding principle was not forged in some self-help parenting book but written in the Holy Book by the eternal God of everlasting love.

If you have been in this situation, you understand the feelings involved. Somehow, this circumstance makes you feel like rotten parents who failed miserably as role models. You battle worry and fear and anxiety as you pray for your daughter's welfare and that of your grandchild. You cringe at the prospects of telling your family and friends. It all feels so embarrassing and shameful.

The enemy accuser of your soul bombards your mind with thoughts that this is God's punishment for your past sins. There are accusations that you and your child do not match up to those "perfect" families all around you in the neighborhood and church. The devil torments your mind with guilt and shame with suggestions this is beyond God's willingness to forgive, but the accuser has it all wrong!

God never turns His back on His children; He is always involved for their good. That is a life lesson all parents should imitate as the parents in this story did.

Be willing to settle the issue with God. The pregnancy is not the problem. Neither is that child in the womb. Be honest with God and radically reorient your whole life under His lordship. Whether it be good or adversity, let God take care of the details. In spite of wayward actions, God takes full responsibility for what goes on in the lives of His children.

This was a desert place for Carol Ann's family. Maybe you have been there too or perhaps you have just arrived; the swirling dust may not have even settled. What do you do? How do you go on? How do you mend the broken heart of your daughter when your own heart is broken beyond description?

Perhaps you are traveling down the same path as Carol Ann's daughter; come to Jesus, run back to Jesus. You will discover what she found; there is no condemnation. You will find forgiveness, acceptance, love, and hope. Please do not abort your baby. Give your child life in your care or the care of loving adoptive parents. Let God's love lead you to the best decision for your child.

If you have already experienced an abortion, there is still a loving God ready to take you in His arms. You may or may not be ready to share that chapter of your story, but you do not have to carry the guilt or nagging hurt any longer. Jesus died on the cross to separate your sins from you as far as the east is from the west and to bury your guilt in the depths of the sea, never to be held against you. The God of forgiveness specializes in weaving our misery and mess and mistakes into a beautiful tapestry of His goodness. Run into His loving arms and start a new chapter in life, a chapter free from past guilt, one written with the message of God's forgiveness. Forgiveness powerful enough to reunite you in heaven with the child you conceived.

> "Come now, let us settle the matter," says the Lord. "Though your sins are like scarlet, they shall be as white as snow; though they are red as crimson, they shall be like wool. If you are willing and obedient, you will experience good." (Isa. 1:18–19)

This is a journey, a journey through a desert wilderness. The way is unclear, the heart is unprepared, but one thing is sure—you cannot go back. The path is not easy, but it is worth traveling. Carol Ann and her daughter can help you. They have been there with their mouths and hearts full of the desert dryness, but God led them to the oasis of grace. The flowing fountain is free and unlimited for anyone who is thirsty. It was life-sustaining to them and will be for you. They found hope there. You can too.

Springs of Hope

And we know God causes all things (or just some things?) *to work together for good to those who love Him and are called according to His purpose.*

God has wrapped His goodness around all your sufferings and all your sins, all your choices and all your circumstances. That is worth repeating in this story as well as yours. There are not *some things* that make God's promises untrue or ineffective.

Suffering can be a consequence of sinful actions, but not all suffering is self-inflicted. Parents might not be responsible for their child's actions, but they can still suffer for them and with them. Likewise, a child might suffer for the parent's choices, yet it is not the child's fault. Sometimes suffering is no one's fault, but however it comes and whatever pain it entails, it has a divinely designed duration and purpose. Great hearts are made with great suffering.

Hope shines brightest in the darkness of despair. In the context of the same biblical chapter of God's promise of good in Romans 8:28, there are some very important accounting principles regarding suffering and hope. You do not need a business degree to apply them to your situation.

The first spiritual accounting principle regarding your suffering is found in the first verse (Rom. 8:1). Your suffering comes with no condemnation from God. Your suffering is not punishment. Your sin counts, but it does not count against you if you trust Jesus. Your sin is not against God's law, but against God's love. Sexual experience outside of marriage is not only wrong; it is not good for you. For your own good and the good of your future marriage and children, please do not do it; stop doing it. No condemnation is not a free license to violate God's love.

God hurts over our sinfulness as parents hurt for their wayward child, only worse. God's love for the sinful child is also similar to a parent's but infinitely greater, and so is God's instantaneous and complete forgiveness. How can we be sure of that? "God demonstrated His love to us when Jesus died for us while we were still sinners" (Rom. 5:8). God does not condemn you. Anyone else who would condemn you is just wrong, sinfully wrong.

There is no condemnation for our sins, but there are still consequences. Sometimes the consequence is private guilt, and sometimes it is public responsibility with lifelong consequences, like raising a child; it will take God's help but there is no condemnation branded on your forehead for all to see. God's love covers any and all our sins. Learn this and love God enough to change.

How do you change? God has already changed you. Something new inside of you started when you trusted Jesus to take away your sin. He gave you a new life, growing inside of you like a baby in the mother's womb. As you focus on the spiritual truths of God's unconditional, unlimited, unending love for you, it changes you (Rom. 8:5). God's love is powerful enough to change you. Always take that into account.

The next accounting principle related to this magnificent promise of hope in the midst of suffering can be found in Romans 8:17–18. Those who follow Jesus are now counted *as children of God and heirs* of God and all His goodness. God adopts some not-so-good children and makes them His very own. Like every child conceived out of wedlock, we were conceived in our own sin but given new life, fully and forever accepted in the everlasting love of God.

That changes everything. *Consider that the present sufferings are not worthy to be compared to the future glory.* The word *consider* is an accounting term meaning to calculate something. Do the spiritual math. Look at your problems from God's perspective. Suffering is light and temporal. Glory is weighty and eternal. God has never failed anyone. God has never shortchanged anyone. No one in heaven wishes His earthly plan for their lives had been different.

Present realities must be seen in light of the future. Every mother embraces that same truth during childbirth. The present sufferings are not worth being compared to the wonderful joy of holding your baby. We live in a world seeking instantaneous gratification. Whether it is Starbucks coffee or premarital sex, the desire does not want to wait. In fact, this culture tells you it is foolish for you to wait to make your own coffee or wait for marriage to have sex. But that is not reality; if you want the glory, you have to wait, and waiting can sometimes feel like suffering.

The suffering of an unwed pregnancy can be difficult, but it is not worthy to be compared to the goodness of God revealed in that coming child. Ask Carol Ann and ask her daughter. Was the shame and suffering worth it? Their eyes will sparkle as their faces break out with the biggest smiles. Ask Carol Ann's husband. That boy is the joy of his life.

Carol Ann shared this verse of hope, one of many which sustained her and her daughter in the darkest moments.

"Suffering produces perseverance, and perseverance produces character, and character produces hope" (Rom. 5:3–4).

God transforms all our suffering into strength of character and then into greater hope. Let's evaluate this hope based on the accounting principles just presented. Most likely, we would place suffering in the negative column. Take a moment to consider…to do the spiritual math.

1. The important words in this description of God's purpose begin with *suffering*, which refers to crushing pressure, being burdened down from severe stress, or to break with trials, tribulations, or troubles. That certainly sounds negative. Suffering comes from the pressures and stress of life, but they have a purpose. Actually, suffering is an invest-

ment. Suffering *produces* something...The common verb means to bring about, to work something out. Suffering squeezes you until it *produces* what God knows is inside you. And what does God intend to bring out of you? Some very positive (good/beneficial) things.

2. Suffering leads to *perseverance*. This word describes the *endurance* needed to bear up under stressful circumstances. You have to stay under the pressure in order for suffering to accomplish its purpose, which is for God to showcase the *perseverance* He built inside of you. God gave you the ability to endure in love regardless of the family crisis or social pressure. That becomes a positive spiritual asset.

3. Perseverance produces *character*. This word refers to something that has passed the test and been proven to be true. The pain of suffering builds Christlike character. There is no other method, no bypass, and no exception. Conformity to Christ is the ultimate goal. *Proven character* is a lasting attribute worth far more than silver or gold.

4. Living and loving like Jesus promotes *hope*, the confident expectation of experiencing all the good God has promised to those who love Him. What is hope worth? Ask the hopeless. Hope is not a diminishing commodity; neither is it subject to stock market volatility. Carol Ann had hope, the hope shared by her husband and daughter. That same hope is available to you.

When you get squeezed, what is on the inside comes out. If you squeeze an orange, you get orange juice; a squeezed tube of toothpaste produces toothpaste. The inside substance becomes visible because of outside pressure. Perhaps you have said or heard someone recovering from an outburst of rage comment, "Sorry. I lost my temper." No, they did not lose their temper; they found it. What is on the inside always comes out under the weight of outside pressure.

When you get the news you did not want or expect, you can grumble and complain, criticize and blame. Show those feelings; blame others, blame God. You can express your disapproval of the unpleasant circumstances or the difficult persons with rage or retreat. You can choose to withdraw into despair or give in to embarrassment, anger, bitterness, even resentment for the present situation. A squeezed life can project a lack of joy, a shortage of love, an absence of hope; or it can exude an overflow of those precious attributes of perseverance, proven character, and hope. Which will be displayed in your life when the stressful situation intensifies? That totally depends upon what is inside when the external pressure is applied.

The unexpected news of an unwed pregnancy will certainly squeeze your life. The main issue now is not what happened, but how you will respond. There is no time to rush to the religious bookstore and stock up on Christlike character. This is the time when the world sees whether Jesus is really inside you or whether your life is just an empty shell with lots of spiritual pictures, placards, and music. God already knows what is inside of you; the pressure reveals the truth to you and others. If Christ is inside of you, then the squeeze brings out the fragrance of Christ's love and the sweet aroma of hope.

Christlike character is more important than temporary relief from suffering. Suffering squeezes our hope, but it also produces endurance which builds character with more hope. That is a very wise and good blueprint for life. Carol Ann and her daughter embraced the process and instead of resistance or resignation, they faced the challenge to their faith. The end result was an even greater opportunity to live and love like Jesus.

Carol Ann shared this part of her story of hope to help someone like you get through the chapter of your life with more joy. Possibly, it will strengthen you to help some other young lady struggling with the consequences and circumstances of her choices. She could benefit from a reminder that she is not alone. She needs to know she is loved and forgiven. She needs to understand there is hope.

Where there is despair, there is hope, really big hope as big as our God!

The Right Understanding of Hope

There is no person and no circumstance beyond the reach of God's goodness. In *all things*, Christlike character is far more important than temporary relief from suffering.

> We boast in the *hope* of the glory of God. Not only so, but we also glory in our sufferings, because we know that suffering produces perseverance; perseverance, character; and character, *hope*.
>
> And *hope* will never humiliate or embarrass us, because God's love has been poured out into our hearts through the Holy Spirit, who has been given to us. (Rom. 5:2–5)

I will extol Thee, Oh God my king
Over all His works, Of which I am truly one
His mercy hovers like a cloud Never raining dry
Sustain me when I fall
Lift me up when I'm bowed down
You are the water never failing to satisfy
You are right in all Your ways
And yet You are kind in all You do
I cried and You saved me
Loving-kindness keeps me
I say the Lord is great, So great, let me search
And never discover how great
As long as Your rule endures, I admire Thee
I admire Thee

—"145 (The Song of a God-Admirer),"
Myles Roberts,
The Critics

8

My Sister's ALS
Love Outside Your Circle

Renee's Story
Understanding *Those Who Love God and Live for God's Purpose*

You sit in the doctor's office while you watch the minutes pass. He has completed all tests and is ready to give you the final diagnosis. He speaks professionally but compassionately when he says you have a terminal illness with no cure. Four months, two years, four years left to live. The room begins to blur as tears build up; sounds are muffled as your brain kicks into denial of what you have just heard. A bomb has been set; the ticking commences; it will detonate on a given day at a given hour. Denial moves to fear and then panic. Every minute is counting. You don't have long left on this earth. You thought you were in control of your life. Not so. Days pass as you battle the anxiety. You realize you cannot live this way paralyzed by fear. You lift up your eyes to your only source of strength and cry out to God. How do I retreat to the green pastures? How do I find the still waters of your peace? The words of a very old hymn come to you. "I come to the garden alone…and He walks with me and He talks with me and He tells me I am His own." I hear another promise. I will walk through this shadow of death with you; I will not leave you. Ever!

Slowly your thinking begins to shift. Living with ALS or any long-term suffering requires you to change your perspective from paralyzing fear to the peace and joy God offers. Your weakened condition necessitates you to think right because things will not always look or feel right. Similar to you and Renee's sister, the Old Testament prophet Jeremiah went through a time when his heart was enormously burdened about the future implications for him and those he loved. He battled bitterness and hardship and adversity; his hope began to perish. He wrote about those feelings in Lamentations, *until I recalled in my mind*—until God refocused my thoughts on this—*why I have hope*. "The Lord's great love never ceases; His compassions never fail. They are new every morning. God's faithfulness is always great" (Lam. 3:21–23).

From time to time, we all wonder what the future holds. Will we be in a car wreck, will we live many years in a nursing home, or will the pain from cancer ravage our body? There are important guiding principles for stepping out into the unknown future: You belong to God. His love for you will *never* cease. He will be faithful to you forever! What is your response to the God who loves you this fiercely, who has designed the *best* possible life for you, and will walk ahead of you to reveal His divine purpose?

Love the Lord your God more than ever and embrace His plan of loving others.

Whatever the future has for you, at some point, there will be some lows with the highs, some adversity with the blessings—but whatever is out there in the future and whenever it comes, know this: God is *always* there. God is *already* there. Whatever debilitating illness might come, God has *already* designed it to maximize your platform of influence.

There is absolutely no reason to be anxious, afraid, or worried about the future, because God has gone ahead of you, just as He did for Renee's sister. Whether you plod along at a snail's pace or race into the future faster than the speed of light, God is already there. In whatever future event—struggle, suffering, sorrow, sickness, joy, blessing, whatever is out there—God is already there. In your journey through ALS from its early symptoms to its diagnosis to its reality in your degenerating muscles to your dying breaths, God is there with you and for you.

God causes all things to work together for good for those who love God, the called according to His purpose.

What is that purpose? Use your God-given platform of influence to love God and love others with a wide-open heart.

ALS brought a different platform of influence into the life of Renee's sister, one which set her free from the prison of her weakened body. Her story became a beacon of hope to other women imprisoned in despair. If you are drifting through some rough waters, look up toward the horizon. Her lighthouse still stands and it continues to shine on a safe course to hope's harbor.

Renee's Story

We shared a room from the time my younger sister was born until I left for college. Our twin beds were so close we could hold hands at night, tell secrets, or just giggle ourselves to sleep. We even shared wedding dresses when we married three months apart. We shared pregnancies and all the celebrations of our children as they grew. I loved my sister dearly. We planned to grow old together, and she was going to be the primary caregiver for our mother who lived around the corner from her. Then ALS struck my sister.

Those three letters ripped into the hearts of every family member—devastation, tears, questions, sorrow, unfulfilled dreams, emotions that could be shared with God alone assaulted all of us, for we knew the disease was terminal. It's as though we began to mourn for her loss four years before she died.

But God...

But God, probably two of the most powerful words in scripture, began working all things out for good for those who love Him and are called according to His purpose. My story is what He taught us during those four years. Yes, there was an unspeakable sadness in our hearts; every time I drove back from Madison, I cried half the way home for the sister I would lose. Her husband, children, mother, and friends can testify to the tears they shed as well.

Charlotte prayed that God would honor the desires of her heart, and the desire He placed in her heart was to bring glory to Him in the time she had left. We were all witnesses to an outpouring of the Holy Spirit as God worked in Charlotte's life. He poured out His love on her and through her. Love poured in from friends and her church family—cards, flowers, food, money, time—whatever gift God had bestowed on these people He moved in their hearts for them to share. Showers of blessings rained down on my sister. She and her husband were in awe of the overwhelming acts of kindness. This encouragement on a daily basis was God's grace upon grace given to my sister.

One Sunday as her preacher talked about what ministries they could be involved in to show God's love to others, God called my sister to go to the prisons and work with women's Bible studies through the godly leadership of Buried Treasures Ministry. Once again, we saw His hand at work. Red tape waiting time was cut through; guards moved prisoners to accommodate the wheelchair.

God held her close on the very difficult days when she would be in pain from a fall or she could no longer feed herself, or every muscle in her body began to give way. She told me once she was determined Satan would not rob her of the joy of living; she disciplined herself to put on the necessary armor every morning as she prayed and read God's Word with her caregiver. From her wheelchair up to five days before she died, she shared God's Word, His promises, and His love with these inmates. She sought no spotlight for herself, only to lift Him up. Once again she told me she had never known the power of the Holy Spirit as she did on those days when she prayed with those women behind bars. She wanted them to find the bread of life. It was a beautiful picture of one common, ordinary clay vessel emptied of self as weak as could be being used by the almighty God.

God provided other audiences. She was asked to share her testimony to the church and in her women's Bible study groups. She sought reconciliation with anyone with whom there had ever been hostility. She wrote letters to every family member to leave her legacy of love.

This earthly life is not our own.

God held Charlotte's every tear in His hand throughout the four years. Of course we all prayed for healing. But as her body continued to fail her, her heart grew stronger in her love for God and others. On December 26, God took Charlotte's spirit to be with Him. We gathered at the funeral home a few nights later to welcome over five hundred people who came to say how Charlotte had touched their life in some meaningful way. Then we gathered again in her church sanctuary the next day to celebrate her life. Charlotte had planned the service. It was not designed to spotlight her. During our time of family tragedy, God had taught her and all of us that our life is not our own; once we become His child, we walk with Him in obedience. We serve and love others to model the grace God so freely gives. We know that He brought all things together for His glory in Charlotte's life—even the dreaded ALS. So how fitting at her funeral that the choir and audience stood in unison to sing the song Charlotte had picked, "Worthy Is the Lamb."

Hallelujah! For the Lord God Almighty reigns!

Desert of Despair

How you see God predetermines how you respond to everything else in life.

If you see God's love as bigger than every challenge you will face in life, then you will respond to those challenges with hope in His love and trust in His purpose. God's purpose for your life is for you to love God and love others, so God uses suffering to stretch your heart into a great heart. Whenever you love as God loves, you reveal the glory of His goodness to those around you. All God asks of you is to let Him love you with His magnificent love until that love overflows out of you to others. Showing a life of love remains God's purpose in sickness and in health.

Charlotte was called to a divine purpose which included ALS, Lou Gehrig's disease. ALS is a progressive neurodegenerative disease affecting nerve cells in the brain and spinal cord. The muscles get no nourishment causing them to atrophy, to waste away. The disease progresses while physical strength digresses. Little by little, the brain loses its ability to control muscle movement. Patients lose the ability to move, eat, speak, and eventually, breathe. Currently there is not a cure or treatment to halt or reverse the disease.

If you or a loved one suffers with ALS, you do not need a primer on its effects, and if you suffer from some other debilitating disease, a comparative list of symptoms is unnecessary. Suffering hurts in any and every form. Charlotte suffered just like those of you with similar battles. Her sister Renee suffered just like all of you with hearts torn apart by your loved one's progressive weakness and your inability to lessen the struggle.

No suffering defines your life. ALS does not change your identity in Christ. ALS and other diseases might affect your abilities or strength; they might confine your movement or location; they might limit your access or independence. They do not change your purpose. Sickness might make you more of a recipient of others' care, but it never lessens your opportunity to love. If anything, suffering should increase your love for God and for others. Sometimes, it even increases your opportunities to showcase love.

God never allows suffering into your life without an eternal purpose for your good. Never! Even ALS serves that purpose. Charlotte saw and embraced that even before her family did. Charlotte knew God, and she discovered through her faith journey that amyotrophic lateral sclerosis would get them even better acquainted. That does not happen without questions. She had questions; her sister and others had questions. Wouldn't you? God does not forbid us to ask questions; He just uses suffering to teach us how to ask the right questions that have the most beneficial answers for our life's journey.

"Why?" "Why this?" "Why now?" "Why me?" Those are usually our first questions, followed by reflective queries for some explanation. "Why would God take away the health I need to make an impact in this life? How can this possibly be for my good or the good of my loved ones? Why does this feel so bad, if it is meant to be good?"

Or you can ask, "What now?" Where do you find God's purpose for your life now that circumstances have dramatically changed? Remember the guiding principle: You find God's will for your life in God's Word. The verses immediately following this glorious all-encompassing promise in Romans 8:28 describe God's ultimate purpose for us which can be summarized as becoming conformed to the likeness of Jesus (Rom. 8:29–30).

God designed you to be able to live and love like Jesus. We all know it is difficult to think of others first when we are feeling well. In sickness, it is definitely not easy. How about when you are dying? God led a dying ALS sufferer to think of loving prisoners. Charlotte spent the final years of her weakened life sharing the love of Jesus with strangers in prison. What a beautiful picture of hope!

Even though Charlotte's body was imprisoned by physical weakness, her spirit could still soar closer to Jesus and become more like Him. That kind of freedom needed to be shared with others chained to the darkness and despair of their physical and emotional prisons.

God's purpose is for you to practice the same kind of love Jesus shares with you. Charlotte loved God and her love for Him kept growing even as the ALS took over more of her body. Charlotte loved others as her life journeyed from holding her sister's hand at bedtime to holding the hand of an incarcerated woman in need of prayer, hope, and love. The prisoners saw what Renee saw when she sat with her sister to share their life stories. This woman loves God.

Springs of Hope

For those who love God, the called according to His purpose...

The purpose of God was on display in Charlotte's life for everyone to see. Her life serves as a blueprint for your suffering. Your story might not include prisons and Bible study groups, but it should trace the same steps of love to someone in need of help and hope.

What are those steps? They begin with understanding the magnificent love of God in His promise and purpose for filling your life with His goodness as revealed in His Word in places like Romans 8:28. When the chapter titled ALS was written into Charlotte's life, she had to decide if that dreaded disease is included in "all things" of God's promise. That is always easier in theory than reality. What would this mean for her future and for those she loved?

Why didn't God just heal her in this life? Many people were praying, so why did the disease continue to progress from the nerve cells in the brain to the spinal cord to the muscles throughout her body? We should pray and we should believe God is able to miraculously heal. God has proven He can heal, and God encourages us to pray for healing. God was able to remove the ALS suffering from Charlotte's life at any moment just as God can heal you instantaneously or take away your suffering immediately. However, God's ways are not our ways, and the faith that pleases God might include trusting Him when He chooses not to lessen our suffering. In truth, it might take greater faith to continue to hope in God through the suffering. It did for Charlotte.

Ultimately God removes sickness and sorrow and suffering from you forever, but for now, God knows the exact amount and the precise duration of time for those things to serve their purpose in your earthly life, just as ALS did for Renee's sister. In God's plan for Charlotte and for you, there is the hope of a heavenly future with greater good and greater glory. That hope is not some wish list, it is as sure as the sun rising each morning.

The glory of God's goodness is inside those who love Him, like a treasure inside of an earthen vessel, unnoticed by most of the world (2 Cor. 4:7). To others, you and Charlotte look like a version of everyone else suffering from ALS. Maybe you are battling a different disease or disability. You might look like any other patient, but somehow you know the glory of God is inside you now and ahead in your future. God gave you spiritual DNA that continues to hope while every muscle wastes away. The brain may quit sending signals through the nervous system, but hope never stops flowing through the spirit.

God's love is so powerful that nothing separates you from it. Not ALS. Not anything. God takes whatever threatens to separate you from His love and turns it into greater good for you. God's love for you is so strong that you actually triumph over the trouble; you conquer the fear of the ticking bomb; you banish the panic that once consumed you, and your suffering becomes a platform for loving more people with that same kind of powerful overcoming love. ALS threatened to tear down Charlotte's life, but God's love raised her up higher on a platform built with ALS materials.

Right now counts forever whether you suffer with ALS or not. Right now is the time to love others, not when you feel better.

The Psalmist proclaims, *"My times are in God's hand."* Do you see your times in the hand of God? Let me phrase this question another way. Do you see God in your times? Whatever might be happening in your life, learn to look for God, because He is there. God is there to help and to give hope for every moment no matter what season of life.

Preach this truth to yourself until it becomes part of every breath. Wherever you are, God is always there.

Wherever life will take you, God is *already* there. Whatever suffering or debilitating illness might come, God has *already* designed it to maximize your platform of influence.

I want to encourage you to do two things: embrace and enjoy. Embrace your struggle and enjoy your God. Embrace your story and enjoy your life, each and every chapter. Embrace your suffering and enjoy your loved ones.

Great hearts are made with great suffering. Embrace each season in your life, each event in your life and enjoy it as a gift from God. No matter how it is packaged, it is designed to maximize your platform of influence for God's glory and the good of others. The delivered package of suffering can lead you to frustration and fighting against God, or it can lead you to a greater love for God. Every specific season of suffering is a gift of God's blessing. Charlotte embraced God's purpose in the new chapter of her life; you can too.

How do you embrace and enjoy a loved one suffering from ALS or some other debilitating illness? Understand suffering for what it truly becomes in the hand of God, gain for her and good for you. There is a time to mourn. There is nothing wrong about crying. There is a time to grieve and a time to sorrow, but this is also the time God gave you to express love for a sister or mother, for your children and friends, and for those most in need of love's expressions: widows, orphans, and prisoners. Look beyond your normal circle of love. You might just discover God's purpose for your life.

We all feel apprehension about the future, for good reason. Some suffering just will not go away. Shadows multiply and darken. Night falls. Winter comes. For too many of us, we can see only as far as our present problem and its accompanying anxieties. Our horizon becomes our fear of the future. We cannot see anything beyond it.

Let's look at an interesting word found in Romans 1:4. The context is about the fulfillment of all the promises God made in the Scriptures, like Romans 8:28, promises pointing to Jesus *who was declared the Son of God with power by His resurrection from the dead*. Take note of the word *declared*. The root Greek word can be translated in English as "horizon." So the verse concerning Jesus could be understood as *who was "horizoned" the Son of God with power by His resurrection*.

The horizon represents the full range and scope of our comprehension. The horizon is a boundary. It is the boundary of your environment, the boundary of your world. The horizon encompasses all your vision as far as you can see but also where you cannot see beyond.

Jesus is our spiritual horizon. By His resurrection, Jesus stands as the first and the foremost of a new creation. Jesus has become the full range and scope of its comprehension. The resurrection power of God has come to souls dead in sin (2 Cor. 5:17). Every member of this new creation possesses a new life produced by the same exceeding power of God that raised Jesus Christ from the dead. That God-given eternal life is not just the hope of a future heaven; it is the horizon of hope for this present life.

What does that have to do with ALS and all other forms of suffering? Everything. As a new creation in Jesus Christ, you are not bound to the old creation. By the same power of Jesus's resurrection, your spirit can break through and out of shame, suffering, and even death. The new creation lives and loves without the restrictions of sight and feelings. The spirit of sufferers can rise above and beyond physical limitations. You are not bound to medical prognosis and human weakness. The surpassing power of resurrection fills and frees your soul. You have hope on the horizon!

For the follower of Jesus, that horizon of hope is Jesus Christ our Lord (1 Tim. 1:1). He is over us, beside us, in us, around us, and underneath us (Isa. 41:10). He is the new boundary we see through the eyes of faith. His love is all-encompassing of every problem, anxiety, and fear.

"Faith goes up the stairs that love has built and looks out the windows which hope has opened." That is the description applied by Charles Spurgeon. We do not know what the future holds, but hope has eyes of faith that look through the opened windows to see the One who is there on our horizon. Jesus encouraged us to look beyond the horizon of our fears to the horizon of His love, love greater than our fears. Maybe you are fearful of your future because your horizon is too limited. Look beyond your problems, sickness, and sorrow. Lift your eyes to see the risen Lord who is here with you causing all things to work together for your good.

What is on your horizon? What is ahead for your life's journey? What stops you in your tracks, muscles weakened and paralyzed in fear? Is it the fear of following God into the unknown future? Is it the fear of sickness or death? Jesus has become the horizon boundary of those who love Him and live for His purpose.

Jesus became Charlotte's horizon. That was the key to her hope. She saw beyond the ALS to a horizon of unending goodness. Look around you, just as Charlotte did. This ALS stuff is not about you; it is about those you can see. ALS can aid your spiritual vision. The horizon is full of people for Jesus to love through you.

God designed a perfect plan for you and me to display faith to a faithless world, hope to a hopeless world, love to a loveless world, and life to a dying world. If all the good God promises always comes true, then *why not me? Why not you?*

All your future lies within the Lord's horizon of goodness. Learn to look past or through your problematic circumstances to Jesus Christ, your help and your hope. Look to no one else and listen to no one else but the Lord of your horizon. Spend time in your garden walking and talking with Him. Embrace and enjoy this chapter of your life. Make it count now and forever.

When the going gets rough, preach to yourself the truths of God's Word. Your lamentations can guide you to the springs of hope where God's loving-kindness never ceases, His compassions never fail, and His faithfulness is always great!

Where there is despair, *hope* is on the horizon.

The Right Understanding of Hope

The promise in Romans 8:28 is *only* for those who love God and live for His purpose to use their platform of influence for the glory of God and the spiritual welfare of others.

"But those who *hope* in the Lord will renew their strength. They will soar on wings like eagles; they will run and not grow weary, they will walk and not faint" (Isa. 40:31; emphasis added).

Alleluia
Alleluia
For the Lord God Almighty reigns
Alleluia
Alleluia
For the Lord God Almighty reigns
Alleluia
Holy
Holy are You Lord God Almighty
Worthy is the Lamb
Worthy is the Lamb
You are holy
Holy are You Lord God Almighty
Worthy is the Lamb
Worthy is the Lamb
Amen

—"Agnus Dei (Worthy Is the Lord),"
Michael W. Smith

9

My Mom's ALS Love Inside Your Circle

Kim's Story
Understanding *Those Who Love God and Love Others*

A baby, an invalid, a quadriplegic, a special needs child. They all need someone to care for them. Sometimes in life, we become that person in need of care; sometimes we become the caregiver. The strain, the time, the effort become a daily routine. The tears, the tough days, the troubled nights are just part of caring for a loved one who cannot care for herself.

This is another ALS story and another side to the purpose in suffering. The symptoms are similar, but each individual has her unique story, deserving to be told. We will pick up the lessons from Lamentations and the emphasis on God's faithfulness much like a jeweler studying the beauty of a precious diamond as its dazzling light bursts through the different prisms, dispersing light rays across its spectrum of colors. An experienced jeweler will place a diamond up against a black velvet background and then shine a light on it to enhance the brilliance of the gem. Sometimes we cannot understand God's love because we have not seen it in its best light. From God's point of view, His love shines brightest in suffering and is best appreciated for its magnificent beauty when paired with our helpless condition.

In the previous chapter, the focus was on what God's love did through a woman suffering from ALS to bring glory to the God she loved. In our companion story, the focus is on God's love being showered on the ALS sufferer by her family, which also glorifies God. Suffering is a great tool for learning to take love to a higher level in both the one suffering and the family of caregivers.

The suffering woman does not want to be there in that condition with everyone having to help her. She has always been the helper, the worker, the caregiver for everyone else. She knows how hard this is on her family. This was not her choice. She feels regret for disrupting the lives of those she so dearly loves. Her heart aches for others even more so than for her own loss.

That same heartache is shared by her family. They hurt for her heartache. They cry for her pain, not their difficulties. They labor in love just as she has done for them for so many years. The roles are reversed now. The caring mother needs to be cared for, the nurturing wife needs to be nurtured, the loving sister needs to be loved, and everyone needs hope.

If you are the one incapacitated, then God plans to use you to help teach others how to love more and love better. Accept your role. Hopefully you have set a good example of selfless service. Now you are the practice field, although that is hard for any independent-minded person to acknowledge.

If you are a loved one of someone becoming more dependent, then God plans to use you as His instrument of love. Embrace your role with joy and hope. Learn from God's love how to be selfless. It is not drudgery; it is not an interruption to your life. For this chapter in your journey, caring for your loved one is your life. God placed you together for this purpose. You need to love as much as they need to be loved.

The life of Kim's mother, Billie, became a special light of hope and love shining radiantly against the backdrop of the ALS shadows. The weaker she became physically, the stronger the bonds of love held her family together. The darker the circumstances developed, the more brilliantly the hope diamond sparkled.

What will be said of you when that time comes? Will the angels declare that you suffered in faith, hope, and love? I pray that might be said of all of us. But what will be said of you when you are the one left to serve the one suffering? Let it be written in the heavens, "She joyfully served in faith, hope, and love. It was her finest hour!"

Kim's Story

Like most people, my mom had made plans for her retirement years. She had dreams of moving to the family lake house with Dad to enjoy a simpler, slower paced life. After working full-time at a very demanding job for most of her adult life and raising four children in the process, it was time to slow down and enjoy life at the lake house on a quiet cove of the lake. She filled her time with sewing, fishing, gardening, and spending time with her kids and grandkids on the weekends. Dad planned to work several more years until they could both live more comfortably during retirement. Life was good.

The good life can be dramatically altered without warning.

Life, however, took a different course only one and a half years after this move. At the age of fifty-three, Mom began experiencing strange symptoms, slight muscle pain, and slurred speech. Mom thought she was "just getting older," but the family began to fear that something more serious was taking place. First the family consulted with local physicians to find an answer. The process was incredibly frustrating as tests were run, but no diagnosis was made. As Mom's condition worsened, the family experienced more fear. If the problem could be diagnosed, it could be treated; however, finding a diagnosis seemed impossible. Mom was sent to Houston to have extensive neurological testing completed.

There, we received a diagnosis—one that would change our family forever.

Mom had ALS (amyotrophic lateral sclerosis), more commonly referred to as Lou Gehrig's disease. We were told she would have three to five years to live, and during that short time, she would rapidly lose the ability to use basically every muscle in her body. She would not be able to walk, talk, eat, or even breathe. ALS would essentially rob Mom of doing the things she truly loved and would ultimately end her life at a young age. This strong, courageous, and compassionate woman who had taken care of her family her entire life would be rendered completely and utterly dependent on others to care for her.

During the next two and a half years, our family stood by Mom's side and watched her physical body deteriorate, as she lost ability after ability. Mom continued to display her selfless attitude, as she stated on several occasions, "This is going to be so hard on each of you." She knew this life was short, and her future held an eternity with God; however, she also knew her family would be heartbroken as they dealt with her physical decline and the loss of her presence on this earth. Mom decided shortly after diagnosis to have a peg feeding tube installed. Doctors urged her to do this before her body became too weak since she would inevitably lose the ability to eat. She was admitted to the ICU on several occasions for respiratory failure, and the family made a decision early on to provide breathing support by ventilator. After being in ICU on two separate occasions, she completed long-term care rehabilitation. After the third trip to ICU, the doctors made the determination that Mom no longer could be rehabilitated and that final, end-of-life planning needed to take place. Since Mom required a facility that could accommodate a patient on a ventilator, the options were limited; however, God led us to a special place where we felt she would receive excellent care. She did, in fact, receive excellent care there for a year and a half before she left this earth at the age of fifty-six.

God always reinforces the reality of His presence and faithfulness.

From her diagnosis to her death, our only hope was in our God. He reinforced His faithfulness and presence during these last three years of her life. Mom had lost her ability to speak, but she was able to write for a considerable time. One time in ICU when my brother and I were visiting, her eyes continuously drifted upward. My heart knew what she was seeing. When I asked her, her expression became very serious; she picked up her board and wrote ANGELS. The significance of this was indescribable. My Mother was so important to her Lord that He sent angels to comfort her during this time in her life. What reassurance for the family to know she was not alone, that our Lord was with her at all times.

God prepares and provides for every moment.

God prepared our hearts when we were faced with deciding when the machines should be turned off. She had struggled too long and suffered too much, and we wanted her to rest in the arms of her savior. It was a blessing when He took her home and He gave us peace with our decision.

God also provided our family with tremendous strength during Mom's stay in the nursing home. My dad would work a full day, drive an hour to the nursing home, spend time with Mom, and then drive an hour home. Not a day went by that my mom did not see Dad's face.

Mom has been gone for several years. Once again God's provision and timing has been perfect. He replaced death with life, and sadness with absolute joy. Less than a year after Mom's death, we were blessed with our first child—three years later, our second. Though Mom is not here to guide me, I have the gift of an amazing mother-in-law to hold my hand through this journey—another example of God's provision for which I am incredibly grateful.

Plans change, but there is great comfort in knowing that God controls the master plan.

God will always provide us with what is needed, when we need it, to endure any hardships that come our way. At times it was difficult for me to see the light during the struggle, but I believe God used this experience to further mold me into the person I need to be to fulfill only a small piece of His overall plan. To this day, He continues to teach me to pray about situations that arise in life and to leave the outcomes to Him, for it is in His will that He accomplishes what is truly best for us.

Desert of Despair

Kim said what we all feel when our loved one is suffering. Sometimes it is difficult to see the light during the struggle. We hurt for our family member's pain. We hurt for our own heart's loss. The dark clouds all look ominous. We dread the present and fear the future, but the Lord promises that His mercy will burst forth from those dreadful clouds to shower us with His goodness.

All of us need strength for today and hope for tomorrow. Kim's mother set her sights on the same horizon as Renee's sister. Hope grew brighter as the days drew darker. Hope always finds the light of day in the darkness of despair. These sufferers of ALS and their families also shared many of the same lamentations as the Old Testament prophet, Jeremiah. Life can take a sudden and difficult turn from independence to total dependence, from strength to weakness, from self-sufficiency to powerlessness. Those times call us to take love to a higher level, both love for God and love for one another.

God often uses the backdrop of our "helplessness" to highlight His love for us. "For while we were still helpless, at the right time Christ died for the ungodly" (Rom. 5:6). The word *helpless* literally means "weak." It comes from two Greek words meaning "without strength." The Bible depicts our terrible state of despair; we are without physical strength, without emotional strength, and without spiritual strength. But Jesus came to help us at exactly *the right time.* When is the right time to help a loved one in the way Jesus helps us? At the time when the other person is most helpless.

Where do you find the wisdom and strength to help your loved one when things appear so hopeless and you feel so helpless? I want to elaborate on one of the biblical passages of hope introduced in the last chapter. In the Old Testament book of Lamentations, the writer, Jeremiah, found himself and those he loved in the darkest place he had ever known. The circumstances left him facing a crisis of faith. He was experiencing an unimaginable amount of physical and emotional suffering. He found himself growing weaker. He was absolutely helpless. When he considered all he had been through, he was overcome with despair. He was wrestling with the most baffling questions of life—the same questions with which we wrestle when we face sorrow or suffering or tragedy.

If God is not responsible for what happened, then who is? Why did the all-powerful and all-knowing God not stop it? If God is behind all that happened, how can we believe in a loving, caring, good God, when so much of what has happened to us is filled with grief and anguish and sorrow and suffering?

Those are haunting questions that are addressed in this portion of Lamentations. The questions turn into instruction and encouragement. Perhaps some of you are facing a similar crisis of faith to the one faced by Jeremiah's or Kim's family. What are you to do? What did they do in the darkest hours? They learned to think in terms of God's character, not their circumstances.

> Surely my soul remembers…I recall to my mind, therefore I have hope. The Lord's lovingkindnesses never cease, for his compassions never fail. They are new every morning. Great is Thy faithfulness. The Lord is my portion, therefore, I hope in Him. The Lord is good to those who wait on Him, to the person who seeks Him. (Lam. 3:20–25)

Confidence in the faithfulness of God is something to be shared. When your despondency is at the lowest and your bereavement is the greatest, join with Jeremiah in singing his lamentations which evolve into a sweet hymn of hope.

The foundation of hope is based on the character of God. Learn to think in terms of God's character, not your circumstances.

This I recall to my mind; therefore, I have hope. What is the "this" that Jeremiah remembered? God's loving-kindnesses, His never-failing compassion, His unending mercies, His faithfulness, and His goodness. When Jeremiah began to think about the character of God, he realized that the God holding the other end of the rope of life could be trusted regardless of the unwelcomed circumstances. Kim and her family came to that same realization.

The Lord's loving-kindnesses indeed never cease. God promised He would never walk out on His people; He never has and He never will. In Jeremiah 2:2, the same word is used in the imagery of a divine marriage. The Hebrew word cannot be expressed by any one English word. The word could be described as unfailing devotion, steadfast love, or loyal love. It is something that is unending. It never ceases. Here it is translated "loving-kindnesses," plural. Again, in the context of a covenant marriage relationship, God has promised us His unfailing devotion and His unending kindness. God's loyalty is unquestionable. As long as you are alive, you still have hope because of God's character.

So when something in life turns out differently from the way you had planned, or you are in difficult circumstances that would not be of your own choosing, how do you get through it? Any crisis of faith needs to be answered by going back to what you *know* (recalling to mind) about God. God has promised you that His steadfast love will never end. There will never be a moment when God's great love for you will end—never!

You may not understand all that is going on in your life, but you can know this: God has not quit loving you. If you give in to the idea that God must not love you anymore, then you end up in despair for no reason except "stinking thinking." The truth is that God's love for you never ends.

For His compassions never fail. God is always compassionate to His people. We need to remember that truth. We need to recall that God's mercies, again plural, flow from the never-ending river of God's heart. God is going to be there with you and for you with multiplied compassions and mercies just like the tender loving care of a mother for a baby. God's compassions are never going to stop and are never going to fail; that is comforting news to the one suffering in sickness and also to the caregivers.

The next verse states, *God's mercies are new every morning.* They are renewed each day. In other words, they never diminish over time. So recall this to remembrance if you truly want to have hope. Each morning, God is just as committed to taking care of you as He was the day before; God's unfailing loving-kindnesses and unending mercies never end; they never fail and they are never diminished. That all adds up to hope!

Pain and problems, suffering and sorrow, despair and danger might steadily intensify but mercy will always have the final say. "His steadfast love endures forever." Why would Jesus do this for you, of all people? Christ did this for the joy set before Him. He did this for love. Understand the gravity and the greatness of this thought.

> "The universe is no longer supremely about you. Yet you are not irrelevant. God's story makes you just the right size. Everything counts, but the scale changes to something that makes much more sense. You face hard things. But you have already received something better which can never be taken away. And that better something will continue to work out the whole journey long." –David Powlinson

There is a lesson in this great truth. God will never allow you to bear suffering beyond what His mercies will sustain. God's grace is always sufficient for you. Each day has enough mercy/

compassion for that day. Instead of a mind full of anxious thoughts about circumstances over which you have no control, think about the greatness of God's love for you.

But what do we do? We tend to despair and worry about tomorrow's troubles. Worry will never erase sorrow and suffering from your tomorrows; it only robs you of joy and strength for today. Jesus said we should not do that, *for tomorrow has enough trouble of its own*. That is what you must recall. In the crisis of faith, we know we can get through the next minute because God has given grace to do that. We might even feel fairly confident about getting through the whole day, but we do not know about tomorrow and we do not know about next week or what we are going to face next year. So we worry and fret. God says that His mercy is sufficient for all you will need today and it will be again tomorrow. God gives you mercy today for today's situations. Tomorrow, the difficulties will be new, but the mercies of God will be new as well.

What should we say to all this? Jeremiah said it for us. Kim repeated it. *Great is Thy faithfulness*. This is the most familiar verse in all of Lamentations because it has been put to song. God is always faithful, and His faithfulness will never end. It will never cease. It will never diminish. God will always be there to strengthen you and support you. If you focus on your problems, your sorrow and your suffering will drag you down into despair. However, if you think about God, you will realize that God's steadfast love, His unfailing mercy, and His great faithfulness are always present to give strength for today and bright hope for tomorrow.

There is a wonderful description of God's character found in the book of Exodus. God was sending Moses to command Pharaoh to free God's people so Moses could lead them out of Egypt into the goodness God had promised them. The promise was not enough to ease Moses's fears of the future, so the frightened and worried Moses asked God to reveal His true identity and character traits. If God truly expected this helpless man to confront the hard-hearted Pharaoh, then Moses needed to know what all of us need to know when faced with our crisis of faith. Who is God and what is He like? God responded, "I am the Lord Sovereign God who is in control. I am a God who is merciful and gracious, slow to anger, abounding in steadfast love, abounding in faithfulness" (Exod. 34:6).

God has told you who He is and what He is like. He is the Lord who abounds in faithfulness. You are not in control of what is going to happen in your life, but God is. You do not know what is going to happen tomorrow, but you can recall and remember what you know about your God that is not going to change tomorrow—His steadfast love, His unfailing mercy, and His great faithfulness. They are renewed every morning.

The love of God, the mercy of God, and the faithfulness of God are like the fresh morning light to those frightened by the darkness of danger, feeling trapped in the sweltering flames of their suffering. Suddenly, hope comes into your fiery trials dressed in asbestos armor. Lying helpless, you are rescued by the God who would not give up. His love feels like breaths of fresh air to your lungs choking from the smoke. Pulled to safety from the fiery furnace, His mercies taste like gulps of fresh water. Then His faithfulness imparts renewed strength to rise up from the dust and ashes. Suddenly you recall to mind, you are still alive, not because of your worries or your works but because of who God is and what God is like, "the same yesterday and today and forever" (Heb. 13:8).

The character of God indicates that all is not lost. We are not totally consumed by the suffering and the tragedy. God's faithfulness is self-renewing each day and this is the historical track record that was given to us to govern our lives; it is recorded in the Scriptures. God has always sustained those who trust in Him. The sovereign Lord of history never changes; therefore, we should wait on God to deliver us with His gracious mercies.

When there is a crisis of faith, remember what is true about God. His daily mercies are reminders of His great faithfulness in the big things. When you see tomorrow morning's light, you need to remember the sunlight is a daily mercy of God. When you take your next breath while you read this paragraph, you need to remember that each intake of oxygen is a reminder of God's mercy. When you get your next drink of water, you need to consider it as a reminder of the daily mercy of God. All the little things that you take for granted in the daily routine of life are to remind you that God is still the God who can and will take care of you.

Since God is great in faithfulness, those who are suffering have hope. Since God is steadfast in His love and unfailing in His mercy, those in the worst conditions still have hope. Since God is a God of unchanging character, then even the ones feeling devastated by their circumstances still have hope. When you face a crisis of faith, remember the character of God—His steadfast love never ceases; His mercies never fail, they are renewed each day, they never diminish; His faithfulness is great, greater than your difficulties, greater than your troubles, greater than your doubts and unfaithfulness.

When you entertain the character of God in your thoughts, the great and good God of the historical, biblical past becomes a present-tense reality. He becomes to you what He was to those in the past. When you face a crisis of faith, God will be just as real to you in His steadfast love, His unfailing mercy, and His great faithfulness. That is why the lamenting writer cannot contain his hope to the written page…"The Lord is my portion…therefore I have hope in Him" (Lam. 3:24).

Expect the goodness of God.

Any expression of hope is grounded in the expectation of the goodness of God. In the Hebrew language, verses 24–27 all begin with the word *good*. The emphasis is on God's goodness based on the tremendous truth: *The Lord is my portion…therefore I have hope in Him.* Our portion in life is the Lord God of goodness. Wow!

The psalmist says, "Whom have I in heaven but you? Earth has nothing I desire besides You. My flesh and my heart may fail, but God is the strength of my heart and my *portion* forever" (Ps. 73:25–26; emphasis added). The word *portion* comes from the root word meaning to divide. God says, "This is your part in life. You get Me." Whether you get a little part of this world or a big part of this world, you are going to leave it behind, and it is not going to last because the things of this world are passing away. ALS will not last; caregiving does not continue without end. But the Lord is forever; His kingdom is everlasting and so is His goodness.

God has given you Himself, "in order that in the ages to come He might show the surpassing riches of His grace in kindness toward us in Christ Jesus" (Eph. 2:7). The sufferings of this time are not worthy to be compared with the glory we are going to experience. In our everlasting life, it will take ages and ages of eternity for God to show you how good He is because His goodness never ends; it is infinite and everlasting.

In the "ages to come," God will do you the very best He can do and in the next moment in eternity or the next thousand years or million years of eternity, you can look forward to God doing something better for you. Every moment of endless days, you will receive the very best of God's goodness; and somehow the very best of His goodness is still to come. Never-ending goodness; that is *your portion*. Your God gladly gives all the riches of His eternal kingdom to His children (Luke 12:32). In the moments of suffering and caregiving, recall to mind that God's steadfast love never ceases. His mercies never fail. His faithfulness is great.

Where there is despair, *hope*; the Lord is your portion. A writer from the past, Thomas Brooks, equated *"having the Lord as your portion"* to being the happiest person in the world. He compared its reality to the morning star in the midst of the clouds, or the moon when it is full, or roses in the springtime. He associated its beauty with lilies by the springs of waters or gold set in a ring filled with numerous, precious stones of various worth.

What more could you want than for the Lord to be your portion in this life and the life to come? The essence of faith is to cling to God as your portion. The next time you see a full moon or a bright star in the break of the clouds or a budding rose in a spring rain or a beautiful ring on someone's finger, you need to remind yourself, *"The Lord is my portion; therefore, I have hope."*

Just because you cannot see hope in the way ahead does not mean that there is none. Often during a crisis of faith, you do not know what to do; you cannot see how this can work out for good. Much like driving a car at night in a fog, it can become difficult to see the highway or its surroundings. The road signs are hidden from view. You are driving along and you cannot see the turn in the road. You can lose perspective of where you are. The street did not move; you just cannot see it at that moment. In the same way, your circumstances in life might hinder you from seeing the promised goodness of God, but it is still there! You have to believe that the goodness of God is not going to move out of your life because of a diagnosis or disease or distress or danger. God's goodness is in pursuit of you and will surely overtake you; you are just in the fog's darkness today.

Even when Kim's mother was too weak to speak, she looked beyond her present pain to that same horizon of hope mentioned in the last chapter. Jesus was there with her and He was in control of all things. Hope became her reality. When the fog clears, you will realize that you have that same hope. Whether you are the dependent sufferer or the loving caregiver, the Lord will be your portion, now and forever.

God's divine design is to renew your confidence in God. In a crisis of faith, remember the character of God and expect the goodness of God. He is great in faithfulness. There is no end to His goodness. This suffering will not last forever. These troubles will be over; the tough times will eventually pass and the blessings of God will come as sure as the morning sun.

Springs of Hope

For those who love God, the called according to His purpose...

Love for God and love for others are inextricably linked in an inescapable bond. We are embedded in Christ, and Christ lives in us for the sake of loving others the way we are loved. The glorious, omnipotent God of glory stooped down to become one of us in order to embrace us in His love. God's long-suffering love becomes the example for both the patient and the caregiver.

Loving God is made visible by loving others. Those who love God, love others with that same kind of long-lasting, long-suffering love. At our best, our words are so small and our actions so minimal compared to God's love for us. We are like busy little ants carrying particles of dust from the Mount Everest of God's love. We are not close to running out of His endless supply; we have not exhausted the innumerable ways to demonstrate His infinite love.

When caring for someone who is limited in caring for herself, there are some extremely vital elements to learn, live, and share. One is hope, the theme of this book. The other two factors are love and faithfulness; each fuels the other. Together they resemble the life of Jesus and His heart overflowing with compassion in the midst of a world of sufferers. You are the representative of Jesus as His caregiver to the one in your circle of love to share those same never-ending loving-kindnesses and never-failing compassions that are new every morning.

Jesus said to *treat other people the way you would want them to treat you. Do unto others as you would have them do unto you.* Consider these two action provoking questions. "If I were in need right now, what would I want that person to do for me? How can I make the love of God visible to this person right now?" Listen for the voice of God in response; He will show you ways to love that person that you never thought possible. Love requires effort. It will cost you time. It will cost you things. But you will never give away more or anything better than what God gives back.

Even when you are in the darkest place of your life, you are never outside the sphere of God's grace. There are some very practical things you can do while your loved one is in the midst of suffering and sorrow and sickness. Share joy, not misery. Respond with thanksgiving and not resentment. Value each new day. Appreciate each new breath.

Let us all make sure that our care for others does not come across like clanging cymbals full of sounds but no love. Use kind words clothed in beneficial actions. "Kind words bring life... soothing words are a tree of life" (Prov. 15:4). The little things matter. A smile, a laugh, a tear, a hug are powerful expressions of hope and love. A cup of cold water or a clean bedsheet are of far more worth than it might appear. A note of appreciation or time spent going through family pictures can be priceless. Read, sing, talk, or just hold hands. Say, "I love you." Say it often.

Love endures through space and time. If distance or responsibilities or important moments in other family members' lives prevent you from being there with the one suffering, do not feel guilty. She would want you to enjoy life and those precious moments. You will need rest as well. God understands. Just do what you can, when you can. Today's technology makes staying in contact much easier. There are many ways to help; just communicate your love in words and actions. What will you need to take your love to a higher level in the time of their declining independence?

Ask the Lord for perception, patience, and perseverance.

1. *Perception* is a conscious awareness and detection of those around you. As we go through a day full of concern for our own needs, we tend to be dull of hearing and blind at

perceiving the needs, difficulties, distresses, and attitudes of others.

In the midst of busy days and hectic weeks, our awareness of others can become very weak. In fact, we can become completely cold, numb, and hardened to the struggles and difficulties of others. Sometimes a serious situation with a sick loved one forces us into a greater awareness. We no longer overlook the needs of others while staring into the oblivion of our own problems, we actually see someone who needs love.

2. *Patience* is a characteristic that only the Spirit of God can produce in you (Gal. 5:23). The biblical description for *patience* means long-suffering. You must be willing to suffer long with the frustrations and demands of caregiving. An appeal to God's preeminent long-suffering toward us puts things in proper perspective. How long must you suffer with this person? For as long as God has suffered with you. Long-suffering patience comes across in gentleness. Your presence soothes and relieves the sufferer from worry and fear. In a time of pain, it is pleasant for them to have you near.

3. *Perseverance*, the ability to remain and perform under pressure, must be added to perception and patience. Strengthening the weak is taxing. Serving in lowliness is emptying. Caring for those struggling is wearying. Truly being invested in loving care for someone else will be consuming and tedious. There will be many times that it looks unrewarding, unending, and maybe even unappreciated. Love pushes on and pulls through. Patient love demonstrates a *stick-to-it-iveness* that is altogether different from our common, culturally influenced interactions.

"Be kind to one another, tender-hearted, forgiving the way Jesus Christ has been to you" (Eph. 4:32). *Kindness* is the outward expression of a tender heart which shares others' emotions and pain, a character trait perfectly exampled by Jesus Christ in His empathy for our hurts and heartaches. To *be kind* is to be of the same kind as someone else. It is to put yourself in their position ("like them") to personally relate to them. See things from their perspective; meet them where they are. Be perceptive. Be patient. Persevere.

One thread of truth has been seamlessly woven into our lives—God's faithfulness. God's faithfulness is universally transparent yet immeasurable in its greatness, extended to everyone yet beyond the reproach of anyone. Be faithful to your God. Be faithful to your loved ones.

God's Word exhorts us to hold fast to the confession of our hope in the faithfulness of God. *Hold fast* is a nautical term meaning "to steer toward" and "to maintain a direct course." The God who promised is faithful. His purpose does not change and He cannot lie—those are the two unchangeable realities that make our hope sure and steadfast. Our trust in God's faithfulness is demonstrated in our faithfulness to love those in need of help and hope.

> For God will not forget your *work* and the *love* you have shown Him as you have helped His people and continue to help them. We want each of you to show this same diligence to the very end, so that what you *hope* for may be fully realized…through *faith* and *patience* inherit what has been promised. (Heb. 6:10–12; emphasis added)

We must make opportunity to love, take every opportunity to love, and seize the most of every opportunity to love. If we want to make the most of every opportunity, we must discover ways to take our love to a higher, longer level and do so without delay. You can always love better, you can always love more, and you can always love longer. Follow Jesus's example. "This is how we know what love is: Jesus Christ laid down his life for us. And we ought to lay down our lives for our family" (1 John 3:16).

Love "lays down" self in order to serve rather than be served. On the night before Jesus would die on the cross in ultimate demonstration of love for His followers, our Lord washed His friends' dirty feet. No one asked him to do that; in fact, no one expected Him to do that. Jesus saw an opportunity to show love, so His example matched His actions to His words. "Let us not love with words or speech, but with actions and in truth" (1 John 3:18). Love becomes visible in actions.

Where do you discover that the Lord's loving-kindnesses never end? Is it not when you are too weak to return any love? Where do you find that the Lord's mercies are new every morning? Is it not when you have used up all the mercies from the previous day? The same is true in caregiving. When the caregiving needs of your loved one have left you physically drained and have exhausted your mercies, then you are ready to showcase the inspirationally radiant diamond-like beauty of God's great faithfulness.

You are inside God's circle of love where hope shines the brightest. God's never-ending love lifts your spirit and His new mercies come bursting forth like the sunrays of a new morning. They give you the daily strength and hope you need for your acts of unselfish love inside your circle.

Some suggestions:

1. Pray in faith. I like to describe prayer as depending on God and cheering God on in His promise to do us good. Depend on God's love to be with your loved one who is going through this time of suffering. Pray the promises of God. Pray for God's will to be revealed, whether by miraculous recovery or by miraculous faith to endure. Pray for God's love to overflow out of your life onto your loved one. Ask the Lord to give you opportunities to love more and love longer.

2. Share hope in patience. Whether you are the sufferer or the family member of the sufferer, your story is being written on the hearts of those around you. Your life story will live on in their memories. It is also being written in heaven in everlasting ink designed to highlight God's faithfulness against the backdrop of your life story. Your life still makes a difference whether you are at full force or worsening weakness. Make every day count. Love suffers long. Time and effort never lessen the impact of long-suffering love; they increase its joy.

3. Practice love. You cannot change the serious situation, but you can change your attitude for the better. Find ways to encourage. Notes, cards, flowers, pictures, music. Trips to the store or the doctor will be needed. Help around the house from clothes to cleaning. Listen to her life lessons; take notes; you might even consider inclusion of her story in the back of this book as tribute to her life and her God. Most of all, just be there as much as you can, even if it is just sitting there taking in the afternoon sun or watching her sleep.

Faithfulness is a precious and diminishing commodity in a world filled with lovers of self and lovers of money rather than lovers of God. Be faithful in love. There is nothing more important now or forever. Where there is despair, *hope*. This world will pass away. Suffering will end. Faith will become sight. Hope will become reality. Love will last—forever.

God will always provide strength for today and bright hope for tomorrow. You will never regret how much love you give. Never! Do what you can while you can to show your love and when you get too weak for anything else, may your soul still sing of God's great faithfulness to you and your loved ones.

The Right Understanding of Hope

The foundation of hope is the character of God.

"The Lord is good to those whose *hope* is in Him" (Lam. 3:25; emphasis added).

Pardon for sin and a peace that endureth,
Thine own great presence to cheer and to guide;
Strength for today, and bright hope for tomorrow
Blessings all mine, with ten thousand beside.
Great is Thy faithfulness!
Great is Thy faithfulness!
Morning by morning new mercies I see
All I have needed Thy hand hath provided
Great is Thy faithfulness, Lord unto me!

—"Great Is Thy Faithfulness,"
Thomas Chisholm

10

The Most Unlikely Person to Be Saved

Pattie's Story
Understanding *Called for God's Purpose*

You are about to read the story of a young woman who someone thought was the worst person in the world, but even then, not out of the reach of God's love. Maybe you would be voted the worst woman in the world in someone's poll or perhaps someone actually said that about you. You do not have to be the worst girl in the world to need a Savior. A young woman can be strutting and dancing her way to hell or sitting in pretense inside a church but with a heart far away from God; both need a personal loving relationship with Jesus. Both need to be rescued from Satan, sin, hell, and mainly themselves. Both need a new life.

There is an emptiness and loneliness which the heart feels without God. Your life can be full of material things, crowded with professed friends, and overloaded with carefree fun, yet your soul (the real you) can feel incredibly void of love and so isolated from real companionship. Your life might appear busy and fashionable while your hidden heart remains dead and messy.

Your soul was created to be full of God; your life purpose is to share the love of God. The most important chapter of your life begins when you let God love you, an undeserving sinner in need of help and hope to make it in this life and into eternity. How much does God love you? "God demonstrated His own love toward [you] in that while [you] were still a sinner, Jesus Christ died for [you]" (Rom. 5:8).

Hopefully, you are already well acquainted with the Savior Jesus. This chapter should remind you of how that wonderful relationship started. If you are not yet a lover of Jesus, there is no better time than this very moment to give your life totally to the One who loves you the most. His love is unconditional, unlimited, and unending.

There is only one love that has the power to totally and radically change a life for the better. Even if your life is really messed up, God can still transform you into a beautiful woman of grace. If you are still lost, someone is searching for you. If your life is coming apart at the seams and wasting away, there is a God who can fix you better than new.

Pattie's story gives every woman hope of a new and better life. Your story might not seem as dramatic as this story, but it is just as amazing. Rescued. Redeemed. Changed. Wow! Saved from a wasted life to live a life of real love that does not fade or end when someone turns out the lights and the party is over.

There is no reason to feel as though you are the worst woman in the world.

We already found her.

She confessed.

Pattie's Story

I carried a childhood shame with me until I was twenty-three years old. Gradually I began to trust no one; I became a person who had to be in control of every situation. I promised myself no one would ever have power over me again. With each year that passed, I erected a taller wall, and then one day all the anger, rebelliousness, and hatred came pouring out of a depraved heart.

I was strutting and dancing my way to hell.

The first chapter of Romans tells us because we did not see fit to acknowledge God any longer, He gave us over to a depraved mind to do those things which are not proper being filled with all unrighteousness, wickedness, greed, evil, envy, murder strife, deceit, malice, haters of God, unloving, gossips. Psalms 12:8 says "the wicked strut on every side." I strutted. I ran as fast and furiously as I could into a self-centered, self-indulgent way of life. I partied, I danced the nights away, I destroyed the hearts of men, and I loved every minute of it.

For several years, I was involved with the leader of an outlaw motorcycle gang. It gave me power I had not had. People feared me. Drugs, drunkenness, prostitution were considered normal. I didn't need anyone; I was in control of my life. I didn't want anyone, especially God, telling me what to do.

There was a young man, Bill, who was a singer in a local band. We ran in the same circles. I loved to dance to Bill's singing, and he loved to watch me dance. Then I didn't see Bill anymore; I did not know God had saved Bill. He had given up his bar singing for singing in the church choir.

Go find the worst sinner you know.

Bill's pastor preached a message: "Go find the worst sinner you can think of. Go show the love of Christ to the unlovely. Never give up until you see the Lord work."

Bill chose me. It took Bill two years to find me. He would call or come by; I made fun of him, laughed at him, hung up on his calls, and did my best to humiliate him. He never gave up.

New Year's weekend I went to Galveston, Texas, to celebrate. Something happened this time. I was confused because everything I did left a bad taste in my mouth. The excitement wasn't there. My date dumped me, and I spent New Year's Eve in a lady's roach-infested basement. There was no way to get back home. I had no one to call to come to my rescue.

I was not in control of the situation. I did not understand what was happening to me. I spent New Year's Day walking alone, and for the first time, I saw who I really was. The shallowness of my entire life passed before me for hours. All the words Bill had shared came pouring out. All his pleadings would not leave my mind. I became desperate. My first day back in town, Bill called, and this time I listened.

Often, I have asked what if Bill had not listened to his pastor. What if he had not taken that message to heart and run with it? What if Bill heard but didn't obey? Suppose Bill thought I wasn't worth the risk. He was not only risking his reputation but also his very life. What if he had said he was just too busy with his own life? Or better yet, what if he had just gossiped about me? He could have fled. The Word of God tells young men to flee from the woman sitting at her door post. I reveled in my sinfulness and did my best to bring others down with me. I laughed when they fell.

God's grace is much greater than my sin.

Bill should have fled, but instead, he obeyed. He didn't isolate himself from the world; he looked for the most wicked; he looked for the unlovely. Next to my husband, I am most thankful for Bill. He is a dear brother in the Lord. He cared for me just as Christ had cared for him. I, the rebellious, self-indulgent, controlling sinner, was in need of God's grace, and because of the love of my Heavenly Father, I was not beyond the reach of His grace.

Tell me, how great is the love of the *God who causes all things to work together for good, to those who love God and are called according to His purpose*! I am eternally grateful that God called me to Himself through the Christlike love of someone who considered me the most unlikely candidate for salvation, perhaps the worst woman he had ever known. "The gospel is the power of God that brings salvation to everyone who believes" (Rom. 1:16).

Desert of Despair

Pattie's story is a testimony to the overcoming power of God's love. God providentially orchestrated all the events, people, and circumstances in her life to get her attention and then magnified her awareness of His powerful love. God connected all the ordinary things in her life to His extraordinary goodness. Without spiritual eyes, the divine intervention "just seemed to happen." In reality, it was all part of God's purpose for Pattie's life, a purpose that connects her story to yours.

You do not have to be considered a bad girl to need help and hope in this life. Good girls get their lives messed up and their hearts in the wrong places. The good news is that salvation is not earned or deserved; it is a gift of God accepted by faith. God uses faith to unite your soul to Jesus. God's Word describes that life connection as being born again, a new spiritual beginning.

The Bible also uses the metaphor of marriage to explain your new union with Jesus. In marriage, the bride and the bridegroom become united as one with all things in common, for better or worse. Jesus takes you, the poor worldly sinful prostitute, and gives you a new life with a new identity, forever loved by Jesus. For those of you united to Jesus, there is a great exchange where all Jesus has is given to you and what you have now is transferred to Him. Everything good and loving is given to you while your sin and its messy misery now belong to Jesus.

That is Pattie's story, the story of all the redeemed who live with hope in God's promise of no condemnation for sin now, no separation from His love throughout eternity, and all things in between worked together for good. That hope is exclusive to those who are united with Jesus *to love God...to live according to God's purpose.*

With Jesus, you are not without hope; you are never unloved. Your life can be radically transformed. Your problems do not all disappear, but your joy is no longer dependent upon your changing circumstances. You are loved...always and forever.

Springs of Hope

Called according to God's purpose...

We all need God; we all need to find our purpose in life. Whether you are still a fashionable rebel or a grace-dressed daughter of God, there is a divinely called purpose for you to consider.

Jesus lives in you to lead you to others He intends to love through you. This purpose statement will be reiterated throughout this book. Jesus saved Bill so that He might lead him back to Pattie where Jesus would love her through Bill's concern for her spiritual welfare. Bill found his purpose in life, so did Pattie. It is the same purpose God has chosen for your life. Jesus will live inside you to lead you to others He intends to love through you. God will providentially orchestrate everything in your life to make you aware of that purpose. Everything? Yes, everything.

Here is the question about Pattie's story as it relates to you. Is it possible for God to take the worst thing that has happened in your life and turn it into a good and beautiful purpose? God's great love is powerful enough to change your perspective about this chapter of your life. All these things in your life that just seemed to happen were orchestrated with a divine purpose. We have introduced you to Pattie; are you acquainted with her sister, Ruth? She was also on the worst women in the world list.

One of the beautiful examples of the power of God's love expressed in the Romans 8:28 promise can be found in the Old Testament account of Ruth's story. It just so happened that Ruth grew up in the land of Moab, a nation of descendants from an immoral incestuous sexual encounter initiated by a woman's seductive deception and a man's mindless drunkenness. The resulting culture laughed and scoffed at the God of the Bible, preferring their own "destroyer" god. They hated God and despised those who believed in God. Even the Bible referred to them as the most unlikely people God would ever save.

Ruth grew up in an immoral culture whose worship of their false gods included sacrifices of young women. It was not an environment conducive to wholesome character or loyalty. Prostitution was an accepted way of life. Somehow, Ruth became one of the most revered women in the Bible, quoted at innumerable Christian weddings throughout the centuries.

"I will not leave you or turn away from you. Where you go I will go, and where you stay I will stay. Your people will be my people and your God my God. Where you die I will die" (Ruth 1:16).

The first chapter of Ruth's unlikely story as God's Cinderella begins with the spotlight on Naomi, her future mother-in-law. What is Ruth's story *and* Naomi's story *and* how does it connect with Pattie's story *and* your story?

Surprisingly, at least to many back in Bethlehem who would have voted the younger Ruth as most unlikely to ever be saved, Ruth becomes the great-grandmother of David, Israel's greatest and most beloved king. Even more shocking is the prominent place God gives her when the eternal Jesus's earthly lineage is listed. Ruth's story *and* David's story *and* Jesus's story *and* Pattie's story *and* your story are all connected by God's divine conjunctions.

In the next chapters, we will follow Ruth's story in more detail, but for now, I want to summarize the circumstances and then take a panoramic view of the bigger picture from God's perspective. Because of a severe famine, a family of four Israelites leaves their hometown of Bethlehem to relocate in the foreign land of Moab. The husband dies, the two sons marry Moabite women but have no children; then both sons die. The widowed mother and wives are left behind to deal with the suffering of survival in a male-dominated society. Filled with grief and bitterness, the mother, Naomi, decides to go home to Bethlehem; against her wishes, one of her daughters-in-law, Ruth, returns with her.

Ruth's story highlights her wholehearted devotion to family and to the God to whom she had been introduced. While working in the Bethlehem barley harvest, Ruth finds favor with the rich and prominent owner of those fields. They fall in love, marry, and have a son. As time goes by, Ruth becomes the great-grandmother of the giant-killer David, the greatest king in Israel's history.

As you pull back to see the work of God on a bigger scale, Ruth's name is recorded in the Gospel of Matthew as connected to the birth of another child one thousand years later, our Savior Jesus Christ. In the larger landscape, we see how the beauty of God's grace to the most unlikely recipient fits into the mosaic of His glory. Inside the ordinary life of an unlikely to be saved woman was the hidden treasure of God's extraordinary love.

The suffering childless widow Ruth moved to Bethlehem with her embittered mother-in-law, *and* it just so happened to be the time of the barley harvest *and* it just so happened she fell in love with a young man who owned all those fields where centuries later shepherds watching their flocks by night would be startled by the light and sound of angels celebrating the birth of Jesus.

Jesus was born in Bethlehem because his earthly father, Joseph, a descendent of King David, had gone back to his family's hometown with his wife, Mary, to register for the government ordered census. Why was Bethlehem the place of their family roots? Because centuries earlier, God called Ruth, a most unlikely to be saved Moabite woman, and connected her love and hope to His ultimate purpose.

Before we look more closely at Ruth's unlikely story, please note that the difficult chapter in your life is connected to your good and God's purpose. I realize you might not feel this is possible right now, but when this chapter of your life is completed, someone in the future will call you a beautiful, blessed woman. It might be months, decades, or centuries before the connected stories will all be told, but how God worked it all together for good will bring hope to some other woman voted by her peers as most unlikely to be saved.

Ruth's story provides encouragement and hope to people who feel as though their ordinary lives are insignificant. This is a true story directed at women who think they have lost hope, women ready to give up in suffering and give in to despair. For now, you probably feel like the woman most unlikely to have any hope. Welcome to Ruth's world. It was a world very familiar to Pattie.

Ruth was strutting and dancing her way to hell. God came and rescued her. She did not go looking for God, but God sent someone after her. Ruth fell in love with Naomi's son and her exposure to his family and their faith awakened her soul to God's purpose for her life. Her story features an ordinary girl called by God for an extraordinary purpose. I hope you are well-acquainted with it, because the rest of the story is one of the great love stories in history.

This story conveys how God works for your good when your times are at their worst. It pictures the grace and love of God in your life, especially when you cannot see any help on the horizon. Whether you are voted Ms. Goody-Two-Shoes or Most Likely to Go to Hell, this grand love story has a wonderful message for you.

"For God so loved the world that He gave His one and only Son, that whoever believes in Him shall not perish but have eternal life" (John 3:16).

God has a master blueprint for everyone He calls to be His follower so we can share in the life and love of Jesus (Rom. 8:29–30). It is an unbreakable chain of love where even the future things are discussed in the past tense as if already accomplished in God's eyes.

At first glance, it might read like a boring seminary textbook full of theological terms and irrelevant babble. However, I strongly encourage you to read the next paragraphs like a Valentine's Day card from the One who loves you the most. His choice of words is rich with meaning intended to convey His invincible love, incredible goodness, and incomparable glory promised to you.

The biblical text uses five verbs to describe God's glorious love in action.

1. *Foreknew:* I have known you and cared for you before you ever knew or cared about Me.
2. *Predestined/*prepackaged: I made plans for you to become like Jesus, in direction in this earthly life and in perfection through all of eternity.
3. *Called*: I arranged our meeting and introduced Myself for the purpose of winning your heart by the sheer magnitude of My love for you.
4. *Justified*: I will never keep a record of wrongs and I will treat you as if you are as perfect as Jesus, now and forever.
5. *Glorified:* I have showered all My goodness on you, and it will take me endless ages of eternity to show you all the incomparable riches of My goodness and expressions of kindness to you.

Now, in case you zoned out for a minute, what does all that have to do with you? I offer two primary, but not exclusive, reasons.

1. *God's faithful steadfast love is available to you, making your hope as durable and unchangeable as God Himself.* God had a plan to pursue you even while you were still dancing your way to hell. God surrounded your life with His everlasting goodness from before history to beyond the future and, in between, used divine conjunctions to turn your life around to His life-changing love.
2. *No one, including you, is beyond the reach of God's love.* God's love has made a place in His family for you, just as God did for Ruth and Pattie. It does not matter how bad you have been or how bad your circumstances are now. You are not beyond the reach of God's love.

You will never find unselfish, unconditional, unlimited, unending love in the dance clubs or social blogs of this world, but God's love can find you there. This kind of life-transforming love does not exist in a darkened car or neighborhood bar, but God's love can find you there. Everywhere you snap a selfie, God is there, calling you to live for a greater purpose.

Sin and selfishness have no substance. That kind of life is empty; it is vanity, already proven to be a foolish, futile, and even fatal investment of your time. On the other hand, God's love has substance, a lasting weightiness about it. It builds you up, instead of tearing you down; it fills you up, instead of leaving you empty.

Everything changed the day Pattie ran into Jesus's loving arms. She found the same love and hope Ruth discovered. Can your heart make that same confession? *"Your God is my God."* When you have the same God, then you have the same love and hope. Just as in their lives, there will be dark nights questioning the reality of God's love. Circumstances change. Losses mount. Things look as though they can prevent a happy ending. Then it just happens…a divine conjunction comes along…But God…

God has called you. Turn to Jesus. Trust Him. Follow Him. He loves you with a promise of no condemnation for your sin and no separation from His love. He specializes in taking the most unlikely and unwanted to be His very own beloved. Then He causes all things to work together for good, for Ruth, for Pattie, for you, for yours. Even in our despair, we have hope.

God's love story is the greatest one ever told. Its chapters include the stories of Ruth and Pattie. They were surprised at how good God is to the most unlikely girls. This glorious romantic narrative also incorporates a beautiful account of your story with an amazing ending and surprising connections to God's bigger story about the life and love of Jesus.

God blessed you by connecting other people to your life. Someone has shown you God's love through tears and prayers, through actions and not just words. Someone wanted you to read this book. Take some time to express your gratitude to the Lord and to them for sharing God's love with you. God purposes to use you to share love and hope to someone else, maybe some most unlikely to be saved woman waiting for you to introduce her to God's amazing love. Share your hope in God.

Jesus Christ specializes in calling the worst women in the world to experience a complete makeover inside and out. He offers a love with life-transforming power and a hope with invincible goodness. Right now, wherever you are physically, emotionally, and spiritually, fall into the loving arms of Jesus. He understands your situation, cares about your concerns, comforts your hurts, and gives you hope. He sees the bigger picture. Trust Him to fill your emptiness, to clean up your mess, to change your life.

This chapter in your life is only part of your story. The best is still to come.

Where there is despair, *hope* in God! Someday you will dance with Jesus in glory.

The Right Understanding of Hope

No one is beyond the reach of hope. No one. Not the worst woman in the world and certainly not you.

Your hope is as big and as real as your God!

"For in this *hope* we were saved" (Rom. 8:24; emphasis added).

Amazing Grace, how sweet the sound
That saved a wretch like me
I once was lost but now am found
Was blind but now I see
The Lord has promised good to me
His Word my hope secures
He will my shield and portion be
As long as life endures
When we've been there ten thousand years
Bright shining as the sun
We've no less days to sing God's praise
Than when we've first begun

—"Amazing Grace,"
John Newton

How to Follow Jesus

Stop here. This is a moment to examine your faith, hope, and love.

How do you know if you are really following Jesus or just pretending? Biblical salvation is described by what it produces, not by what one says or promises.

Salvation is a living and loving personal relationship with the Lord Jesus Christ.

God offers salvation as a free gift. You cannot earn it or ever deserve it. You receive salvation by believing in the Lord Jesus Christ. "God demonstrated His own love for us in that while we were still sinners, Christ died for us" (Rom. 5:8). God promises that *whoever believes* (right now, present tense) *in Jesus has eternal life.*

Do you believe in Jesus right now? Is He your horizon of hope in every circumstance? Have you received His unconditional, unending love that fills your heart until that same love overflows to those around you? That all begins with the right understanding of what happened when Jesus died for you.

On the cross, God treated Jesus, His perfect and loving Son, as if Jesus had lived your selfish, sinful life in order that for all of eternity God might treat you as if you had lived Jesus's perfect, loving life.

Wow! That is great news! "If you confess with your mouth that Jesus is Lord and believe in your heart that God raised Him from the dead, you will be saved" (Rom. 10:9).

Here is a biblical checklist to examine your own heart for faith, hope, and love.

"Therefore, if anyone is in Christ, the new creation has come. The old has gone, the new is here!" (2 Cor. 5:17).

1. Do you have a new direction in life? *If there is no new direction in life, there is no new destination for eternity.*
2. Do you have a new Lord in life? *If there is no new Lord in your life, there is no new life in you.*

3. Is your life changing to live side by side with Jesus and for Jesus? *If there is no change in your life, there is no Jesus Christ in your life.*

    So where are you spiritually? Have you ever received Jesus as your personal Lord and Savior? Accept what Jesus did for you on the cross and receive Him as your substitute. Place your name into the verse. God said, *"Whoever (your name) believes in Jesus has eternal life."*

God is merciful to perishing sinners, even the worst ones. God's gift of undeserved grace is what saves you, not your performance. God will stay side by side with you in this earthly life and He has already reserved a place in heaven for you. God's love for you is so great that He will never, never, never, never let you go. That is your blessed hope.

This is God's love gift to you, not because of anything you have done or earned on your own. God did this so in the future heaven He might show you how truly good and kind He is to you, because it will take God forever to give you all His infinite goodness and never-ending love! (Eph. 2:1–10).

Here is a sample prayer for trusting Jesus as your Lord and Savior.
The important thing is to follow Jesus. This suggested prayer is not a formula. There is no magic or spiritual power in these words. God is looking at your heart. Use your own words or use these words if they express what your heart feels and desires. Jesus is inviting you to love Him and follow Him side by side forever. Will you? Why not pray right now? It is vitally important for today, for every season of your life, and for all of eternity.

Dear God, thank you for loving me. Thank you for sending your Son Jesus to rescue sinners from perishing under the responsibility of their sins. I am definitely the worst sinner I know, so thank you for paying the cost for my sin on the cross and conquering my sin by rising from the dead. Thank you for the gift of a new beginning with everlasting life.

I believe in Jesus as my Lord and Savior. I want to have a personal relationship with Jesus. I want to follow Jesus side by side. Change me. I want to learn how to love you with all my heart, soul, mind, and strength. Show me how to love others as I love myself. Use my life as a platform of influence for your glory and the good of others. I love You. Amen.

Christianity is simply following Jesus. This life is all about direction, not perfection.

Love the Lord your God with all your heart, soul, mind, and strength while learning to love others as yourself. Live your life as a testimony to the value of knowing and loving Jesus Christ.

I pray you have a better understanding of what a great promise there is for those who love God and are called for His purpose.

And we know God causes all things to work together for good.

The next chapters will focus on the right questions and point you to the right applications of this marvelous promise of hope. It is not difficult to understand, but it only becomes possible when Jesus lives inside of you to lead you to others He intends to love through you.

PART II

The Right Questions

What, then, shall we say in response to these things?

—Romans 8:31

11

The Interrogation Interlude

If God causes all things to work together for good, then why do my present circumstances not look or feel good?

What should you say in response to this?

These women had so many questions. Crushed dreams, broken hearts, tragic circumstances, and loss of loved ones can trigger countless uncertainties. You probably ask the same questions. They usually begin with, "Why?" "Why this?" "Why now?"

The Hebrew expression for *why* most frequently used in the Psalms is both a cry of grief and protest. It means "to what end" or "for what purpose" did this happen. We desire and often demand an explanation for everything, particularly the circumstances which seem to go unfairly against us. Have you ever considered that you might be asking the wrong questions?

You might not get all the explanation you request, but God assures you that He has a wise and good reason for everything He does. All of our suffering is linked to a larger and higher purpose. Darkness, despair, and depression are valid spiritual experiences. Check out the Psalms. Read Jeremiah and Isaiah. *Let him who walks in the dark, who has no light (no explanation), trust in the name of the* LORD (Isaiah 50:10).

It is easier to philosophize about suffering when you are not experiencing any of it. When suffering actually comes just as God told us it would, we are surprised. Our minds are immediately flooded with so many questions, but what are the right questions?

What answers do you absolutely need to make this journey in life endurable? Enjoyable?

Amazingly, God points you to the right questions for your situation. They can be found in the verses following His promise of good (Rom. 8:28) and His purpose for your life (vv 29–30). God even asks, "What should you say in response to this?" (v 31).

God provides four rhetorical questions we should all ask when things look and feel bad (vv 31–39). Whether you experience the loss of health or the loss of a loved one, ALS, cancer, coronary disease, heartbreak, depression, or an accident, these are the right questions about suffering which come with God's seal of approval.

Q1: "Since God is for us, who can be against us?"

God is for you. The devil is against you, sin is against you, this world is against you, circumstances may feel as though they are against you, but God is not against you. God is not out to get you. God is not neutral toward you. God is for you. God will never, never, never, never, never be against you (Heb. 13:5). God is always loving you and connecting all the circumstantial dots to do you the most good. Personalize the verse. Put your name in the prepositional phrase. God is for *you*, and His goodness to you is undeserved, unearned, and not based on some performance treadmill test. God is always watching over you to do you the greatest good. Write it on your heart. Tweet it to the world. #Godisforme.

Q2: "He who did not spare his own Son, but gave him up for us all—how will he not also, along with Jesus, graciously give us all things?"

God's love for you is unlimited and unending. God did not spare His Son at the cross. He gave His very best and all He has to you. He gave you the most precious and costly gift He could give. God will not shortchange you now. God is not hesitant or reluctant to be good to you. There is no limit to the good God will give you. God promised He would never withhold any good from you (Ps. 84:11), and God promised it will take forever for Him to show you all His goodness (Eph. 2:7).

Q3: "Who will bring any charge against those whom God has chosen? Who is the one who condemns you?"

Not God. What is happening in your life right now is not punishment for your sins; Jesus has already been punished for them. Jesus Christ died on the cross to demonstrate God's love for you and satisfy God's judgment for your sin. There is now no condemnation of you and no condemnation for the rest of your life or on judgment day. Jesus continues to intercede for you in the courts of heaven. God does not condemn you, so any charge from someone else will be thrown out as inadmissible in heaven's courtroom.

Q4: "What can separate us from the love of Christ?"

Nothing and no one. Not trouble. Not hardship. Not persecution. Not being without food or clothes. Not danger or threats. No, in all these things, we are more than conquerors through Jesus's love for us. For I am convinced that neither death nor life, neither angels nor demons, neither the present nor the future, nor any powers, neither height nor depth, nor anything else in all creation will be able to separate us from the love of God that is in Christ Jesus our Lord. You are always loved.

Summary: God is for you, never against you. God will give you everything that is good for you with nothing left out. God never condemns you; He perfectly and permanently accepts you. No matter what happens in life, God will keep you surrounded by His unlimited, unending love.

That sounds so wonderful. Is it believable? Is it true for your life?

The next chapters will interweave this glorious promise of Romans 8:28 with its beautiful picture in the lives of Ruth, Naomi, and some precious women of our time who happened to share the same church family. Together, their life stories will illustrate how the truths of these promised assurances work in our ordinary lives. You will read stories of fear, family crisis, loss of loved ones, reconciliation, chronic sickness, love for the impoverished and imprisoned, depression, desperate tears for acceptance, and the heartache of childlessness.

Then there is still your story. Where there is despair, hope.

The Right Questions about Hope

Since God is for us, who can be against us? He who did not spare his own Son, but gave him up for us all—how will he not also, along with Jesus, graciously give us all things? Who will bring any charge against those whom God has chosen? Who is the one who condemns you? What can separate us from the love of Christ?

"Therefore, with minds that are alert and fully sober, set your *hope* on the grace to be brought to you when Jesus Christ is revealed at his coming" (1 Pet. 1:13; emphasis added).

We pray for wisdom, Your voice to hear
We cry in anger when we cannot feel You near
We doubt your goodness, we doubt your love
As if every promise from Your word is not enough
And all the while, You hear each desperate plea
And long that we'd have faith to believe
'Cause what if your blessings come through rain drops
What if Your healing comes through tears
What if a thousand sleepless nights are
what it takes to know You're near
What if trials of this life are Your mercies in disguise
When friends betray us
When darkness seems to win
We know that pain reminds this heart
That this is not
This is not our home
'Cause what if your blessings come through rain drops
What if Your healing comes through tears
What if a thousand sleepless nights are
what it takes to know You're near
What if my greatest disappointments
or the aching of this life
Is the revealing of a greater thirst this world can't satisfy
What if trials of this life
The rain, the storms, the hardest nights
Are your mercies in disguise

—"Blessings," Laura Story

PART III

The Right Application

What, then, shall we say in response to these things? *If God is for us, who can be against us?* He who did not spare his own Son, but gave him up for us all—how will he not also, along with him, graciously give us all things? Who will bring any charge against those whom God has chosen? It is God who justifies. Who then is the one who condemns? No one. Christ Jesus who died—more than that, who was raised to life— is at the right hand of God and is also interceding for us. Who shall separate us from the love of Christ? Shall trouble or hardship or persecution or famine or nakedness or danger or sword? As it is written: "For your sake we face death all day long; we are considered as sheep to be slaughtered." No, in all these things we are more than conquerors through him who loved us. *For I am convinced that neither death nor life, neither angels nor demons, neither the present nor the future, nor any powers, neither height nor depth, nor anything else in all creation, will be able to separate us from the love of God that is in Christ Jesus our Lord.*

—Romans 8:31–39 (emphasis added)

12

A Rough Road through Childhood

Rebekah's Story
Application of *God Is for Us*

Why do we look around and think all the other families are perfect and our family is the only one messed up? We desire for everything to go smoothly as it seems to do for everyone else, especially those in our church. Instead, we feel ashamed of the difficulties in our family travels, and we fear the rough spots along the way.

Some families break up; some fall apart. Others just hide the cracks. Family crisis fuels anxiety. Threats of abandonment fly like cruise missiles in a nighttime fight. Sometimes the threats are carried out. Sometimes the bomb hits without warning.

There are fears from without and fears from within. A young Rebekah grew up surrounded by fear and anxiety. She was well acquainted with the heartache of childhood abandonment. Perhaps you are as well. Sometimes all we can do is cry as we peel away the onion skin layers of fear upon fears.

What is it that you fear? Do you live in a perpetual family crisis? Maybe you have been abandoned or spent years fearing whether a parent or spouse might leave without warning, never to return. Perhaps you live in fear that your child might never come home again.

Like pain, fear also comes in all shapes, sizes, and colors. Some fears loom large while others fade. Some fears are big, like giants and monsters and cancer; some fears are little, like terrible two-year-olds and intrusive mothers-in-law. Some fears are as tall as skyscrapers, others small as spiders. Some fears are laughable but certain fears rob you of sleep and sanity. Some fears contribute to depression and some to anxiety.

Fear is a strangely haunting thing. Rebekah feared abandonment, which fueled her feelings of being unloved and unwanted. The struggle with fearful feelings often leads to a lifetime of anxiety from abandonment or the return of its heartache. You grow up in fear of rejection, hurt, loneliness, or separation caused by death.

Feeling unloved and unwanted, too many children grow up without the stabilizing love of a safe and secure family. You might be a member of this invisible segment of our society. Statistics do not make it feel more personal although they might raise greater awareness of the powerful impact on young lives abandoned by parents. In America, the numbers are shocking for children living in foster care. Even more young lives are strained and scarred by divorce, left with unanswered questions about love and loyalty. Some are raised in single-parent homes or by grandparents or extended family members. Too many have no caring person watching over them. Worldwide, the abandoned children (with names and feelings and futures) stagger the senses. Orphaned, abused, neglected, homeless, unwanted, unloved. I am sure there are some "abandoned or neglected or abused" children living not far from you. It's a harsh, rugged, lonely road. Get involved someway. Pray. Give. Go. Teach. Adopt. Love. Give help and hope.[1]

The orphaned and abandoned are always near and dear to the heart of God. Rebekah's story is just one of those accounts. Thankfully, she has shared her story of the rough road she journeyed through childhood along with God's plan for good in her life. This is what hope looks like to a hurting child awakened to its reality.

Rebekah's Story

At the tender age of fourteen, my mother discovered she was pregnant. Scared and ashamed but "in love," she married the father of the child she was carrying. On a hot August day, my brother was born, and these two children, now fifteen and seventeen years old, were parents. I came along just fifteen months later, and my sister two years after me.

Shattered dreams and bitter pills are hard to take at any age, even more so as a child.

For several years, we all lived with my mother's parents. They selflessly provided love, guidance, and financial support for our family. Although my parents had support and help from their family, the stresses of life and caring for three small children crushed them. It crushed all their hopes and dreams of what their lives would have been if they had not been "tied down" to this life they never would have chosen for themselves.

So, when I was seven years old, my mom left my dad. She packed all three of us up in our tiny car, and we drove away that horrible day. We said good-bye to an empty house and to our childhood. That day was my first memory of a feeling of sadness and emptiness that perhaps only children of divorce can understand. From then on, the things I heard, saw, and experienced made me grow up sooner than any child should.

Anxiety and fear can become a child's sleepover guests.

The next several years were filled with custody battles, the back and forth between houses, and arguments that once ended with my father being taken away by the police. They were also filled with anxiety, fear, loneliness, and despair. There were weekends that my siblings and I would be packed and waiting by the door to spend the weekend with my dad, and he would never show up. The feelings of abandonment were so unbearable at times that it would make me physically ill.

Eventually my dad moved out of state; my mom and my brother, sister, and I moved in with my grandparents. Our lives seemed to settle down for a while, and I was thrilled to be living with my grandparents again. They both were incredible rocks of strength and a welcome refuge from the storms of my parents' lives. My grandparents loved the Lord and were always pouring the truths of God's Word into us. In God's grace and mercy, my brother, sister, and I all came to a saving faith while we were under my grandparents' care.

It hurt to feel unloved and unwanted.

It wasn't too long before my mom met someone and they were married. We all packed up again and moved in with our new stepdad. My stepdad was cruel and controlling, and he kept us from ever seeing our grandparents. Those days were some of the darkest of my life. We lived with them a year, and my mom decided we should move back in with our grandparents. Even though I was ecstatic to be leaving that situation, I wondered, how could my mother let us go? How could she choose this awful man over her own children? The walls of anger and bitterness were built up in my heart stronger and higher. I felt abandoned, unloved, and unwanted.

Just one year later, my father told me that it was becoming too difficult to keep up the long-distance relationship with us. I was eleven years old at the time, and I did not see or speak to him again until I was nineteen.

Your past does not control you.

Though it was painful, it was just as equally freeing! Finally, my siblings and I were in a godly, loving, stable home. I felt freedom to be a kid again, and all three of us began to flourish! By God's grace and in His infinite wisdom, my past did not cause me despair. In turn, it strengthened me and allowed me to see and experience God's goodness in an intimate way.

My freshman year of college, my friends and I were getting ready to go celebrate my nineteenth birthday. Right before we left, the phone rang, and it was my dad. I was in shock; I had not heard his voice in eight years. I don't think I spoke more than a couple of words, and when I hung up the phone, so many of the feelings I had been suppressing for years came rushing back. The hurt, the anger, and the bitterness hit me hard and all at once.

We have a Heavenly Father who will never abandon us.

The following day, I was in my dorm room, and I cried out to God as I had never cried out to Him before. I begged Him to take these paralyzing feelings away. I pleaded with Him to be to me what my earthly father and mother never had been. I was desperate for healing and His tender fatherly care. Even though my grandparents had been wonderful, they could not fill the loss I felt: loss of innocence, loss of a childhood, and loss of love from my parents. God came, and He came in a powerful, tangible way. I felt the arms of a loving father around me that day. He pulled me close and sheltered me under His wings.

In Romans 8, Paul says that all those in Christ have received a spirit of adoption as sons and daughters. We can call Him "Abba, Father." What precious words these are to the hearts and lives of the abandoned and the fatherless.

Now that I am an adult, I can look back on my childhood, and I can empathize with how difficult it must have been for my parents. In recent years, both of them have apologized for the mistakes they made, and by God's grace, we have restored our relationship. It is not always easy and it's definitely not perfect, but thankfully, those are not qualifiers for forgiveness.

Thank God if you have been led down a rough road.

Charles Spurgeon wrote, "Thank God, then, if you have been led by a rough road: it is this which has given you your experiences of God's greatness and loving-kindness. Your troubles have enriched you with a wealth of knowledge to be gained by no other means." I would not have chosen this story—a story of loss, heartache, and abandonment; however, Christ has transformed my story into joy and peace everlasting in Him. I thank God I was led down a rough road.

Desert of Despair

Hope. What does hope look and feel like to an orphaned child? What if they see no hope on their horizon?

Rebekah was abandoned. It left her feeling unloved and unwanted. The abandonment by loved ones was not her fault. She did nothing wrong to cause it and neither was it because of some defect in her personality. The abandonment happened because of reasons beyond her control. All parents are faced with tough decisions regarding the welfare of their children. Sometimes they later regret some of their choices. Children often do likewise. Thankfully, there is forgiveness for all of us.

Nevertheless, abandonment breeds fear. Rebekah's fears ruled her life until God's love cast out those fears from her heart. Those monsters still come knocking, but they are unwelcomed guests where Jesus lives. Fear visits all of us. I confess that if I did not believe God's faithfulness to be for me and with me always, just as He promised, I would go mad from fear. I have learned to preach to my soul. God is for me, so where there is despair, *hope*. Rebekah learned that as well; she just traveled a rough road.

What do you fear? Abandonment? Being unloved and unwanted? Do you fear suffering? Sickness? Cancer? Many women wrestle with thoughts of worst case scenarios which rob them of present enjoyment. Perhaps your early life events of loss have fueled fears of future anxiety and apprehension.

Pastor and author Chuck Swindoll has been credited with the saying, "Life is 10 percent what happens to you and 90 percent how you respond." Many women would say the opposite. They feel as though their future happiness is largely determined by the 90 percent of what happens to them. They are trapped in thoughts that how they respond makes no difference in life, but in reality it is the response that shapes the heart, not the outside pressure. Great hearts are made with great suffering.

Since God is for us, who can be against us? God is for us and with us, but sometimes the journey travels down a rough road.

Rebekah learned that the Lord was all she needed. Jesus Christ was the faithful love and everlasting joy that could never be taken away. His promised presence would throw out those unwanted visitors of fear and replace them with thanksgiving and hope.

Ruth experienced many of the same challenges as Rebekah. Ruth understood fears and family crisis. So did Naomi, her mother-in-law. Their lives would ultimately be defined by their responses to God, not the pressure of what happened to them. They were both widowed and childless, abandoned by death. Their story begins with their fears (Ruth 1). They lived in a time of rampant lawlessness and unfeigned selfishness. There was no governing authority. Everyone did what was right in their own eyes. It was a time of immorality, greed, and crime. It was a time similar to ours where laws are used to justify lifestyles so people can do what they want, not what they ought.

They lived in a time of social chaos, moral chaos, religious chaos, and in many cases, family chaos. All of the peer pressure and every cultural influence led people further and further away from devotion to God. Parents did what was best for themselves, without consideration of their children's welfare. There was a leadership vacuum in the government, the places of worship, the marketplace, and most importantly, the home, a world with which Rebekah and many women today can identify. Ruth grew up in Moab and Naomi in Bethlehem, but famine and fear would soon unite their life stories.

Naomi described her life story as bad and bitter. She blamed her husband's decisions, but ultimately she came to the conclusion that God was against her. God was to blame for *all things* in her life which made her bitter. What happened?

It just so happened that there was a famine in the land of Israel, and a God-loving man had to make an extremely agonizing decision regarding the welfare of his wife and two young sons; he moved his family from Bethlehem to Moab, far away from their home and culture. Once a prominent family in their homeland, they now were starving refugees with nothing but what they could carry.

They looked like the refugee families seen on TV. Whenever you see those thousands of refugees seeking a better life for their family or just hoping to survive, please care. Each family has a story of suffering, different from how you hurt, but it is still suffering. Pray for them to be guided by God to a place of provision. If possible, help in some tangible way.

Naomi's husband decided to relocate his wife and their two little boys to a foreign land. It was a heart-rending transition away from family and friends, away from prominence and normality, away from the only life she knew. Did her husband know what he was doing? Why Moab? Naomi had nothing in common with those ungodly people. What mother would want to raise her sons in that environment, even if it were just temporary?

Then plans changed. Naomi's husband died while the family was still in transition. He did not plan to die or leave Naomi and his sons alone in a strange land far away from relatives and friends. Most often, life does not go according to our plans. Circumstances outside of our control can change the best conceived plans and leave a family in crisis. Parental choices can have lifelong consequences.

The changed plans evolved into crushed dreams as Naomi's sons died. Naomi's dreams of sharing happiness with her sons and grandchildren were shattered. Everywhere she looked, Naomi saw bad things. She saw her life go from full to empty. What happened to her began to define her life. She became bitter and hopeless. She arrived at one misconceived conclusion: "God is against me."

Naomi was blinded by her own perceptions. Naomi believed God was against her. Family life probably looked that way to Rebekah. Do you think that Rebekah had those same feelings when her parents gave her, her brother, and her sister away to her grandparents? Do you think she ever felt as if the God her grandparents talked about was against her? Did her family crisis leave her feeling unloved and unwanted by God?

How do you feel right now? Do you feel as though all the other families are perfect and yours is the only one messed up? Do you feel as though family harmony and happiness have abandoned you forever? Go ahead and say it. You think God is against you. At least, it must feel like it, especially if you are wearing those feelings on your face the way Naomi did. Until she learned the truth.

Abandonment can cause despair; despair can blind perception. However, even when someone walks away and turns out the lights on your lonely heart, God is still there with you. In every family crisis and challenge, God is for you, not against you.

Springs of Hope

Since God is for us, who can be against us?

Rebekah would discover the protection and provision of God's love for a family in crisis. It was a hope shared by Ruth and Naomi whose life stories cannot be told without the wonder of the unseen God working all things together for good. That same hope can be yours. God is for you, not against you.

Most of the time, we have to wait until the smoke clears to see God's favor in the fiery trials of life. Circumstances usually do not change overnight. God could change them immediately, but there is an amazement to the providential timing of God's blessings that would be missed. Ruth's and Rebekah's stories are good reminders not to expect things to change overnight, but over time and not always in the ways we imagine. Why? God's ways are infinitely higher than ours and substantially better.

You can overcome fear with love and hope. Do they sell that stuff at the store? Pesticides, pharmaceuticals, or the frozen section? Love and hope are always available in God's Word. And it's free! I highly recommend one of my favorites, Isaiah 41:10.

It conveys an all-inclusive promise that addresses the subject of dealing with fears associated with abandonment. This verse serves as a lifeline for those feeling unloved and unwanted. Grab hold and do not let go.

"Do not fear, for I am with you; do not anxiously look about you, for I am your God. I will strengthen you, surely I will help you, and surely I will uphold you with My righteous right hand" (Isa. 41:10).

I think about this verse often because of its powerfully reassuring promise.

1. God is over you.
2. God is with you.
3. God is in you.
4. God is all around you.
5. God is underneath you.

God is wherever you are. He will take care of you. He will provide every need. God has you covered, so you can live without fear and fall asleep without anxious thoughts. Joseph ended the book of Genesis by saying to the descendants of faith, "God will surely take care of you." I do not know what the future holds for you, but God will surely take care of *you* in times of fear or family crisis.

Learn to look at your future through the lens of God's presence and promises.

Whatever your circumstances are and however they might change, there is a way to look at them through the lens of God's presence and promises, like the ones in Romans 8:28 and Isaiah 41:10. God is for you. Being in God's presence should not only give you assurance, it should also leave you awestruck in worship and filled with hope.

God said to Abraham and Isaac and Jacob, "Do not fear. I am with you," to Joseph, "Do not fear. I will surely take care of you," to Moses and Joshua and David and Isaiah, "Do not fear. I will be with you." Jesus promised the first disciples and all His subsequent followers including you, "Surely I will be with *you* always" (Matt. 28:20; emphasis added).

We think no one has ever experienced a family crisis like ours. The Bible is full of accounts of families in troubles from within and without. God will always be for you and with you as your divine Protector. Always. There is refuge under the shadow of His wings. "This I know, God is for me..." (Ps. 56:9–11).

Learn to look at your life through the lens of who God truly is. There is nothing to fear, except forgetting the promises of God. The God of those promises is personally present with you. God is directly involved in everything concerning your life. God did not abandon Naomi, Ruth, or Rebekah. He will never abandon you.

Too often, we become afraid we cannot overcome our fears. The prescription for overcoming our fears is remembering God is with us. The eternal almighty Creator God stepped into our time and space to dwell among us and in us with promises to help us. God sees us and notes every individual hurt and heartache, every struggle. We are never alone in our suffering and never without hope. He will never abandon us.

Pour your life into a verse like Isaiah 41:10, as you listen to the voice of God speaking to *you*: "Do not fear, for I am over you and beside you and in you and around you and underneath you to help *you*."

The God who controls and creates and chooses says, "This is why I have united you to Jesus. I chose you before the foundation of the world to be Mine. You have a Father who will never abandon you and a family to whom you will always belong. I called you out of darkness and death. You are Mine forever. I will always be over you, by your side, inside you, all around you, and underneath you, so that everywhere and in everything I might be your God."

Throughout the Scriptures, the fearful become the faithful when they turn their eyes to the horizon of the Lord Jesus Christ. *There is no place so lonely, no place so dark, no place so deep, and no place so frightening that the Lord will not be with you to help you.* Ruth and Rebekah learned to look past their fears to the horizon of God's love.

"When I am afraid, I will put my trust in Thee" (Ps. 56:3). We taught this Bible verse to our little children early in life. I pray that they and I will remember to embrace its reality day by day, week by week, whatever we face. I hope you will as well.

> Since God is for us, who can be against us?...For I am convinced that neither death, nor life, nor angels, nor principalities, nor things *present*, nor things *to come*, nor powers, nor height, nor depth, nor any other created thing, shall be able to separate us from the love of God, which is in [our horizon] the Lord Jesus Christ. (Rom. 8:31, 38–39; emphasis added)

Whatever gives rise to anxiety and fear in your life is certainly controlled and limited by the God who is everywhere, all the time, all at once. You and I need to learn to live in the awareness of God's presence and power. We need to practice shaping the perception of our suffering with the awareness of God's help and hope. God has something for you to do. Whatever it is, there is no reason to fear, for God will be with *you* and God will help *you*.

You do not have to climb higher to get closer to God and should you sink into the depths of despair, you are not farther away from God. You might feel that way, but no matter how dark it feels, the psalmist says, "When the darkness overwhelms me, and I feel like I cannot go on, God is right there with me. The darkness that frightens me is like light to God. He sees me;

He sees what is going on; and God is taking care of me" (Ps. 139:11–12).

Learn to strive for peace in your circumstances, not perfection. Life is never perfect for anyone. Families will have problems and challenges. When your world feels as if it is falling apart, God's presence steadies your soul and calms your heart. When you are afraid, put your trust in the God who is over you, beside you, in you, all around you, before and behind and underneath you.

The Lord is on your horizon for one reason, to help you. Rebekah's tears flowed much like those of Naomi and Ruth. Traveling down the rough road, it sometimes felt as though God was against them until time replaced perception with the reality of God's goodness. God is always loving you and connecting all the dots in your life to do you the most good, even the dots marked chaos and crisis.

Every child needs the love of parents. Where that is absent, the heart suffers—for a long time. You do not have to carry that hurt forever, and you do not have to repeat the cycle to another generation. If you are still in tears over your fears or family crisis, do not give up to the despair or give in to the fear. God is a caring father and a healing physician who loves you. He gives hope for the helpless and love for the brokenhearted. All the children around the world without a home deserve to hear and feel this hope and love. Do something to help.

Because God promises his absolute faithfulness and indestructible love will see you through to a good end, then you are able to walk a very rough road. If you traveled a rough road through childhood, be thankful, not resentful. You have found healing and hope in your God. You have experienced the greatness of God's love and gained a wealth of knowledge that could not have come by any other means. Your Heavenly Father will never abandon you. God is for you, and He will always help you.

Our God specializes in bringing good out of a family crisis. Ask Ruth and Rebekah. Your story is not over. Maybe someone will ask you to share it.

Where there is despair, *hope*.

The Right Application of Hope

Write it on your heart. God is for me. Tweet it to the world.

#Godisforme.

"You are my refuge and my shield; I have put my *hope* in your word" (Ps. 119:114; emphasis added).

> This is my Father's world
> O let me never forget
> That though the wrong seems oft so strong
> God is the Ruler yet
> This is my Father's world
> The battle is not done
> Jesus who died will be satisfied
> And earth and heaven be one
>
> —"This Is My Father's World,"
> Maltbie D. Babcock

---

[1] Read UNICEF reports for current statistics. In addition to the larger, more familiar organizations dedicated to these causes, I recommend checking out these trustworthy nonprofit groups making an enormous impact on the lives of at-risk children in some of the most impoverished places: Faces 4 Hope (Africa), El Sadai (Moldova), Passion for the Poor International (countries in the eastern hemisphere), Global Heart Ministries (Iran, Central Asia, and Turkey), and One Hope Tulsa (Inner-City USA and Mexico). God works through individuals in these organizations and others like them as part of His plan to bring help and hope to children in need. Get involved someway…today.

To everyone who's lost someone they love
Long before it was their time
You feel like the days you had were not enough
When you said good-bye
And to all the people with burdens and pains
Keeping you back from your life
You believe that there's nothing and there is no one
Who can make it right

There is hope for the helpless
Rest for the weary
Love for the broken heart
There is grace and forgiveness
Mercy and healing
He'll meet you wherever you are
Cry out to Jesus, cry out to Jesus

For the marriage that's struggling just to hang on
They lost all their faith in love
They've done all they can to make it right again
Still it's not enough
For the ones who can't break the addictions and chains
You try to give up but you come back again
Just remember that you're not alone in your shame
And your suffering
When you're lonely
And it feels like the whole world is falling on you
You just reach out, you just cry out to Jesus

To the widow who suffers from being alone
Wiping the tears from her eyes
For the children around the world without a home
Say a prayer tonight
There is hope for the helpless
Rest for the weary Love for the broken heart
Cry out to Jesus! There is hope for the helpless.

—"Cry Out to Jesus," Brad Avery, David Carr, Mac Powell, Mark Lee, Tai Anderson

13

Death Came Sooner than Expected

Belinda's Story
Application of *God Gave Us His Own Son*

Death is a certainty. Sudden death to a young husband and father is a tragedy.

Death never synchronizes its arrival to our man-made calendars. Belinda's husband was an answer to my prayers. He quickly became a teacher and role model for hundreds of teenage boys in our neighborhood ministry. I asked him to pray about becoming copastor of our church. We agreed to talk about it again when I returned from a couple's weekend getaway.

I received a call on the second night. It was Huey. "Pastor, I need your prayers for my family and me. The doctors just told me I have been diagnosed with stomach cancer. They say it is terminal." We prayed together as we would many more times. It was not a question of faith in God but rather sweet surrender to God's will. We prayed for a miracle, confident God was able. We prayed for courage to hope in the face of obvious physical deterioration. We believed death was gain. We both looked forward to being face to face with Jesus and living in the joy of the heavenly inheritance the Lord has promised His children.

Maybe you are facing a similar challenge. Maybe you are caring for a loved one, or maybe you are the surviving spouse.

Hope in God. Hope in God for this life and the one to come. God is faithful, yesterday, today, tomorrow, and forever.

Okay. That sounds like the words of a preacher. Now let me ask the question this preacher asked God. It has probably crossed your mind. Why do some of God's people die in the *prime* of life when their effectiveness in His kingdom seems to be at it greatest usefulness?

I do not have an answer for you, but I have discovered a better question when death comes too soon. *What should you say in response to all this?*

He who did not spare his own Son, but gave him up for us all—how will He not also, along with Jesus, graciously give us all things?

Because God did not spare His own Son, there is special significance to any death-too-soon journey. Our hope in the extraordinary and everlasting love of God connects our ordinary lives with all the tragedies and triumphs into an extraordinary narrative descriptive of something much greater than ourselves. God lovingly paints our life stories into the beautiful landscape of His grace and the mosaic of His grandeur and glory. This magnificent masterpiece is the consummate creation of God's endless love highlighted against the backdrop of our darkest circumstances.

Belinda's story is one of those heavenly designed illustrations of a spouse's death, too soon to make any sense. Many of you carry in your heart your own personalized version. Her story will not lessen your pain, but it can heighten your hope.

Belinda's Story

Huey became my high school sweetheart. We continued to date throughout college until we both graduated. We married and had two wonderful sons, John Paul and James Caleb.

My husband was handsome, athletic, smart, and loved Jesus. He loved me and our two sons, both handsome, athletic, smart, and in love with Jesus. Huey was a lifelong firefighter, recently retired to give more time to our own start-up business. We lived in a beautiful house in a great neighborhood.

We had a good life with big dreams of an even better one.

A big part of that dream included traveling to do mission work without needing financial support from the local church or others. Some city political groups were even courting Huey about running for mayor. His primary reservation was how that would take away from his time following his sons from one sports field to another as well as his time teaching God's Word to inner-city youth and gang members. Those relationships were extremely important to him.

Death came too soon.

In mid-September, Huey went to the hospital because of stomach pains and bloating. The doctor who saw him prescribed a medication for possible stomach ulcers. He continued to have the pain and bloating so he went back to the hospital; this time an x-ray was done. The doctor who reviewed it saw an immediate red flag. Huey was called back for an endoscope to confirm the diagnosis of stage IV stomach cancer with less than six months to live.

Six months? We were shocked. But we did not have even six more months together; it was three. The diagnosis came in October, and Huey would be with the Lord in heaven before Christmas.

There was much sadness for our family although we did not shed many tears. Huey was the poster boy for fitness, literally; his picture was on billboards across the city promoting a fitness center. Now he was dying. We would watch his physical stamina weaken as his body wasted away to just a thin shell. But that was what someone might see on the outside. Inside his spiritual strength rose to new heights as God reminded us of His sovereignty and faithfulness.

We hoped in God. Hospital counselors thought we were in denial. We had struggles, but we understood God was in control.

Our souls were anchored to the promise that God causes all things to work together for good to those who love Him and live for His purpose. All things. That includes cancer. And death. So our family began the journey of trusting the outcome to God.

We also began the medical journey. The oncologist told us there was a drug that might help, but because we had no insurance, "We could not afford it." Those words stung. A dear friend flew Huey to Houston for advanced alternative cancer treatments at the Burzynski Clinic and offered to fly him to Germany for a new experimental treatment that was to be made available in January.

Did we have low days? Yes, of course. Cancer saps your strength and threatens your faith. Once treatment started, Huey would be better one week and then face a setback the following week. Were there fears and disappointments? The unknown and the unexpected always start there until faith gets refocused. We talked and prayed a lot for our sons. We shared our past joys and regrets. God was with us. Whether the days were marked by prosperity or adversity, we remained confident that God was with us and for us.

Ironically, we had for many years what most would call security—great jobs, two incomes, insurance, and 401k. At this critical time in life, there was no insurance, great jobs, or steady income. Our savings would be quickly exhausted, but God's provisions began to pour in.

We were amazed at the support we had from friends and family. Though we were without income, how rich we were in Christ. Loved ones had begun to give unconditionally: they took care of our sons, they hired people to come in and help, they paid our bills; they insisted my job was just to focus on taking care of Huey.

We had the opportunity to go to MD Anderson, but we had to be a resident of Texas or pay $2,000 to be admitted without insurance. Because we did not have the cash, we returned home, and Huey was admitted to the local hospital. Shortly after, he was placed in hospice care. After phone calls to officials in Washington, DC, and with the help of senators, Huey was admitted to MD Anderson one day prior to his death.

Cancer took the life of a seemingly healthy physically fit man who had won first place in a body building contest a few years before. Now it was a challenge to even eat. The cancer ate away at his body; he aged thirty to forty years in a few months. Yet nothing altered His faith in His beloved Heavenly Father. His last words were, "Seek the Lord, while He can be found, call upon Him while He is near." Then Huey entered into eternal rest; he went home to be with His Savior.

The boys and I returned home to begin the procedure to file for bankruptcy. One year later, there was the foreclosure on our home. Once again, God's provisions began to pour in. Dear friends offered to let us live with them for six months, men from our church lined the streets with trucks and trailers to help move our things to a storage unit, and I moved into my friend's house.

I would pray earnestly to God each day for the needs of that day. I learned to trust God like the children of Israel as they waited on their daily manna. We were adopted by a family who mentored me in the business dream that Huey and I had shared. The business has grown and my sons have flourished. Both have graduated from college. They both could share stories of God's faithful provisions.

It has indeed been a journey for all of us through a crisis in unchartered territory. I have been physically and spiritually transformed. I was once extremely independent, trusting in self. I am now Christ dependent. I have learned that God is faithful, He has given us all that we need in Christ Jesus, He is Sovereign over all things, His Word is true, and He is always with me. His plans are not our plans, but I can trust Him no matter what because He causes all things to work together for my good. I can be still and know that He is God.

My greatest loss has become my greatest gain.

I can now see our God in everything. I see and live life with eternal eyes anticipating the Lord's return. I lost my husband, but I will see him again in glory, full of life and joy and love. Huey left a legacy of trusting God no matter what. In life and death, hold on to Jesus. I am thankful my sons witnessed that. I pray they will carry their father's legacy into new arenas of faith.

Desert of Despair

Any life journey contains detours and setbacks. Invariably, there are sudden turns and road blocks. The steps of ordinary people in their ordinary days will include suffering and, at some point, death. Hopefully, you get to grow up, fall in love, find enjoyment in hard work, and struggle in the joys of raising a family. Because we live in a sin-infested world, tragedies are part of that journey. They often cut short our plans and dreams.

The death of a spouse is never an easy event no matter what his age. Your world changes immediately. Fears and anxieties rush in. Emotional, financial, and family decisions are suddenly dumped in your lap. You might even feel as if you are walking around in a fog, a daze, a dream. There is no timeline or finish line for grief. Go at your own pace. Be patient with yourself. Sometimes it might be a struggle to just get through an hour at a time while still dealing with your emotional loss. You will never forget but you will heal. It just takes time, and that amount of time is different for every person.

I cannot offer a satisfactory answer as to why this tragedy happened. Whether the death of your loved one was caused by disease or accident, it never comes as good news. *What should I say in response to all this?* I will offer you the promises of consolation from God that permeate the Scriptures, promises designed to create a great heart out of great suffering. I also will point you to four bedrock truths that I can glean from the right questions regarding God's goodness in the loss of your loved one.

1. God is not against you. *Since God is for us, who can be against us?*
2. God is not withholding good from you. *He who did not spare his own Son, but gave him up for us all—how will He not also, along with Jesus, graciously give us all things?*
3. God is not punishing you for something you did or did not do. *Who will bring any charge against those whom God has chosen? Who is the one who condemns you?*
4. God will not forget you or leave you alone in this new chapter of your life. *What can separate us from the love of Christ? Not trouble. Not hardship. Not needs for food or clothes. Certainly not death.*

There will be more reflection on the ramifications of these truths later in this story and in subsequent chapters related to your heart's struggle with feelings of depression and emptiness and its search for renewed purpose and love. But first, let's unite your heart with Belinda's heart and walk this journey together. Along the way, we will pick up Ruth, with her surprising confidence in God's promised provision, and Naomi, who really struggled with her thoughts that God was against her.

Belinda's story shares similarities to the experiences of Naomi and Ruth in the loss of their husbands, too soon, so unexpected. The tragedies interrupted meaningful lives. But in each case, the end result led to greater significance. As you navigate this incredibly difficult period in your life, their inspirational stories show you how to think right. They give hope that you can live again, not just cope with the loss. Most importantly, they remind you that you are not alone in this journey, and the Lord has not finished your story.

For Naomi, one blow followed another. It all felt like too much. Her life was tragic; she did not see how God could possibly cause all these things to work together for good. Her suffering clouded her faith with cynical feelings. *The hand of the Lord has gone forth against me.* Everywhere she looked, everywhere she went only reminded her of what she had lost.

Naomi's husband had not planned on dying and leaving his wife to raise two sons alone. Neither did Huey. They were both prepared to die, having placed their hope in Jesus for this life and the next. They just did not plan to die so soon.

Death would be gain for Naomi's husband and Belinda's. The hope of being with Jesus forever was the way they lived and the way they died. But Naomi and Belinda would be left behind to raise two sons without a father. The resulting struggles would only magnify the difficulty. Naomi would cry out that God was against her and life was hopeless.

Did either of those ladies ever feel as though the departed husband got the better end of the tragedy? Did they ever think that things would have been easier had they been the one to die first? There is no doubt that when a believer in God dies, it is gain. They are better off in heaven where hope is now the substantive reality of all God's goodness. They are where all the dots are connected to showcase a greater purpose. They are lost in praise, not questions. They are swimming in an endless ocean of love, not drowning in sorrow and debt.

Naomi and Ruth were left here without a husband just as Belinda would be. The social and financial burdens would take a tremendous toll on their souls. They would all lose their homes, be forced to relocate, and seek new provision. If you have come to a place in your road where you feel sorry for yourself or find yourself angry and bitter toward God, or thinking your journey is just too hard to go on, look again at their stories.

They had no partner, no provider, no protector, no pleasantries to share, yet they were full of hope. Hope is in your future even if you cannot see it today. These ladies can loan you some spiritual binoculars.

It is understandable for your vision to be clouded by your sorrowful loss and your mind flooded with questions concerning why these things happen. If you feel bad and bitter, I want to give you a break today. I ask others to do the same. This is not easy. Tragedy is a bitter pill to swallow, and its aftertaste can linger long. In the short term, you do feel "empty."

You are not alone. God is with you and for you. Holding on to that promise is easier when the difficult circumstances belong to someone else. When tragedy suddenly knocks at your door, does the promise of God's goodness fly out the window? Sometimes it feels that way.

There is a thin line between sweetness and bitterness. In cooking, it could be the amount of sugar. In spiritual things, the difference is hope. In a multitude of unanswered questions seasoned with blame and bitterness, you can still hope in God. When hope gets fully mixed into the recipe, you cannot see it, you just taste it.

Belinda tasted hope. Ruth tasted hope. It took longer for Naomi, but the bitter taste in her mouth was eventually sweetened with that same hope. The good news for you is there is still plenty of that sweetener in God's pantry. "Now faith is confidence in what we hope for and assurance about what we do not yet see" (Heb. 11:1).

Springs of Hope

Why was Huey so healthy and then suddenly facing a terminal disease? Why did he leave us when his impact in God's kingdom seemed to be at it greatest point? I do not have the answers. I am as confounded as anyone. I could not answer Belinda's questions because I had no answers to my own. But God asked me the same question He poses to you and anyone in your situation to whom He has promised to cause all things, even cancer and death, to work together for good. It is the right question for your situation, and it comes with a sufficient answer to strengthen your faith, hope, and love.

What should you say in response to all this? God is for us. So whether you are the preacher or the cancer patient, the caregiver, or the surviving widow, here is the right question. "He who did not spare his own Son, but gave him up for us all—how will he not also, along with Jesus, graciously give us all things?"

God did not spare His Son at the cross, even though Jesus was at the height of His earthly ministry of helping others. God gave His very best and all He has to you. He gave you the most precious and costly gift He could give. God will not shortchange you now in the face of cancer or calamity. God is not hesitant or reluctant to be good to you when the diagnosis is terminal or the accident is tragic. There is no limit to the good God will give you. In truth (that cannot be repeated too often), it will take forever for God to show all His goodness to you (Eph. 2:7).

What should you say in response to all this? God's love for you is unlimited and unending. That is the answer to the right question. Ruth and Naomi would discover that truth in the midst of their grief. Belinda and her two sons would sense the presence of God's love in new and more tangible ways than ever before. I have the opportunity to share their story. *And God* will connect all the dots to your life!

God purposes to use this earthly life to transform you to live and love like Jesus. God guarantees you will be with Him throughout this life and the eternal one to come. We do not know what the future holds. The prognosis might arrive in a pink slip, a doctor's report, or a death notice. We do know God will never abandon you or His purpose. He promises to be with you every step in life including cancer and the death of a loved one.

> God has given us *a living hope* through the resurrection of Jesus Christ…into an inheritance that can never perish, spoil or fade. This inheritance is kept in heaven for you, who through faith are shielded by God's power until the

coming of the salvation that is ready to be revealed in the last time.

In all this you greatly rejoice, though now for a little while you may have had to suffer grief in all kinds of trials. These have come so that the proven genuineness of your faith—of greater worth than gold, which perishes even though refined by fire—may result in praise, glory and honor when Jesus Christ is revealed. (1 Pet. 1:3–7)

The living hope we have in Jesus is strong enough to endure the reality of trials and suffering. We live in a fallen, broken world that is the polar opposite of our heavenly inheritance. In this world, things perish, spoil, and fade in value and substance. Our health or the health of someone we love grows weak. Something we value is taken from us and defiled. Our best dreams and greatest successes fade, but that also describes our sufferings in this world. They will all perish, spoil, and fade.

The common element of all these various multicolored trials is the experience of grief. The Bible is very honest about the reality of suffering. It never promises we will have suffering-free lives. Instead, it guarantees a living hope that is so real and so powerful it shines brightest in the face of trials and death. Huey and Belinda never shined as brightly as they did in their toughest trial.

Grief has an expiration date, so do trials. They remain *for a little while, if necessary*. Even a lifetime of suffering in this world is only "a little while" compared to the everlasting joy of heaven. God promises you an eternal inheritance with everlasting blessings full of all God's riches. Your inheritance is imperishable; it will never be used up. It is undefiled; it can never be messed up. It is unfading; it will never lose its value.

Your heavenly hope is resistant to death, sin, and time. Your hope is reserved in heaven for you, and you are personally protected by God to guarantee you get there to enjoy it. How can your feelings move from resentment to rejoicing in a difficult, stressful battle with cancer? No one is saying that is easy, but it starts with learning to think right about the foretaste of glory.

Sometimes you have to climb up on the mountaintop to see it; sometimes being plunged into the depths of darkness provides the best view of just how great and glorious God's love for you truly is. You not only have a reason to hope, but you also have a reason to rejoice.

Our hope is not wishful thinking or positive confession or some mystical religious concept. Our hope is a Person. His name is Jesus. The purpose of trials like cancer is to test and prove the genuine nature of our faith and showcase our hope to the watching world. If our faith in Jesus becomes only a ticket to better health and increased wealth, how could the unbelievers know our faith and hope were real?

Trials reveal reality. Hope in Jesus shapes how we live and how we die. It colors the picture of the trials of cancer. Suffering does not suffocate hope; it breathes new life into it so that "we entrust ourselves to a faithful Creator" (1 Pet. 1:19).

To *entrust* means to give someone something of value for safekeeping. A dying cancer patient can be entrusted to God. So can the surviving spouse. Take note of Belinda's hope in the midst of grief. It is the same hope that sweetened the lives of Ruth and Naomi. God will provide all the good things we need, and it will be blessings beyond our imagination just as the next chapters of Ruth's story will reveal.

Belinda's story recounts how she and her husband followed in the footsteps of Jesus through the valley of the shadow of death. Together they leave a legacy of faith. A legacy of hope. A legacy of love.

In our culture, *legacy* is often a misappropriated word. In this context, *legacy* refers to something passed on to the next generation. Any legacy begins with one step in the right direction followed by a whole lot of continuous steps in that same direction. A legacy never just happens; it starts with someone making a positive impact in the midst of their trials; it is sustained by those who follow in those same steps with that same hope.

The Lord Jesus Christ started this legacy and carries every one of His followers from start to finish and through everything in between. What God did for Huey and Belinda He does for you and me. Your story might be similar to these widows, but it is as unique as you. Through whatever circumstances or tragedies make up the chapters of your life, you can share the same testimony. "I know in whom I have believed and I know that He is able to guard all that I have entrusted to Him until that day He brings me safely home" (2 Tim. 1:12).

Huey was a great dad and role model. He was a successful firefighter who began a successful business. He could have been a mayor or a pastor. However, he never wanted those things to define his life. He understood that humility was a virtue, not a weakness. Huey embraced life and faced death with a simple purpose, to glorify God. He understood that losing your reason for living was far worse than losing your life. Those are steps that lead to a legacy of faith, hope, and love.

We have to be careful that the pursuit of our life goals, no matter how important they seem, do not cause us to lose sight of our real purpose, to glorify God in how we live and love and die. I was blessed to know a young man and woman whose journey through the dark days of cancer reminded me of that. I saw the heart of a giant and the courage of a champion. I saw a faith-filled woman walk each step with her husband into a legacy worth following.

One of the frontrunners of our faith wrote these words in his last letter: "I have fought the fight. I have run and finished the race. I have kept the faith" (2 Tim. 4:7). The writer used a very emphatic adjective to highlight his focus on the ultimate objective. I fought *the* fight! I finished *the* race! I kept *the* faith! The goal is not just to finish but to finish strong with an ecstatic burst!

Huey did not limp into heaven. He burst through that finish line! His body had been weakened by the cancer and his physical strength horribly deteriorated, but his eyes were fixed on the prize. His soul was set on its purpose. His spirit was ecstatic as he crossed over the line from hope into glory! That is how I am determined to finish. With an ecstatic burst of joy!

In life, we do not know exactly where the finish line is. We might get to a point where we know it could be in a few days, but most of the time it sneaks up on us. All of us know we are going to die, but none of us expect it to come when it does. It usually comes too soon in our timetable of life expectancy. So the issue becomes how to finish strong with an ecstatic burst when you do not know the location or time of the finish line.

Finishing strong never just happens; it is empowered with wholehearted purpose.

What is your motivation for finishing strong? There is a crown of righteousness for all who are faithful to Christ and hope to see Him as their coming King. Listen to Huey and the ones he followed describe the victory. "Now there is in store for me the crown of righteousness which the Lord, the righteous Judge, will award to me on that day—and not only to me, but also to all who have longed for Jesus' appearing" (2 Tim. 4:8).

What is that crown of righteousness? Theological scholars offer several ideas. For me, biblical righteousness is the "life and love of Christ" placed inside of me by the grace of God. This *righteousness* is the essence of being in a right relationship with God and being committed to a right relationship with every other person in my life through the expression of Christ's life and love. My practice of that life and love of Christ is still flawed here on earth because of the remaining seeds of self-love which continue to dwell within me and war for the control of my soul.

However, the victor's crown (*the crown of righteousness*) will be the "perfection of the life and love of Christ in me," which will be fully displayed throughout the rest of eternity. What joy for me and what joy for others who will then be loved by me! I will love them without any selfish tendencies, without any selfish motives, without any selfish expectations. I will love God and love others perfectly, just as Jesus loves me! That is a goal worth an ecstatic burst for the finish line!

That is the championship reward for which we entrust ourselves to the *God who causes all things to work together for our good*. That is the joy for which we agonize and suffer now. This championship crown is for all who are in love with the Jesus who appeared on this earth to save them and who will appear again to take them home with Him forever.

How do you prepare for that ecstatic burst across the finish line when you are kept unaware of when and where it is? Develop a mindset of present-tense enduring loyalty to Jesus. Do something today and each day thereafter to build the foundation of your life on faith, hope, and love in Jesus. Your legacy in life is determined by the direction of your daily steps. "I eagerly expect and *hope* that I will in no way be ashamed, but will have sufficient courage so that now as always Christ will be exalted in my body, whether by life or by death. For to me, to live is Christ and to die is gain" (Phil. 1:20–21).

Where there is despair, *hope*! In the midst of loss and heartbreak, Ruth, Naomi, and Belinda all got to the place of hope. You can too. Your greatest loss can become your greatest gain. Leave a legacy of loyalty to Jesus. Leave a legacy of relentless hope in God.

Fight the fight! Finish the race! Keep the faith! Finish strong with an ecstatic burst into heaven!

The Right Application of Hope

Nothing speaks so profoundly about a person's life and legacy than what is remembered of him or her after death. God always writes the last chapters, but in reality we help write our own obituaries while we are alive. God has given you everything He is and all He has so that you can finish strong and faithful. Hope empowers the ecstatic burst.

Finishing strong does not just happen. Start today!

"Be strong and take heart, all you who *hope* in the Lord" (Ps. 31:24; emphasis added).

> One day the trumpet will sound for His coming
> One day the skies with His glories will shine
> Wonderful day, my beloved one, bringing
> My Savior Jesus is mine
> Living, He loved me
> Dying, He saved me
> Buried, He carried my sins far away
> Rising, He justified freely forever
> One day He's coming
> Oh glorious day, oh glorious day
>
> —"Glorious Day,"
> John Wilbur Chapman

14

Living in the Darkness of Depression

Martha's Story
Application of *God Does Not Accuse You*

Have you ever felt you were hanging on by a thread? A thin, thin thread unraveling in your hands? But in that moment, you realized that there was Someone bigger holding on to that thread and He would never let you go under. In that darkest time of your life, you knew the God of hope was there with you.

In times of deep depression, it is almost impossible to see any signs of hope. Your spiritual vision is impaired; your thinking is clouded. Despair becomes your constant companion. You cannot just "snap out of it" and feel better. Something is wrong. As negative things continue to mount for weeks, months, or even years, any future prospects dim darker and darker while your emotions sink lower and lower.

Depression is a strange sickness. It does not discriminate between young and old, rich or poor, black or white, spiritual or ungodly. Ironically, it traps you in a prison of extreme loneliness where you imagine no one cares, while you battle anxiety and fear that someone might care enough to check on you. Others do not understand. You feel ashamed, confused, and overwhelmed by even the most routine parts of life. You feel judged, condemned. Competing worries vie for your mind's attention. Feelings of helplessness and uselessness and worthlessness weigh you down with self-imposed guilt. You begin to emotionally shut down in your dungeon of despair, too weak to even lift your eyes toward the horizon of hope.

Sometimes all you can do is sit in the darkness of your hurting heart and cry. Sometimes your prayers feel frozen in time and space. Those feelings which overwhelm the depressed also threaten to drown the family caregivers. They sense the sky falling as they watch that thin thread slipping from their loved one's hands. In the midst of that discouragement, the God of hope sits down beside you in the darkness, takes your hand, and holds you through the night. You are not judged; you are loved.

It is vital to the welfare of your soul that you learn to preach the truth to yourself. There will be times you feel down emotionally, mentally, physically, and even spiritually…perhaps extremely downcast. Feelings are not facts; they can change with the circumstances, but they never control the final outcome. Your feelings do not determine reality. Only God is truth and God never changes or loses control.

Even when you do not see God, feel God, hear God, sense God, God is still there, with much love and much understanding, with no condemnation and no accusations. God has been in this place before with many of His sons and daughters. Some of those experiences are recorded in the Scriptures to give us encouragement and hope. Some are buried in private closets. God understands. God never leaves a depressed heart unattended. Where there is despair, *hope*.

Martha's Story

Our family lived with a child who suffered from the disease of depression. Everyone's life was affected. It seemed as though a thief in the night came and stole the very essence of our precious daughter. She became someone we could hardly recognize.

Who understands depression?

After the birth of her second child, postpartum depression became a way of life for her. As her parents, her father and I tried to counsel with her but with no results. After all, how could we help her when we didn't understand depression at all? During a session with our pastor and dear friend, we became aware of what this disease could do to change one's personality and life as we knew it.

After much prayer and begging, we convinced her to see a psychiatrist, and for the first time, we heard the words *severe clinical depression*. At last, we knew what we were fighting but did not have a clue what that fight was going to bring to her or our family.

Our dark nights never seemed to end. Our tears never exhausted their supply.

Many of our days were filled with prayer and supplication for God to bring about an end to the nightmare and pain, while each night was filled with tears that never seemed to run dry. After being ostracized and very misunderstood by friends and several close relatives, our daughter moved to another city and tried to "start over."

I had to learn something very important; depression is a disease, just as real as cancer or heart disease. I had thought of it as just an emotional pity party or spiritual weakness. This was something beyond my daughter's ability to prevent or control.

The big D continued to chase her with a vengeance. Appointments with counselors and physicians, coupled with medicine changes, along with the hospital stays kept her dad and me constantly on our knees before our Lord. Our thoughts were never far from her, but at the same time, we were drawn more deeply into our relationship with Him. Since she was away from us, my prayers daily were pleading with God to place a hedge of protection around her as there were days and sometimes weeks without contact with her.

The Rock of Refuge is the only Anchor for the soul.

God had a plan for us all. We know God can miraculously and instantaneously heal, but He chose not to in our situation. God did lead us to doctors who slowly, very slowly, came up with a combination of medications that gave her some good results, and today she is living a much better life. Remember though, this took a number of years to find this combination, and though her depression has never been cured, it can be treated; we now have a lull in the storm.

Psalm 94:3–23 has been a great solace to my heart during very anxious days, especially verse 22: "The Lord has been my defense and my God the rock of my refuge." As our rock, God can always be found faithful. He can provide safety until problems pass. The psalmist reminds us "under His wings you shall take refuge" (Ps. 91:4).

With God defending us, we don't have to fear. We can trust that He will keep us when trouble comes. I sincerely believe this because my Redeemer is faithful and true.

"Thank you, God, for your strong and unchanging nature. Help us to hide ourselves in You when trouble comes our way. Remind us that we don't have to fight our own battles. You are here, with us and for us."

Desert of Despair

Depression can have a physical or mental or emotional or spiritual cause. Many times, it involves all these areas. Certainly, depression generated from one region will eventually negatively affect the other capacities. This book is not dedicated to the diagnosis and treatment of depression. See a doctor. Talk to a friend or counselor. Saturate your mind with God's Word. Just do not give up. There is hope despite your feelings to the contrary. The writer of this book has seen that hope on display in the darkest of nights. I do not have a cure, but I am well acquainted with the challenges to the depressed and to their loved ones, and with the hope they can find.

Depression is a cruel monster. It lurks in the darkness of the mind ready to trap its victim into an intricate web of anxiety, fear, and despair. The beast grows in size, pressing down on the chest with the weight of a massive boulder, blocking out the light rays of hope, demanding you give up on life.

The fury of despair rages unmercifully. Bound with the cords of depression and blinded by its darkness, you become drained of all thoughts of happiness. You cannot move, see, or feel anything. You are empty. Empty of everything good, everything joyful, everything worthwhile. Surrounded by nothing but empty shadows, you hang by a single thin thread, the only thing between you and the bottomless abyss of empty darkness from where no one returns. Sometimes you hang on that perilous ledge for hours, days, even longer.

But God—the God of divine conjunctions—connects the thin thread, unraveling in your hands to the mighty promise of hope held in the hands of the One from whom the monsters of depression flee. You feel alone, *but God* is with you and He will never let you go. You become lost in the darkness, *but God* sees in the darkness. You feel hollow, *but God* fills the empty mind and heart with hope. God is for you. God gives you all the good things you need, *and God* never condemns or judges you, not even for feeling so depressed you cannot read the Bible or pray a prayer. When you cannot say a word or feel a thing, God is right there with you, understanding every unsaid word and feeling every untouched heartache. God understands your weaknesses and brings you comfort, compassion, and closeness.

God was with Martha and her daughter in those times of great darkness. Martha knows what Ruth went through with Naomi. Naomi was depressed over the losses in her life. She told her daughters-in-law she felt hopeless. Happiness was a stranger, but she was well acquainted with sorrow's gloom and doom. She felt useless with no future significance to her life. Her sorrow overflowed to others. Her foreboding fears encompassed her loved ones in the same darkness.

Naomi was not condemned by God for her feelings. As we walk through the story, we see that God does work things out for Naomi, but for the first chapter of their story, Naomi is allowed to wallow in her grief and stumble through the darkness of her despair.

God does not promise some simple sudden fix to our problems. He never promised that life would be easy and carefree, but God does promise that he will never abandon us. God did not say we must be happy all the time, rather He says we must trust in Him all the time, even in days of anxiety and nights of despair.

"Weeping may tarry through the night, but joy comes in the morning" (Ps. 30:5). The night is often long and dark. Sometimes it feels longer and darker as you hang on the verge of losing all hope.

That is why we need someone with us in the depression of the emotional darkness, someone who can see the hope we cannot see. It is not the time for someone to tell us to shake it off and get going or command us to just praise the Lord and the darkness will disappear.

There are no easy solutions. If it were a matter of the will, most depressed women would choose a different life, but they cannot. Why? Depression hides hope, it weakens ability, it destroys confidence, it clouds the mind, and it shakes the senses. Depression is powerful, but it does not mean you are spiritually defective. It can be overcome, but it is generally not the quick fix hoped for by the oppressed or by the family members caught up in its wake.

It really helps if family caregivers understand that depression makes people feel desperately alone and misunderstood. If your loved one were battling cancer or ALS, you would be understanding of her weakness. You certainly would never condemn her for her sickness. Those suffering from depression need that same compassion and understanding. This is your opportunity to practice the servant love exemplified by our Lord Jesus Christ. This is your time to shine with patient, long-suffering, unconditional love in the darkest moments of her physical, emotional, and spiritual weakness. There will be feelings of frustration and failure for you and her, but those are false readings.

To the one suffering under the burden of depression, look beyond the accuser's stare to the Guardian of your soul. Where there is despair, *hope*. You are not condemned; you are greatly loved even in your lowest moments. *Who will bring any charge against those whom God has chosen? Who is the one who condemns you?* Certainly not God. Your feelings of frustration and failure are inadmissible evidence in God's courtroom. God does not accuse you of spiritual failure because you struggle with depression. There is a divine purpose to this trial in your life. Faith, hope, and love will be vindicated, and joy will be freed from its imprisoned darkness.

Hope in God is always conveyed in love whether it comes from Jesus in the Scriptures or the life of Jesus in a loved one's soul. We readers can see the God of hope in Naomi's story when she could not. Ruth knew there was hope, and that is how she helped Naomi through the depression. It was not by lectures or reprimands but by the demonstrations of love fueled by her own hope in God.

Depression is never just about the one who is depressed. It is also the story about the opportunity to love as Ruth did, as Jesus loved us in our helpless and hopeless state. In every situation of depression, there is a great need for remarkable steadfast love in defiance of its circumstances, obstacles, and discouragement.

Ruth could trust God when Naomi could not. In those moments, Ruth trusted God for both of them. In the worst times, Ruth buoyed the whole family with her own faith. That is the mission of the caregiver. Is that easy? No, definitely not.

Depression ruthlessly seeks to choke out all hope. The lungs gasp for breaths of hope. The heart sinks and spiritual lifelines become clogged. In that emergency, the Paramedic of our soul is always there in time to perform love's CPR.

Even when you do not see God, feel God, hear God, sense God, God is still there.

This glorious truth needs to be relentlessly repeated in every possible way until it permeates your thoughts and feelings. Depression is a disease whose advancement is curtailed only by the truth.

Life is hard with or without depression. God is at work in the darkest of times for the good of His people. Accept God's unconditional love; you are not condemned. Do not be so hard on yourself; in fact, be kinder and gentler to yourself. Where there is despair, hope. God's love resuscitates, it empowers; it outlasts the worst and longest depression.

> My heart was grieved and my spirit embittered…Yet I am always with you; you hold me by my right hand. You guide me with your counsel, and afterward you will take me into glory. Whom have I in heaven but you? And earth has nothing I desire besides you. My flesh and my heart may fail, but God is the strength of my heart and my portion forever…As for me, it is good to be near the Lord. (Ps. 73:21–28)

Is that what despair feels like? Does it feel as if your body is failing and your heart cannot go on? Sometimes God can seem strangely silent, far away, disinterested, uncaring. Blindly, you grasp for straws, search for clues, cry for answers. Your prayers sound unheard, your feelings unfelt. You are caught up in a swirl of chaos, confusion, uncertainty. You want to retreat into the shadows of your sorrow, out of sight, checked out of life.

However, this questioning and search for answers to understand what is happening from within your own thoughts is *anxiety*. It is an endless and futile cycle that always leads to more despair, confusion, and hopelessness. It is important to learn that this cycle does not work; it only creates more worry, greater misery, and bigger fears. You can never find answers from within your own limited reasoning. Trying to make sense of life and how you feel apart from God's truth will always be futile.

We will suffer *many kinds of trials in life* (James 1:2). Some are comfort-shaking, others life-altering: incurable cancer, debilitating depression, challenging disability, unfair treatment, painful afflictions, panic attacks, impending death. Life is full of weakness and worry, guilt and grief, disappointment and despair. Who chooses to live that way? No one really.

If people could just snap out of it, they would. If they could just think positive thoughts and move on in life, they would. Depression can hold the most spiritual among us in its death grip. It is a force to be acknowledged, but it is not a power greater than God's hope. No matter how far down it drags you, it cannot separate you from God's love.

The winter of the soul is never a comfortable season. The sharp blasts of the cold winds of adversity are painful. The frost can chill the spirit and numb the senses. Maybe you are experiencing uncontrollable weeping or inability to concentrate, difficulty to just get out of bed or to read God's Word. God has not abandoned you in your icy arctic of despair.

This book is not able to take the pain out of your suffering, but God can make your suffering purposeful.

Hope does not have seasonal restrictions. God controls the winter as much as the springtime. There is no one more loving, no one more merciful, no one more compassionate, and no one more patient, powerful, and faithful than our God. Even when joy stays out of reach and spiritual darkness embattles the soul, *hope never, ever, ever disappoints* (Rom. 5:4).

God gives you enough faith and hope to hang on. Take it; embrace it. God sees your struggle and feels your pain. God will always give you enough strength to take one more breath and make it through one more day. In the darkest moments on the battlefield, that is victory.

You are not a spiritual failure because you struggle with depression. This is your suffering. In and of itself, it is not good. In the hands of God, it will work out for good somehow... someway...sometime. Do not give up.

The best encouragement to my faith in the soul's struggle with spiritual darkness has been the assurance found in Psalm 27:12–13: "I would have despaired unless I had believed that I would still see the goodness of the Lord in the land of the living. Wait for (Hope in) the Lord. Be strong and let your heart take courage. Hope in the Lord."

Springs of Hope

Who is the one who condemns you? Christ Jesus is the one who died—more than that, who was raised—who is at the right hand of God, who indeed *is interceding for you.*

What is despair? Essentially, *despair* is the opposite of hope. *Despair* becomes a hazard-warning sign declaring you have given up on God. Hopelessness is an enemy to faith. Too many of us fail to understand that the spiritual condition of our soul is usually in a worse situation than our health. As the wait lengthens, the situation often worsens.

If you take your eyes off the Lord and focus only on your circumstances, the tendency will always be to swerve toward the ditch of despair. Hopelessness gets stuck in that ditch, and it takes more than a tow truck to get out. God is a very present help to get you back onto the highway of hope where every billboard reminds you that God is for you. God will not withhold any good thing from your life. Get your Goodyear snowtires of truth on now and prepare for the winter season of the soul.

What can you do when you feel depressed? Look at your God, not your circumstances. "Faith does not look at the things which are seen, but faith looks at the things which are not seen; because the things that we can see are just temporary, but the eternal things are things we cannot see" (2 Cor. 4:18).

Despair might give up on God, but God never gives up on your despair.

I want to introduce you to a man whose life was far worse than the worst and darkest days of your despair. I realize you might consider that to be impossible, so let me ask you to consider him as messed up as you feel when that thin thread of help and hope is slipping through your fingers for the last time.

In the fifth chapter of Mark's Gospel, Jesus took His disciples to meet a man no one wanted to be around. Those who loved this guy the most now considered him a lost cause. This man's life was messed up physically, mentally, emotionally, and spiritually. He was so miserable that he screamed and cried through the night.

He said his name was Legion. He was the poster child of a soap opera world of despair. He became an example of someone beyond all hope. He lost hope in himself, others, and God. Others lost all hope for his recovery. Jesus wanted His disciples to understand that this person was without God, without help, and without hope.

Legion had lost all hope. There was not one moment of anything but despair in a life filled with conflict and torment. Not one ray of hope ever penetrated into his darkened soul. Legion made the lives of others so miserable he was now ostracized and avoided at all costs.

Legion was on the road to self-destruction. He roamed the wilderness. He ran through the graveyards. He hid in the caves. Sometimes he was like a raving maniac, others times a recluse. He acted as if he were bi-polar. He endangered the lives of others while he was in the process of ruining his own life. There was a depressing cycle to his life: circumstances would get out of control, he would get desperate and downcast, depressed and dangerous. Someone would try to get him help or lock him up, but it never worked. Circumstances would get worse; he cycled back into depression. Some nights were filled with screams of frustration and other times only the silence of hopelessness.

Even when he was on his own, Legion was not free. His desires and dreams were crushed. His mind retreated into a world where everything was wrong. He lived like the walking dead on a road from worse to worst, imprisoned by the darkness in his soul. He was driven by the unrest that was in his mind.

His emotional state left him socially alienated, spiritually unfit, culturally unacceptable. He had come to the point where it was humanly impossible to love him. He was incapable of loving anyone back. His moods fluctuated wildly, from crying to screaming, from extreme highs to below bottom. Legion was in perpetual torment. You might be very familiar with his feelings.

Depression and anxiety cause that same kind of mental turmoil. It is *torture*. Whether it comes from without or from within, it is still torture. There are many times that the depressed person would gladly trade the mental pain and emotional torment for the most severe physical pain. There is no way to describe it to someone who has never experienced it. Your own mind attacks you in the most frightening and horrific ways; you experience desperation beyond anything you could possibly imagine. There is nothing good about it.

Depression challenges God's promise in Romans 8:28. Not only does it cause questions about "all things" working together for good, it even raises doubts about the "we know God" part. Doubt the existence of God? Scandalous thoughts and yet depression questions everything you were ever taught or believed about God. At times, you might not even be able to have a Godward thought. It certainly does not feel as though God is there with you and the fear of being alone in that mental-emotional-spiritual darkness is terrifying. Many even begin to fight against the idea of God's reality and presence. Legion did.

Legion's mind was tormented night and day in a way that tormented everyone else around him. His despair was contagious. No one knew how to help him. At this point in his misery, no one believed he could be helped. No one, except Jesus.

Jesus went looking for Legion, just as He does for you in your depressed condition. This is what the disciples were supposed to learn. It was humanly impossible to love this man, and yet Jesus went to where he was. Jesus was not afraid of Legion's condition. Jesus never condemned Legion for being in that state of mind. Instead, Jesus gave Legion hope. (Loved ones, please take note and hope.)

What is the lesson of Legion's amazing life story from despair to hope?

1. *No one is ever beyond the help and hope of Jesus Christ.* Jesus might end up as someone's last hope, but Jesus will always be a lasting hope. Jesus changed Legion forever. Now of sound mind, he could reunite with his family and friends.

2. *There is great value in loving one hopeless person.* Loving someone in the midst of their despair is of much more value than fortune or fame. It is more valuable than anything else in this world, even if it costs you all that you have. Love them the way Christ loved you, even if they say they have no hope. Ruth loved Naomi. Martha loved her daughter. They both chose to not let their loved one sink into depression alone. As much as it hurt, as much as it cost, they would be with them and for them. Why? Because no one is beyond hope and loving one hopeless individual is of infinite worth to God.

3. *When you give love, you give hope.* Jesus's love changed Legion's life. Legion would not be perfect, but his life was now permanently set in a new direction. The man who

did not know how to love himself, much less love others, now went back home to love a family that had given up on him. There is power in going back home to love people who thought you could never change. (Dear depressed lady, please take note and hope.)

We need to live out what we learn. Our lives have been changed by Christ. Your change might not have been as dramatic as Legion's. The circumstances might have been much less traumatic, but the changes were just as real. What should you do? Show the life and love of Jesus to your spouse and to your children and to your extended family. Love the helpless and love the hopeless.

You might feel hopeless by human standards and worldly evaluations. Nothing is impossible to God. In the darkest hours of the soul, God will still be there. You will never go to bed alone. You will never face a day or sail through any storm alone. You will never be so depressed or care for some loved one so deep in despair that you are left to fend for yourself. The Lord will never leave nor forsake you. Never alone! Never without hope!

Your *flesh* may fail. The physical part of you might grow weak and fatigued leaving you despondent and without energy. Your *heart* might fail. You can get emotionally and spiritually worn out and discouraged. All of you and all that makes up your *life* might fail, totally exhausted of resources. Depression might bring you to the very end of being able to go on under its oppression or stay around it as a caregiver, *but God* never gives up on despair.

But God...there is the divine conjunction for depression whatever its cause. But God never fails! Depression is not a sin. Unbelief in God becomes the problem. Faith in God when you cannot see the help and do not feel the hope is the answer. Do not give up even when your flesh and heart fail you.

Naomi had faith, hope, and love, but in the darkness, she could not find them. But God found them and returned them to her through the tenderness and tenacity of Ruth's steadfast but nonjudgmental love. Martha learned to do that for her daughter when the times were tough. That is the place and time for steadfast but nonjudgmental love! (Let us all take note and hope.)

"Why are you cast down, O my soul, and why are you in turmoil within me? Hope in God." These words of comfort and encouragement come from the same voice of the one filled with tears and turmoil. His circumstances had not changed. His feelings of despair had not gone away. But the psalmist did not give up. Neither should you.

In the midst of the soul's darkness, it can feel as if God might have forgotten you. The "Why?" questions fill your thoughts. But the steadfast love of God will never let you go. Do not let go of that anchor for your soul. God's love for you is sure and steadfast, inseparable and unending.

It has been written elsewhere in this book, but it cannot be emphasized too many times. Learn to preach to yourself the beautiful truths of God's love for you. In his book, *Spiritual Depression*, the physician/preacher Martyn Lloyd Jones highlighted the importance of learning to preach to yourself instead of just listening to yourself.

> Have you realized that most of your unhappiness in life is due to the fact that you are listening to yourself instead of talking to yourself? Take those thoughts that come to you the moment you wake up in the morning. You have not originated them but they are talking to you, they bring back the problems of yesterday, etc. Somebody is talking. Who is talking to you? Your self is talking to you. Now this (Psalm 42) writer's treatment was this: instead of allowing this self to talk to him, he starts talking to himself. "Why art thou cast down, O my soul?" he asks. His soul had been depressing him, crushing him. So he stands up and says, "Self, listen for a moment, I will speak to you." Hope in God.

Depression listens to the wrong voices. Hope hears God. You are loved at your worst. You are loved in the darkest times. "Why, my soul, are you downcast? Why are you so disturbed within me? Put your hope in God; for I will yet praise Him, my Savior and my God" (Ps. 42:11).

Hope in God! Nothing can ever be said that will help more than that. If you cannot feel hope or hold on to hope, then ask someone to hope for you as Ruth did for Naomi until Naomi could feel her feet back on the solid ground of God's love. Many nights, Martha did that for her daughter.

What Jesus did for the downcast psalmist He will do for you. What Jesus did for the confused and hopeless Legion He will do for you. Your life might look like a battle with depression, but in truth, it's a struggle for hope. Every grace story is a grateful story. My story may not be great to you, but it is to me. You ought to feel that way about your story. It might not sound great to the TV evening news, but it ought to have your soul awestruck that you have been changed by the grace of God.

You can help the depressed. You do not have the power to relieve them of their despair, but you can stay with them in uncritical love because you see the hope when they cannot. You do not have to take a ten-week counseling course before you can go home and love somebody else the way the Lord has loved you. Your God has power over human helplessness in the storms of life and power over human hopelessness in the darkest times. Our hope is in God.

Since God is for you, who shall separate you from the love of Christ? Absolutely no one and nothing, not even the worst depression ever. Nothing can ever separate you from Christ's love. You are loved by God and you still have hope in God. How can you succumb to despair when the omnipotent God of unending goodness has promised to be your helper? Preach to your soul to trust and praise God until your flesh and heart and spirit recover.

Learn this wonderful song for the downcast soul; it begins with the cry of a soul thirsting for hope. "As a deer pants for flowing streams, so pants my soul for you, O God. My soul thirsts for God, for the living God" (Ps. 42:1–2). The writer does not express his desire for relief from his despair. That would not be wrong, but it is not the solution. He thirsts for the love of God. He longs to get closer to God and to know God better. That is the ultimate source of hope for the depressed.

There is no difference between any of us and Legion, except the clothes and the makeup. There is no depression and no cause beyond the reach of Jesus's love. Jesus will either lift the oppressive burden or He will sustain you through the continued darkness. I cannot promise you there will never be another episode of depression. I can assure you that every new season of darkness can get you closer to the God of hope.

Thankfully, the valleys in life really do enhance the rest of life's landscape. They enable you to see life and God in new ways. Through the spiritual binoculars of hope, you see that nothing is wasted. The clouds of darkness and its bitter rain are divinely designed to make life sweeter than ever before. Days of depression are not wasted days; God will use each one of them for greater good. God specializes in turning sorrow into lasting joy. Maybe you are one of Martha's many daughters of despondency, well acquainted with the desperation of depression. Perhaps only few know of your struggle and fewer understand it.

Your heart feels empty yet heavy, the paradox of hopelessness. Your body grows weaker as the joys of life become a distant memory, if they ever existed at all. You feel trapped by the darkness as you sink lower into the depths of despair.

My dear lady, Jesus is there with you. Where there is despair, *hope*. Depression is not a sign of spiritual defeat. Despondency of the soul is the battleground where you will most glorify God. The fury of despair may rage, but the victory belongs to those who hope in God. You are still loved and not condemned. God cares and understands.

Depression can happen in the best of times and to the most spiritual persons. Certainly it can stem from unmet expectations and disappointments in life, but it also can be as much about chemistry as it is circumstances. Contrary to the lies of depression, life is really not about you. You are a part of God's magnificent story. The final chapters of this good and glorious story are not yet finished.

> Ye fearful saints, fresh courage take
> The clouds you so much dread
> Are big with mercy and shall break
> With blessings on your head.

You are a key character in God's beautiful story! When you grasp that truth, you will begin to view the clouds with a different perspective. The cloudy days will feel a little differently. There is rest for the heart and peace for the mind in the newfound ability to see beauty in God's world and find joy in God's gift of life. Legion discovered this hope just as Naomi and Martha and countless multitudes of women suffering depression. This is not a curse; it is not some spiritual shortcoming. It is the struggle of your story.

No one understands your mental turmoil and torturous grief better than Jesus. Even when He knew that His suffering would be part of God's story of hope, His soul was very sorrowful, even to death. He prayed about the possibility of the struggle being lifted from His tormented mind as His sweat became great drops of blood falling down to the ground (Luke 22:44). However, Jesus understood there was a bigger picture. The winter darkness of the soul always precedes the springtime resurrection of life.

Each one of us is on a unique journey; some will experience seasons of depression while others struggle with different forms of suffering. There is one thing that is certain that we all share in common. God never fails to lead us out of the desert of despair, the deepest pit, or the apparent dead end. Rejoicing always comes in the morning. Even when life feels like just one single thread slipping through your fingers, hang on tightly. It is actually a rope of hope held in the hands of the Almighty God.

Where there is despair, *hope*. Even here…even now…even this.

This war is won one battle at a time. When you do not give up in your struggle with the monsters of depression, you have gained a key victory. When you make it through another day, you have secured a major triumph. Others might not understand, but God has a plan. God will give you days of joy. That is difficult to see in the fog of depression, so put down some signposts in your heart during the brighter days. God is always there with you; God is always there for you. This time of darkness in your soul will work together for the benefit of you and others somehow…someway…sometime.

The Right Application of Hope

Lift up the eyes of your soul. Hope is on the horizon. Just take another breath. Get through one more day. God is with you in the darkness, and He never gives up on despair.

"Yes, my soul, rest in God; my *hope* comes from Him" (Ps. 62:5; emphasis added).

Who am I, that the Lord of all the earth
Would care to know my name,
Would care to feel my hurt?
Who am I, that the Bright and Morning Star
Would choose to light the way
For my ever wandering heart?
Not because of who I am
But because of what You've done
Not because of what I've done
But because of who You are
I am a flower quickly fading
Here today and gone tomorrow
A wave tossed in the ocean
A vapor in the wind
Still You hear me when I'm calling
Lord, You catch me when I'm falling
And You've told me who I am
I am Yours, I am Yours
Who am I, that the eyes that see my sin
Would look on me with love and watch me rise again?
Who am I, that the voice that calmed the sea
Would call out through the rain
And calm the storm in me?
Not because of who I am
But because of what You've done
Not because of what I've done
But because of who You are

—"Who Am I," John Mark Hall

15

Come Home

Sarah's Unfinished Story
Application of *No One Condemns You*

What is your story? It might be similar to one of this book's stories of these "ordinary" women, but your story is still different, unique to you. There are common themes of suffering but individual heartbreak. The pain does not change whether you are the person most likely to go to hell in someone's eyes or the pastor's wife who is supposed to have the perfect life, marriage, and family. The vast in-between spectrum of flawed, fallen, failed women live with those same crushed dreams, bitter pills, and trying circumstances. Some live in the spotlight shining on their glass houses while others just exist unnoticed in the hidden corners of darkness.

Life can be overwhelming. Hope can seem distant or nonexistent. Some women run; some hide. Some just go through the motions physically, emotionally, and spiritually. Some just head for the *far country* like the prodigal in the Lord's story recorded in Luke 15.

The far country can be anywhere you go to get away from God. It might be in a bar or the backseat of a car. It could be in a church choir or on a computer screen. The far country has hosted many women wasting life on things that do not matter and do not last. The prodigal came to his senses about the greatness of his father's love. He returned home to discover he was treated as if he had never been away. No condemnation. No separation. That same great love awaits you.

I know a woman named Sarah who has her own chapter of suffering in an unfinished story. Actually, I know many Sarahs out there, some in the desert of despair, some far away from the home of hope. Some sit in church pews and nice homes; some run in wild circles. What they have in common is a heart out of synch with the heart of their Heavenly Father. I have not walked in these ladies' shoes, but many who read this chapter will know someone who has. Maybe that person is you.

Sometimes life just gets messed up. It is usually not intentional. Perhaps you have been in a hard place for a long time. Maybe like Sarah, you have shown flashes of faith in very difficult trials, maybe even a long record of faithfulness to God and your family, but somewhere your journey took you farther away from the God of help and hope. You focused more on your circumstances; life began to feel helpless and hopeless. So you did what you thought was best for your life; you took matters into your own hands. Life became about you first and foremost.

At its best, this life remains a struggle. Our culture feeds self-love with media images and celebrity testimonials. Other self-lovers cheer for those running in the wrong direction as they seek to legitimize their own lifestyles or to quiet their own consciences. Even when the Lord gives us a new heart, we continue to struggle with our love of self which remains at war against wholehearted love for God and unselfish love for others.

If your struggles have led you far away from where you need to be, I encourage you to turn back to the God of hope. There is no condemnation for anything you have done or not done. There is no separation from God's love no matter how far away from home you have traveled. Your story is not over. God always writes the last chapter. Until then, God has promised to fill your days with mercy and goodness. I still believe that for Sarah and for each of you who find yourself along that same path.

Come home! *Who will bring any charge against those whom God has chosen? Who is the one who condemns you?* Not God. Not those who love you. Just come home.

Sarah's Story

Sarah is a wonderful woman whose journey was hard, made even more difficult by barrenness and marital challenges. Her attempts at adoption and foster parenting were cruelly upended by the judicial system that tortured her heart and saddened the children she had come to dearly love. Her journey of hope took another major hit with the news of her husband's unfaithfulness. Her faith seemed tested beyond human reason, and yet her hope stayed strong in the darkest of nights as ladies from our church wept with her and prayed with her.

Through all the tears and heartbreak and struggles, she retained a glowing countenance, a beautiful smile, and a servant's heart. During one very tough season of life, she chose to separate from her unfaithful husband. There were other factors involved as there are with all relationships. During that time, her husband privately and publicly repented, sought forgiveness, and returned to the church. He sought reconciliation with his wife, but Sarah decided to start a new life without him. She made the decision she thought best for herself. Her independence seemed to open up a whole new world to her. She placed her hope for a better life in other things. Outwardly, she acted happy; perhaps she was although I thought her eyes betrayed her words.

The pain and disappointment overwhelmed Sarah. Her hurt was deep. She felt many had failed her. She began to distance herself from friends who had wept and rejoiced with her through the difficult struggles, ladies who still steadfastly love her and continue to pray for her.

Sarah was very familiar with the springs of hope that once fed her soul in her desert of despair. As time passed, she drifted away into the fog surrounding her heart and mind. Maybe she ran away with the aid of some night-vision goggles. I feared she lost her way. I do not dare represent myself as one who knew all the things in her mind and heart during those days. She does not have to ever answer to me or anyone else for that matter. God knows her heart. I just want her to come home to God's heart. Come home to Hope!

I pleaded for Sarah to come home to her church family even if she chose not to reconcile with her husband. I know our Heavenly Father stands ready to embrace her in His arms and treat her as if she had never been away or ever done anything wrong. Sarah was not condemned nor judged in any way by God, nor me. We met many times to cry and pray together during those months. My love for her led me to write one last letter urging her to come home and trust the God of hope who always writes the last chapter of our lives. I expected that chapter to be beautiful for Sarah and I still do.

Desert of Despair

Sarah's story is unfinished just like yours. At this point in the book of Ruth, Naomi's story was unfinished. It was time for her to come home. Naomi returned to where she had lost her hope in God. She came back empty and bitter. She even admitted she had lost all hope. But something brought her back home to Bethlehem and back home would be where God would write the last chapters of her earthly life, chapters of joy and love beyond anything she could imagine.

The great news is that God always writes the last chapter of our lives. I pray the last chapter and those preceding it will be gloriously beautiful for all the Sarahs who read this book and for all those clinging to hope in their hearts for the Sarah in their life to come home. Home is not about Bethlehem or church or any physical location. It is a place in your heart, a special place of hope in God.

I kept a copy of that last letter to Sarah. Even then, I felt there was another Sarah wandering in her desert of despair who might someday hear the plea to "come home." I pray that it might be you and the time might be now. I pray you will be able to recognize the sound of our Heavenly Father calling for you with the same words of love directed at Sarah and Naomi: "Come home. Come home to the heart of God, home to hope."

Come home where you are greatly loved! Come home to no fear of abandonment and no fear of condemnation with no fear of separation from God's love. You are fully forgiven! Come home with no burdens of guilt or shameful skeletons from your past. You are accepted! Come back home where God heals broken hearts with love and fills empty hearts with hope. You are wanted!

Come home finally and fully freed from the incessant feelings of unworthiness. Flawed, failed, and fallen but wanted just as you are. You are beautiful! Rush home into the loving arms of your Heavenly Father and be clothed in garments of grace, bejeweled with heavenly treasures, radiant with the glow of a woman loved with an unconditional, long-suffering, and even longer lasting unending love. Come home where nothing but hope is on the horizon!

Springs of Hope

Who is the one who condemns you? Not God.

There is a place in the Father's heart and house reserved for you. Come home. God always writes the last chapter of your life.

There are other women besides Naomi and Sarah whose struggles and sufferings have taken them down a path of misery. Perhaps you are one of those women. Somehow your life got messed up. It might have been someone or something else that derailed your dream before it arrived at its destination. The cause of the train wreck is not the issue. There is still help and hope for you. The last chapters of your life are yet to be written. They can be filled with God's mercies and blessings, goodness beyond your imagination.

How do I know and, more importantly, how can you know that God wants you home with Him? God sent His Son Jesus to this earth to save self-deceived, self-loving sinners like you and me. Jesus came to show us the Father's heart and to fill up the Father's house.

God offers you a great exchange, the most one-sided transaction ever. On the cross, God treated Jesus, His perfect and loving Son, as if Jesus had lived your selfish, sinful life in order that for all of eternity God might treat you as if you had lived Jesus's perfect, loving life. That is great news! God's gift of grace is irrevocable; it will never be taken away. Once loved by God, always loved by God.

Grace is not just a power; grace is a Person. His name is Jesus. He comes to live and work inside of you, giving you both the desire and the power to do what pleases God and most benefits you (Phil. 2:13). That is a biblical description of grace, the life of God at work in you. You might have a different life story, but all of God's children have the same testimony: The Lord will always stand by you in every chapter of life and He will make sure you arrive safely home (2 Tim. 4:17–18).

God's Word calls your next step, "repentance" which is a 180-degree turn in the opposite direction, turning from a self-centered life to a God-centered life. Repentance is the radical reorientation of your entire life to the truth that Jesus Christ is Lord of everything, all the time. This Person-driven life is just one breath and one step away from a new direction. Take that one step now.

Get to know Jesus for who He is. He is the Lord God. That means He is sovereign and supreme. He has the right, the power, and the wisdom to rule your life in the way that is best for you. It also means that Jesus is always to be first and foremost in your life. He is above and before everything else. Jesus is your Savior. He offers you a new and better life.

Once you know Jesus, you realize you can trust Him. He has a better plan for your life than you do. The Lord always knows where you are, where you need to be, and how to get you there. So follow Jesus. Whatever He says, you do, and wherever He leads, you go. That is the Christian life. Even a child can understand.

The journey begins with no condemnation for those who trust in Jesus (Rom. 8:1). It ends with proof that nothing could ever separate you from His love (Rom. 8:35). In between and all through life's journey, God promises to work out everything in this life for your good, somehow, someway, sometime (Rom. 8:28). That is not hard to understand either, just sometimes hard to see and feel.

To all the Sarahs out there, "Come home." Come home to our Father's house where there is no condemnation and no performance track treadmill. Come home now. Come home and be loved with a steadfast, long-suffering love that knows no limits and no end. Come home to the God of hope.

Several times I told Sarah that I intended to someday write a book about the God who brought hope to the many women struggling in our church and that I wanted her story to be a purposeful chapter of the book. This version is radically different than the one I envisioned. The real ending is yet to be told.

God has connected Sarah's story to yours with His divine conjunctions. And God…But God…Your story is not over neither is it so messed up that it cannot be put back together, new and improved. It only takes one breath to have new life and one step to change directions. God's mercy is greater than anyone's messed up life. God can change Sarah. He can change you.

Let God write the next chapters of your life. They will far exceed anything you could dream of writing. Springs of hope can be found in the desert wilderness.

Rethink your story. It needs to be told but not just from the private assessment of your personal pain and challenges. It needs to be told from the perspective of the bigger picture. Maybe you need to come home to finish your story. God will make a way and God will heal the hurts. Others might have failed you and hurt you, but God is forever faithful and His love is incredibly long-suffering and infinitely long-lasting.

Wait on the Lord until you begin to see your story under the spotlight of His glory. You might not see it today because of the dark nights, or gray skies, or foggy mornings, but the sun is in its place and fulfilling its purpose. Each morning God's sun rises in the sky like the raising of heaven's flag signaling the King is still on the throne over all His Kingdom. All day long, the sun preaches to us in pictures without words but full of meaning.

The first five verses of Psalm 19 highlight the sun's message with two marvelous metaphors:

1. *The awed beauty in the eyes of a bridegroom.*

    Every day the sun shines in radiance like a smiling groom waiting for his bride on their wedding day, preaching to you, "Rejoice! This is the most beautiful day of your life!"

2. *The important focus in the eyes of a champion runner.*

    As the sun races its course across the sky, it also reminds us of a champion runner making the final turn around the track now heading for the finish line of dreams shaped in painful training and heart-inspiring challenges. Listen to the sun preach to you. Can you hear it? "This is the most important day of your life! Do not lose hope! Do not quit! Finish Strong!"

    Every morning is a call from God for you to come home and enjoy the beauty of this day in your life. Every sunset is a postcard from heaven reminding you of the importance of your life's story. It needs to be finished and then told to honor the God of hope. Your story might not have a book written about it, but it can be whispered in a hospital, shared in tears with a suffering sister, or passed on in the hearts of loved ones. Where there is despair, *hope*. Hope in God.

Come home, Sarah! Please come home!

Look at the sun. Listen to its unspoken message. God's love for you is far brighter and much bigger than the sun. There is nowhere to get away from it. There is no time it does not exist. It was there for your first breath on this earthly journey, and it will still be there beyond your last one.

This is the right time to come home. Do it today. Do not allow another season in life to pass. It's time to come home… even here…even now…even this.

My eyes feel with tears at the prospect of you coming home. My prayers would turn to praise. Embrace the love extended to you. Know you will be treated as if you had never departed. Treasure that love and share it with the confidence that our God will write the last chapter of your life to be beautiful to you and an important blessing to others.

Where there is despair, *hope*. I still hope. That is why I wrote this chapter. I believe God will connect Naomi's story to Sarah's story and to your story. I know with absolute certainty that the last chapter in each of our lives will be written by the incomparable Author of love and hope. It's a must read!

"Now may the God of Hope fill you with all joy and peace as you trust in Him, so that you may overflow in *hope* by the power of the Holy Spirit" (Rom. 15:13; emphasis added).

God's unfinished story gives you unending hope.

The Right Application of Hope

Do whatever it takes to get closer to God because the nearness of God is your good.

If you are away, come home. If you are where you should be, pray for someone else to come back home.

"I pray that the eyes of your heart may be enlightened in order that you may know the *hope* to which he has called you, the riches of his glorious inheritance" (Eph. 1:18; emphasis added).

Everyone needs compassion
A love that's never failing
Let mercy fall on me

Everyone needs forgiveness
The kindness of a Savior
The hope of nations

Savior he can move the mountains
My God is mighty to save
He is mighty to save
Forever author of salvation
He rose and conquered the grave
Jesus conquered the grave

So take me as you find me
All my fears and failures
Fill my life again

I give my life to follow
Everything I believe in
Now I surrender

Savior he can move the mountains
My God is mighty to save
He is mighty to save
Forever author of salvation
He rose and conquered the grave
Jesus conquered the grave

—"Mighty to Save,"
Ben Fielding and Reuben Morgan

16

Live for Something that Outlasts This Life

Charlotte's Story
Application of *No Exclusions from the Love of Christ*

"She looked like hope!" That was how a woman in despair described this lady named Charlotte. Charlotte's life changed dramatically when God called her to labor among those most in need of help and hope. God would use her to pick up the fallen, care for the oppressed, and love those left behind in a self-consumption world. What a challenge God put before this timid, fearful, uncomfortable daughter! He sent her into the worst and hardest places to love. There would be names and faces in places she had never known existed, at least not in her world. Her "family" would grow, some incarcerated, some in another country, and some living in another world right in her own city.

Desperate people sitting in prison cells, on porches in heat waves, or in small huts in an impoverished country did not see her coming. They were not expecting her and certainly did not search for someone like her in the help-wanted ads. This "ordinary" social club member did not look like a prisoner, a porch lady, or a poor country tamale maker. But to women very familiar with those descriptions, she looked like hope! The hope that is promised in Romans 8:28.

This next story is another illustration of an ordinary woman who found the best life possible when she followed Jesus down the service road of life. He called her out of the more comfortable world of garden societies, blood drives, community-fund garage sales, food and clothes collections, and conventional church ministries. All those community and church opportunities are worthy projects which help make many lives better. But God just planned to extend and expand Charlotte's heart beyond her comfort zone. Perhaps you will hear a similar call on your life.

If you really want to walk with Jesus in this life, you will have to get off the main highway, because Jesus walks the service roads searching for those most in need of help and hope. Has the Lord called you to risk loving others outside of your comfort zone? Or are you still in love with the good life on the social highways and expressways where everything is hurried but safe and controllable? When you follow Jesus down the service roads of life, the journey will enlarge your heart and extend your influence beyond your imagination.

As His beloved children, God wants the best life possible for you and me, not just a good life but the *best*. Where does that life begin? When we bow our knee to Him and accept the sacrifice His Son made for us. God's grace not only pardons us but also empowers us to give ourselves fully to Him, to place all our agendas and missions under His call on our life. Simply put, we become available for what He wants. Then, God takes that surrendered, obedient life and like a loving Father, leads us step by step, path by path, person by person to the life that is best for us, the one that will make our inward and outward behavior match that of His Son's.

God's objective for your life is to connect you to something far greater than yourself. Real love does what it does not have to do. Love makes the lives of others better. Jesus showed us that kind of love, and He is calling you to follow Him into a world where that kind of love is most needed.

Charlotte's Story

The way God arranges our lives and guides us down the pathway one step at a time amazes me. He has often had to pull me back when I wanted to run ahead of Him; He has given me a very narrow field of vision when I wanted to see the whole course. He took me from the time of my life that was to be "my time" and turned it into "His time," which at times was a hard, dark, and weary place where I felt all alone. It was an unfamiliar path, and there was no roadmap.

I often felt I was the only one who even knew this road existed. This was a service road, and I frequently wanted to turn and race along the main highway with my clubs, hobbies, travel, and friends, but God moved me toward poverty porches and private prisons.

I desired to make a change; instead, it changed me.

God gave me the desire to make a change. I felt a need to do something of value to help others lead happier and more productive lives, and I was excited to begin my road of service. In preparation, I completed a literacy volunteer class and was given a young man from a different race and dissimilar background to tutor in reading. Great! I would teach him to read and change his life. Instead, he changed my life by making me aware of a world of poverty, corruption, and heartache. It was a world that had no knowledge of God's grace and mercy; it was a world I had never considered a part of my life. God caused me to examine my heart and to feel a responsibility for the precious people living there.

God took me a step further to Porch Church, where I saw children living in deplorable conditions—most with absent fathers, many siblings, and often drug-addicted mothers. Each day I saw and heard things that gave me a deeper burden for these children. They were living in roach-infested houses with holes in the floors; one day, a little one told me she was afraid of roaches only when they crawled across her face at night. Some nights I would go to sleep praying and wake up praying as though I had never slept. I wanted to fix things for them, but I could not and seemingly God who could, would not. I always had such hope that tomorrow He would work a miracle in their lives, but years passed and I could see no change. I would do everything I could to make a better life for them. So many times I would give them to God only to take them back as mine. After much agonizing, I was able to accept that God's timing is His own. Every child is His. He knows the whole story of their lives and will fit the parts together to complete His plan for them.

There are treasures that money cannot buy. There were often tears in the night, but as God promises, joy did come in the morning. Seeing their sweet smiles and hearing them say, "I love you, Mrs. Charlotte," eased every heartache; the wildflowers they picked and pictures they drew for me were treasures money cannot buy. At Porch Church and on each future path, I felt conflict over my personal safety. My family always saw a danger; I understood their fears but resisted them. This also I would turn over to the Lord only to fret over it again. This burden was lifted through the years as we all learned to trust in the Lord for protection.

What carried me through these dark days was our preacher's sermons and God's Word. The Lord was so good to show me His will in His Word and to give me the joy of His presence when I needed it most. Sweet fellowship with Him gave me times of peace and renewed hope. Many, many times, He solved my problems with scripture as though it were specifically for me and often He reminded me to "be still and know that I am God." The sermons always pointed me to God who was my precious solace and brought peace, joy, and light to my darkest hours.

Through my student and the Porch Church people, I heard of many in prison who needed to hear solid biblical preaching. I was working in the recording ministry at our church and saw a great need for a sermon library in the prison, but I had no connection with prison authorities. In His miraculous way, God put in my path the person in charge of religious services and rehab at one of our local prisons, and soon, we had our library there.

This led to the next step on the service road—prison ministry. God spoke to me as clearly as though in an audible voice and told me to go to the prison, and then He placed an insurmountable barrier in my path. After two days of my confusion and questioning, He worked in ways I could not see and completely cleared my way. He gave me a glimpse into the lives of murderers, prostitutes, drug addicts, thieves, and women who had committed all manner of crimes. One mother had killed her baby while in a cocaine rage; another told me of sleeping outside in the cold and often waking her little ones to see if they were still breathing. God gave me love and compassion for these women in bondage as we studied and prayed together. There were times of sweet fellowship, but other times, the sin and corruption in prison caused me to lose hope, and it was only obedience and remembrance of God's clear call that kept me there.

God orders our steps on an unfamiliar path to make Himself more familiar.

One of the most beautiful paths God put me on during these years was to Mexico. He sent me there quite unexpectedly and introduced me to a young Mixe Indian who has become a lifelong friend. He is a missionary among his own people in the Mixe Region of Oaxaca State. I have often gone to his little village of Mogone; they have loved and accepted me as their own. I have seen hospitality, endurance, faithfulness, and a complete dependence on God that has blessed my life in countless ways. God was so precious to let me see our prayers answered by turning a little church of a few faithful women and three old men into a vibrant congregation of families with a growing faith and missionary hearts.

I am forever grateful that God has ordered my steps along an unfamiliar path. He directed my way, carrying me to places I was mentally, physically, emotionally, or spiritually unable to go.

He walked with me through tutoring, Porch Church, the sermon recording ministry, prison, homeless camps, and Mexico.

This was an impossible journey for an ordinary woman like me; it was too long and too hard, but He made it possible and carried me step by step. By His grace, I was willing to make the journey and be obedient to stay wherever He put me. If a difference took place in any life, I can rejoice, but if not, I can still rejoice. The greatest joy in life is to walk in obedience with Him as He loves you and takes you places you could have never imagined going. Along the way, He increases your faith, gives you a deeper understanding of His great love for you and for others, and gives you precious friends who live down roads you would have never traveled without Jesus.

Desert of Despair

Risking to love someone outside your comfort zone creates an impact that outlasts this lifetime.

Jesus always walks the service roads. The blessings of Charlotte's story were directly linked to yielding her ordinary life to God's leadership down that same path. This was Ruth's story as well. It could be the story of your life. These women would have been considered the least likely to get out of their comfort zone. The Lord walked with them and arranged their steps each day so they could learn more about trusting God in the joy of loving others in extraordinary ways.

As you trace Charlotte and Ruth's steps, look for God's providence, His guiding hand. *Providence* comes from the word *provide*, which has two parts in its Latin origin: "pro" (forward, on behalf of) and "vide" (to see). It means "to supply in advance whatever is needed for support." God never sees without acting, and God never acts without purpose. In biblical terms, *providence* describes the provision and sustenance of God's hidden hand working on behalf of those He loves. He does not leave us alone to figure out what is best for our lives. God's unseen hand is always at work to do us good in the way He sees as best.

In Ruth's story, she bowed her knee to Him and committed that Naomi's God would be her God. She left her old life and vowed to serve the Lord. His providence was at work in the darkest days and nights, in the worst of times, in calamity and crisis. The book of Ruth is indeed a source of encouragement and hope for all of us as we watch what "just happens." What irony for the reader because we know God orchestrated every step to direct Ruth to the best possible life for her. Nothing "just happened." It was God's providence.

It just seemed to *happen* that Ruth returned to Bethlehem, and it just *happened* to be the time of the barley harvest. It just *happened* that Ruth saw an opportunity to put food on the table by working in the harvest field, and it just *happened* that she worked in the field owned by Boaz who just *happened* to notice her. It just *happened* that Boaz encouraged Ruth to return to his fields throughout the harvest time, and it just *happened* that he ordered his workers to give her extra food. It just *happened* that Ruth was so excited at finding favor in the midst of her struggles that she came home eager to tell Naomi the news. It just *happened* that Naomi rejoiced that the fields and favor belonged to Boaz who just *happened* to be the family's guardian-redeemer, one who just *happened* to have the right to claim Ruth and Naomi as part of his family, if he were willing to do so. Well, it just *happened* he was willing because he fell in love with Ruth and they would marry and give birth to a son who would just *happen* to become the grandfather of the greatest king in Israel's history. But we will save that love story for another chapter.

God designed this particular journey for an impoverished and oppressed Ruth. Traveling down the service road of life, she grew in her commitment to Him as she learned to love and serve the distressed Naomi when she volunteered to work the barley harvest fields to gather food for their survival. *And God* (another beautiful divine conjunction) showered her with Boaz's love. She did indeed reap what she sowed. Her journey down the service road changed her dramatically for the better. That is exactly what Charlotte discovered. The more you give yourself away, the more it changes you for the better.

Springs of Hope

What can separate us from the love of Christ? Nothing...

Many people think they are separated from God's love by imprisonment, impoverishment, or just plain misery. How will they ever know there is still hope for them to feel the incredible embrace of God's love? Someone has to risk hugging them, caring about them, helping them.

When you listen to Ruth's story, it frees you to live your life in radical risk-taking love for others. This is the love Charlotte discovered inside of her. Love does what it does not have to do. Love makes the lives of others better. How would these encounters change Charlotte? She found a new joy in the midst of sorrows. The more tears she shared, the more she cared. She lost her story in the life stories of others, and in doing so, God wrote a new chapter of love in her life, a chapter of love which will outlast her earthly life.

Lasting love starts with the love relationship we have with Jesus. Has your heart been captivated by Christ? *Captivated* means "to be influenced and dominated, awed by an irresistible appeal or attraction." Would you describe yourself as being in awe of who Jesus is and what He has done for you? More importantly would Jesus describe you that way?

Let's consider another story of just such a woman, an ordinary woman whose heart was captivated by Christ. She took the risk to love Jesus in an extraordinary way.

Jesus was a guest at a house just a few miles outside of Jerusalem, in Bethany, where He was spending the night during the last week of His earthly life. Just weeks before in that same little village, Jesus raised Lazarus, the brother of Martha and Mary, from the dead. Now Jesus is eating at the home of Simon the leper. Anyone infected with leprosy was treated as a social outcast; they were considered as good as dead, excluded to a leper colony. There was no cure, but Jesus healed leprosy so we can only assume that Jesus had healed Simon, and Simon is captivated by Jesus.

A woman came into the room carrying this very expensive jar of precious perfume, valued at fifteen months' salary, perhaps her IRA savings or family treasure. She broke the container, and the pleasant aroma went everywhere. Then she poured the contents over the head of Jesus and over His feet.

What she did could not be undone. It could not be recalled. This was not a slow drip. It was a gushing stream of precious perfume that was a picture of her heart and its overflowing love for Jesus Christ, the One who had given her new life. She poured it on His head. The sweet scent filled the room. In fact, Jesus's body was probably still carrying some of that fragrance when He was arrested, beaten, scourged, and crucified.

This ordinary woman did something quite extraordinary. She gave Jesus the greatest treasure she possessed. The disciples failed to understand the significance of her action, but to Mary, she thought Jesus was worth everything she had. She knew what she was doing and she understood why because she paid attention to the words of Jesus. Every time you see her in the scriptures, she is sitting at the feet of Jesus. That is the best place to listen and learn; that is where you hear His heartbeat.

This was not just some instantaneous thing; she premeditated and prepared how to do it. She willingly endured the criticism of others. Her social circles had their own ideas of how she should invest her life instead of wasting it in acts of extravagant love, but Jesus commended her.

This ordinary woman made a lasting impression on this world and the kingdom of God. *What did she do? She did what she could.*

This woman's love for Jesus was radical, risky, and extravagant. She held nothing back. Jesus said she just did what she could do and strangely enough, to Jesus, that seemed extraordinary. Why would that be considered so extraordinary? Because most of us come routinely, regularly, casually to worship, not captivated by love, not seeking the road of service He has chosen for us.

This woman did what she could. Do you know that the Lord does not evaluate you on what you *cannot* do? You cannot solve all the problems in the world. You cannot feed all the hungry people in the world. You cannot eliminate all the poverty in the world or your city. The Lord looks at you in light of what you could do if you really loved Him. There are so many good deeds that could and should be done. There are lots of hurting, lonely people. There are many struggling children in the neighborhood and throughout the nations. There are people to feed, hearts to comfort, children to tutor. There are women in and out of prison who need a friend.

What would extraordinary worship of Jesus look like in your life if you did what you could do for Jesus?

Jesus demonstrated extravagant love for you. The love of Mary, Ruth, and Charlotte cannot compare to what Jesus did when the sweet aroma from heaven's treasure of love was broken and poured out for us on the cross. The Son of God, the creator of all things, the heir and end of all things, the sustainer of all things, the radiance of God's glory, the exact representation of God's nature, the ruler of all God's kingdom poured out His life for you. Does that captivate your heart? Do you carry His aroma of love with you wherever you go in life?

What might it look like in your life to be engaged in one extraordinary act of worship to Jesus, not caring what anybody else thinks, not even caring if anybody else knows or notices or ever hears about it? Would you risk doing what cannot be undone just to fill your world with the aroma of wholehearted love for Christ?

In Mary's story, we are faced with the same challenge which awakened Charlotte's heart to its purpose in life. What can I do? Jesus calls that an extraordinary life. Ruth humbled herself and took the initiative to help. She stayed at the task even as the days got long and the work seemed tedious. Those are traits which became part of Charlotte's new ministries to the down and out who felt bitter, lost, empty, and forgotten.

God gave Charlotte courage to step out into an unfamiliar world, to become an instrument of divine providence to others in need. Prisons, Porch Church, and the poorest people in Mexico experienced the love of God. Through Charlotte's life, God's divine conjunctions connected those people to our church. It changed us all for the better as we began to know and pray for the women in the prison by name. Family members from the porches became part of our lives.

Charlotte's work in Mexico began its own chapter of God's providence. It just *happened* that one of our young preacher trainees went with Charlotte to minister among the Mixe people. It just *happened* that he fell in love with the sister of the young preacher and family Charlotte adopted as her personal project. Their father just *happened* to be the primary trainer of preachers in that area as well as the sole translator of the Bible into their native language. It just *happened* that our preacher trainee returned to marry his daughter. Somehow it just *happened* he was accepted into medical school in Mexico and would later become a medical missionary among the Mixe people and open his clinic in the village Charlotte had visited. It just *happened* that the Lord is using this medical clinic and all these preachers to spread the Gospel among the poorest people in Mexico living in some of the remotest parts of the country. *It just happened.* Right?

What can you do for the Lord? "He has shown you…what is good. And what does the Lord require of you? To act justly and to love mercy and to walk humbly with your God" (Micah 6:8). This is a summary of how God wants you and me to live. Live in merciful love toward others. Be passionately concerned for the weak, the powerless, the vulnerable. Care about the poor and prisoners. Help those in need, not just financially but also emotionally and spiritually.

"This is what the Lord says: 'Have the understanding to know me, that I am the Lord, who exercises kindness, justice and righteousness on earth, for in these I delight,' declares the Lord" (Jer. 9:24). Reflect the character of God in all your relationships. You have firsthand experience of both his sustaining grace and his purposeful design. The comfort and hope you are experiencing from God can be given away in increasing measure to others.

Find your place in God's story. Your place to risk love might be across the street, which is just as important as the other side of the world. It might be across town or downtown. It might be to women in prison, or the hospital, or far away in another country. It can be frightening to take your love into an unfamiliar field to work around strangers. God will always go with you. You can give them hope, but it will be your life that is changed the most. That becomes the *best* part of the story.

God's purpose for your life is to connect you to something far greater than yourself.

In *Charlotte's Web,* the clever spider, Charlotte, saves Wilbur the pig from becoming someone's bacon for breakfast by spinning her web into visible words above his stall. The onlookers are astonished to read "some pig" and then "radiant" as her admiring endorsement of the pig's worth. At the cost of her life, she saved another life she considered precious. Although this book conjures up images of insects, animals, friendship, and loyalty, the author speaks to all of us as he drives home his point. The power of love often gives hope to the hopeless. In our Charlotte's story, we find that same life-risking love that connects her life to something far greater than herself.

If you are willing to share love and hope for the hopeless, God will guide you to the right field and the right persons. God's providence will guide you into contact with those in need of hope outside your normal circles. Your presence connects them to God's love. Whenever you risk love, your life will always be more significant than you think.

What is the next step in your life? Do you have any idea what God has prepared for you? You may be asking a lot of people about what you should do, but the person you need to ask is Jesus. Do not just assume that you know exactly what to do. Do not treat every day like another routine day, grinding at the mill or the kitchen sink or the social clubs doing the same things. Open your eyes to see all these opportunities which just seem to "happen." Things fall in place, not by chance, not by fate, but by the work of God. The hidden hand of God's providence is at work for your benefit.

"Commit your works to the Lord and your plans will be established" (Prov. 16:3). The word *commit* is the word for *roll*, to take the weight off you and roll it over on the Lord. *Works* is a navigational term descriptive of sailors who handled the ropes of the sail to benefit from the wind or allow them to navigate against contrary winds.

Who can best handle the ropes of your life? Who can best set the direction for what should be next in your life? It is the Lord. *Then your plans will be established* because your plans are shaped by the Lord's plans. The next steps for your life start with God's plans revealed in God's Word which equips you for what God has prepared for you (2 Tim. 3:17).

The implications are enormous. No matter what is going on in your life, the Lord has you prepared for the next step. He has a plan, and His providence will work it out precisely according to His purpose including the steps of others to intersect with you at just the right moment for you to help them.

No matter how trivial the next step might seem to you or how monumental it might appear, the Lord has ordered all your steps to work out just as He promised. *And we know God will cause all things to work together for our good, for all those who love Him and are called according to His purpose.*

Learn to trust God completely for everything. That is basic discipleship. We are saved by faith, we walk by faith, live by faith, serve by faith, please God by faith. In faith, you trust God completely for everything, placing your whole life and all the circumstances into the hands of God to do with you as He pleases, being satisfied that He knows what is best for your life.

All of us need to become more like Jesus and trust Him completely for everything as we take our love for others to a higher level. Care for orphans and widows, help the poor and downtrodden, serve those with needs, and show benevolent love. Demonstrate acts of love for the helpless, the homeless, and the hopeless.

The best preparation for future usefulness in the kingdom of God is face-to-face fellowship with Jesus.

This chapter was never intended to be a guilt trip or condemnation for what you have or have not done. It is a message of hope. This book does not have the authority to tell you what to do with your life; it only serves as your summons to appear before Jesus face to face to find out what your specific ministry assignment is for this time in your life.

Live for something that will outlast your earthly life. Do not waste your life investing your time and energy on fleeting pleasures of this dying world. Start with face-to-face fellowship with Jesus in the living and active Word of God, which is able to get right down into your soul and into your mind in order to guide you to your next step of faith.

God has you in a place for a specific purpose. For some, that place might need to change; for most, it will not. There will be some of you who have invested your life in serving others but now find yourselves with bad backs, weak hearts, and less energy. God understands your new limitations, so do not despair. Be content and find joy in this season of life. Pray more. Write more notes of encouragement. For whatever place you are in, the appropriate question is, "How can I use this present place in life to best showcase the love of God to those most in need of help and hope?"

Jesus said, "I chose *you* to represent Me." Jesus travels the service road to find those most in need of help and hope. Follow in Jesus's steps. Find somebody else who has been summoned by the Lord for the same purpose. Do God's will together whatever it costs, whatever it takes. Share the journey with encouragement, perseverance, sorrow, and joy. When one gets discouraged, the other one is there to lift up.

Dream big dreams for God and pray big prayers and then be faithful in all the little things.

This is your life chapter to work with God. Jesus Christ lives in you to lead you to others He will love through you. There is no more exciting work than that! This is the time in your life to risk loving like Jesus. Are there some things in your life that are holding you back, slowing you down from going where God wants you to go and doing what God wants you to do? Are there some social entanglements which need to be set aside?

Serve others instead of being served. Pour your life out in extravagant love for others who think they have no hope. They live inside and outside the walls of the traditional church and the safety of social clubs. Go find them. Fill their lives with the sweet aroma of Christ's love.

Whether you are a young person, an older person, or what you would like to think as being in the prime of your life, what does God want you to do? Get face to face with God in His Word. Look at the world with His eyes of love. Have confidence in God. Then go find a field as Ruth and Charlotte did. Just do what you can do for Jesus right now at this time of your life.

God will providentially arrange everything. Things will seem to just happen as your life fills up with divine connections on your journey to new horizons.

Loving others is an expression of your faith and hope in God. Make a lasting impact into the lives of others. Seize every opportunity to love like Jesus. Where there is despair, give *hope*.

Sharing love and hope will help others. Most importantly, it will change you.

The Right Application of Hope

Pour your life into something that will outlast it.

"We remember before our God and Father your work produced by faith, your labor prompted by love, and your endurance inspired by *hope* in our Lord Jesus Christ" (1 Thess. 1:3; emphasis added).

> Truly He taught us to love one another
> His law is love and His gospel is peace
> Chains shall He break for the slave is our brother
> And in His Name all oppression will cease
> Sweet hymns of joy in grateful chorus raise we
> Let all within in us praise His holy name.
> Christ is the Lord! O praise His Name forever
> His power and glory evermore proclaim
> His power and glory evermore proclaim!
>
> —"O Holy Night," Placide Cappeau (lyrics),
> Adolphe Adam (song)

17

In Sickness and...in Sickness

Willie Pat's Story
Application of *No Separation* *from the Love of God*

Hope. What does that word mean to you? How would you describe it? Wishful thinking? Mind over matter? No, God's Word describes *hope* as standing on tiptoes waiting in confident expectation of all the future good God has promised. It is like waiting on the sunrise (Ps. 130:6). You can always count on two things—(1) you cannot rush it and (2) it will surely rise. Where do you get that confident hope? It comes from God. Hope is not based on what one sees, but on reality as defined and described by what the truthful and faithful God says in His Word (Rom. 10:17).

How do you focus on living a life of hope based on the future good that God has promised when you are suffering in sickness and drowning in debt? How do you live out hope when the medical reports go from bad to worse, from short to long? What does hope look like when you are lying in a hospital bed with countless tubes attached to your body?

Sustained sickness can challenge your hope. A critical medical diagnosis might shock your hope. Then worse news arrives threatening to kill all hope. You do not see hope, hear hope, or feel hope. Is all hope gone? Does a time come when you should just give up hope? If not, then how do you sustain hope in moments when it looks as though all hope is gone?

Find your anchor in what God says, not in what you see. Walk in faith each day regardless of what you hear. Persevere through each trial. This is not the time to disengage hope from your life. Maintain your confidence in the Lord because of His surpassing greatness. Expect all the future good God has promised. It will come somehow...someway...sometime. Those were lessons Willie Pat had to learn, not sitting in a church but sitting in a hospital day after day after day. She had promised to love her husband in sickness and in health. She had promised God to trust Him in all situations. Now what happened when those promises were put to the ultimate test?

How do you continue to hope in sickness and...in more sickness? Willie Pat will give the same answer found in Ruth's story of hope. God provides. Hope is never just about the promise; hope becomes visible by the practice.

Willie Pat's Story

My story is more than a Patsy Cline "Stand by Your Man" recording. Most assuredly, it resonates with commitment. Gary and I promised each other over fifty years ago that our marriage would survive sickness and health, riches and poverty, the better and the worse until death parts us. But it has become so much more. With each adversity, not only has our love for each other grown but also our love for God. We seek His face now for His strength to sustain us sometimes an hour at a time.

We also look for His purpose. It is a shift in perspective. How will God use this illness to teach us and those around us? What picture does He want the world to see in our lives? How are the Potter's hands molding us to become more like Christ? I see two ordinary clay pots that God has made. Each time there is another illness, I see another crack in both the pots—just another crack for Jesus's light to shine through to others.

God gives you strength for a long journey.

Let's turn quickly through the pages of our life and arrive at our midlife section. Gary was diagnosed with rheumatoid arthritis; he was given several medications to help with pain and slow down the progression of the disease. He did well for several years, but the pain continued to get worse. His doctor then prescribed a medication, which Gary gave himself in shot form. For six months, there was such a relief he thought he was cured, but the pain came back with a vengeance. He was then put on one of the new intravenous medications, which he was to take once a month. That treatment lasted for eighteen months.

One morning, Gary woke me with a severe pain in his stomach. I called 911, and they rushed him to the hospital. After x-rays, MRI, and CT scan of his stomach, they found a mass, which the radiologist said had to be cancer. They took him to surgery and found a hole in his intestines. The doctor removed part of his colon; he warned us his condition would be fatal if he got an infection. I was so scared and in such shock. My husband is my best friend and the love of my life. I could not imagine my life without him. But God gave me a peace that I did not know I could have, and He gave me strength for a long journey of illnesses.

Our family and an elder from the church prayed for healing with no infection. God intervened, and three days later, Gary was moved from ICU to a room where he slowly began to improve. After further testing, they discovered he had histoplasmosis, which is a fungus that grows in the lung. None of the doctors who treated him had ever heard of anyone having histoplasmosis in the colon. He made the medical books. After fourteen days in the hospital, we went home.

Four years later, Gary went to the hospital with pneumonia six or seven times with at least a week's stay each time. One time, we were in twenty-five days, and he developed diabetes. Another stay lasted thirty-one days; he had a bleeding ulcer that resulted in his having to have six pints of blood. Why was he having pneumonia so much? The doctors ran tests to check his immune system. The average numbers are 1,200 to 700. Gary's was 230; he had no immune system. From there, we went to a specialist who started him on IV gamma globulin. His numbers started coming up, and there has been no more pneumonia. God has been so faithful to us through these illnesses. We trust him for each day that we have together. He used the times in the hospital for us to share what Christ means to us, and He is always there when we need Him. Thank you, Jesus.

The greater your weakness, the greater His strength.

Another four years went by before Gary fell while getting out of the shower and hit his hand on the vanity. It did not seem too bad and didn't hurt, so we assumed he was okay. Several hours later, his hand was swollen and blue. We went back to the ER for x-rays. It was not broken but bruised. They wrapped it and sent us home. They told us to come back if it got worse. It got worse. The next day, he was admitted; there was discussion about doing surgery for compartment syndrome (a painful condition resulting from the overgrowth of tissue which produces pressure which adversely affects blood circulation), but we ended up just staying two days so they could watch it. We were released with instructions to go to wound care the next day. When they removed the bandage, there was a huge blood clot that covered his whole hand. The doctor removed the top skin so it could drain. After three months and many trips to therapy, the huge hole in his hand healed. Again, through all the illnesses and traumas Gary has endured, he never complains. He keeps a smile on his face and does the best he can with the pain and limitations he has. He says he will be healed one day—if not here on earth, then when God takes him home.

Another ordeal started in December before the fall. Gary found a small growth on the right side of his face. He went to the dermatologist and had it removed and tested for cancer. The test came back negative. By February, it was twice as large and very painful. He went back to the doctor and had another biopsy, which was positive. The lab had made a mistake the first time. He was scheduled for surgery in the doctor's office. When we arrived two weeks later, the doctor said there was no way he could do that kind of surgery in his office because the mass reached from his eyelid to his eyebrow. We went to a plastic surgeon for the surgery. The mass was so large the doctor had to cut from above his eyebrow to his ear and almost to his mouth. Gary had a gaping hole in the side of his face the size of a tennis ball. That evening at home, Gary woke me because he was having trouble breathing. He has COPD, so I gave him a breathing treatment, which didn't seem to help, so we were back to the ER. After three days in the hospital dealing with congestive heart failure, we went home. In eight days, we returned to the plastic surgeon who closed the huge wound and put Gary's face back together.

Then the oncologist began radiation treatments. Gary was in agony toward the end because his face was burned so badly. For two weeks, his face bled and hurt, but there was no harm to the eye. Four months after the surgery, his face looked wonderful.

We have faced very serious financial difficulties as well during these years. Our medical bills have been astronomical. After the thirty-one-day stay, we owed the hospital over $100,000. They contacted Gary and forgave $90,000. Our Bible study group gave us a love offering of $6,000. *How great is our God!* The song writer reminds me "He is my strength when I am weak, He is the treasure that I seek. He is my all in all. When I am down He lifts me up, when I am dry He fills my cup. He is my all in all." I live by those words.

Gary has RA, COPD, congestive heart failure, diabetes, sleep apnea, neuropathy, kidney failure, skin cancer, immune deficiency, any of which could take his life, but we are ever thankful to our Heavenly Father for His mercy and grace. We do not know what tomorrow or next week or next year will bring, but we know we will walk through it with Him because our *God is great*.

Desert of Despair

The medical journal could write articles about Gary's sicknesses. Actually, I think they already have. There have been other people with worse sickness and some who have suffered with sickness longer than Gary. However, few have been on such a medical roller-coaster. The highs and lows, mostly lows. The unexpected turns and sudden change of directions. It can make you sick to the stomach and cause your head to spin. Oh wait! Those are just a few of the symptoms of this strange journey.

I have visited Gary and Willie Pat many, many times in the hospital. I have greeted them with every return to church. In between, each episode would leave all of us shaking our heads in disbelief and wonder. Disbelief in the newest diagnosis and wonder at the sufficiency of God's grace. I saw a couple whose faith and hope were severely tested. Those tests would have left many people questioning the wisdom and love of God; but their hope, hammered out on the anvil of experience, was authentic.

Throughout the journey, Gary remained upbeat and witnessed of his faith and hope in God. When he was not in excruciating pain, he had a smile on his face, which exposed the love in his heart. He consistently shared his hope in God with medical staff, hospital visitors, and other patients. Willie Pat always smiled and shrugged. She seemingly took the bad news in stride with hope in God and loyal love for her husband in sickness and in health, unto death. Their steadfast love for each other was on display in every hospital room. Their commitment to one another and their commitment to God never seemed to waver. The journey has not been easy; their commitment was challenged many times. They just stuck it out, in hope and with hope.

The promise of Ruth to Naomi and her God would resonate with visible vibrations throughout Willie Pat's story.

Do not urge me to leave you or to turn back from you. Where you go I will go, and where you stay I will stay. Your people will be my people and your God my God. Where you die I will die, and there I will be buried. May the Lord deal with me, be it ever so severely, if even death separates you and me.

Naomi and her two young daughters-in-law were now widows. The three women had no social status and no financial support within the Moabite culture. Essentially they were now homeless and except for Ruth, hopeless. Naomi decided to return to her hometown of Bethlehem. She ordered the girls to stay in Moab and start new lives. While one turned back, Ruth clung to hope, declaring her steadfast love and loyalty to Naomi and to their God. Ruth even invoked the personal name for God, the Lord. This would signal the commitment as a decision of her heart, not some religious ceremonial incantation.

Why do some stay through thick and thin when others kiss and walk away? Why is undying love and enduring loyalty so precious, then and now? Why is wholehearted devotion so beautiful to watch but so hard to live? You can check with Ruth or Willie Pat for an answer.

I am with you heart, body, and soul for better or worse, for richer or poorer, in sickness and in health. How many times have those words been spoken? Ruth was laying down her life and its future to serve Naomi. She declared her intentions of never wavering from her commitment, never departing from the responsibility she took upon herself with the promise. In spite of the loss of her husband resulting in her becoming destitute and homeless, no matter the depths of her grief and the heights of her pain, she committed the rest of her life to God through ministry to a bitter widow who happened to be her mother-in-law.

They would be together—together the way God is with us. Ruth promised to do what the God of the Bible promises us, to *cleave* together. *Cleave* means to stick, to adhere, to cling, to join, to stay close to someone. The noun form yields the word *glue*. They would always stick together.

The more one considers these words, the more amazing they become. Ruth left the only life she had known, to go to a new place, to work among strange people with different customs and language, with no expectations of marriage or children. She went to take care of Naomi, sick with bitterness about her past and sick with depression regarding her future.

When Naomi declared that her God was against her, Ruth spoke up with, "Your God will be my God." Somehow, in spite of others' hopelessness, Ruth would rise in hope and move on with her life, looking beyond the setbacks to the hope on her horizon. In love, Ruth did what she did not have to do. She made all kinds of personal sacrifices and apparently did it with joy and love in her heart.

Fast-forward thousands of years to a different country, a different culture, and different people, but the internal conflicts for Ruth and Willie Pat were the same. The choice made by both women was the same. Willie Pat lived out that same promise she made to God and to her husband. She never bailed, never quit, never surrendered to the sickness nor the emotional and financial struggles which ensued. Gary was willing for the medical staff to allow him to die in order to ease the burden on the woman he so dearly loved. Willie Pat never saw it that way.

Whatever you suffer and wherever you go, look for God's purpose in your life.

I do not claim to know all their feelings during the darkest days and longest nights. Doubts, worries, and fears are part of the journey of faith and hope. They have to be addressed and conquered. Sickness means setbacks. Setbacks cost. They cost physically, emotionally, financially, and spiritually. And yet, for those who love God and are called to His purpose, setbacks come with divine conjunctions that breathe new hope. A better and brighter hope. Ruth and Willie Pat did not just resign themselves to a life of burdensome caregiving; they actively and aggressively gave themselves to love and hope.

Springs of Hope

He who did not spare his own Son, but gave Him up for us all—how will He not also, along with Him, graciously give us all things?... What can separate us from God's love? Nothing...

There is a life-changing principle that gives application to your hope which has been cited in several chapters of this book: Jesus Christ lives in you to lead you to others He intends to love through you.

1. Jesus Christ *lives* in you.
2. Jesus Christ *leads* you.
3. Jesus Christ *loves* through you.

Jesus Christ lives in you. Inside this earthen body, we have a heavenly treasure. "We have this treasure in jars of clay to show that this all-surpassing power is from God and not from us. We are hard pressed on every side, but not crushed; perplexed, but not in despair" (2 Cor. 4:7–8).

What is this treasure inside of us? It is the Gospel of the "glory of God in the face of Jesus Christ" (2 Cor. 4:6). Jesus Christ came into this life in human form and dwelt among us, and we beheld the glory of God. He explained to us who God is and what God does in our lives. Then in His death and resurrection from the dead, Jesus clearly demonstrated God's purpose to live inside these earthen vessels in order to show the glory of His goodness in loving sick, sorrowful, suffering sinners.

We are not the treasure. We have a treasure inside of us. God designed us to be containers. We are empty clay pots. We are empty and expendable. Essentially worthless, our bodies can be thrown away or donated to science. But God (you just have to learn to love those divine conjunctions!) designed us so that we might contain that which is of infinite value, the real treasure, God Himself. Jesus Christ comes to live inside of us. Why?

God has a plan and purpose, to show the world the reality of who God is and the surpassing greatness of His power through dwelling and working in and through people like Gary and Willie Pat. Clay pots. With cracks. Just ordinary, sick, decaying bodies. That is what they look like on the outside, but that is only the window dressing for the beautiful story from the inside.

Jesus Christ lives in you to lead you to others He intends to love through you. God called you for a purpose, not to carry out your work and plans, but God's plan for you to live and love like Jesus. To show mercy, compassion, and care to the helpless, the worthless, the undeserving.

All God asks of you is for you to let Him love others through you. Be His feet, His hands, His arms, His mouth, His heart. Love others with the same love as God has loved you. Love in demonstration of loyalty and steadfast perseverance. Jesus gave His life for you so you can now say, "I no longer live, but Jesus Christ now lives in me. And the life that I now live by faith, I live by faith in the Son of God who loved me and gave Himself up for me" (Gal. 2:20).

This is basic Christianity. It is believing and hoping in what is real, not what you see, not what you feel, but what God says (2 Cor. 4:18). Your words and actions become a living biography of Jesus Christ, beautifully and eloquently written for others to read.

Are you loving your family with the love of Christ? Are you a container, a delivery package, of the love of Christ to your spouse, to your children, to your parents, to your brothers and sisters? We do not lose heart; we do not give up.

Willie Pat had to make a choice to succumb to the constant hardships imposed on her by a husband's prolonged sickness according to the medical prognosis or be sustained and strengthened by God's promises. *And we know God causes all things to work together for good for those who love Him and are called according to His purpose.* We have this treasure in jars of clay to show that this all-surpassing power is from God and not from us.

Wow! The surpassing greatness of God's power. Which one do you choose? Sickness? Surpassing greatness? Hmmm! Now what are you thinking? Do you intend to check out of life and its relationships because of sickness, or do you stay to see the surpassing power of God in and through you?

Surpassing greatness means "beyond limits." What happens inside of you will be beyond human limitations. What is impossible to man is possible with God. Would you like to see what is possible with God in your life? It requires more than just a halfhearted affirmation. The experience of surpassing power inside you begins with hope and faith that Jesus lives in you to lead you to others He will love through you.

Now where is this surpassing greatness of God's power seen in your life?

The surpassing power of Jesus's life and love inside you is most clearly seen in your weaknesses.

When you are weak, God will be your strength. *Those who wait upon the Lord, God shall renew their strength.* God never grows weary; He never gets tired. He is the everlasting God. You are an empty container designed to hold the life and love of Christ, to be delivered to those who are in spiritual struggles. Those cracks in the clay pot become the gateway for others to see the surpassing power of the light and love of Jesus inside.

The life of Jesus is most clearly seen at the end of yourself. This is not a reference to the end of your earthly life but rather when you die to yourself in the midst of this life. When you come to the end of yourself and admit you are too weak and cannot do this by yourself, look to Jesus for help and hope. Look to His love displayed on the cross, "beholding Him we are becoming transformed to be like Him from glory to glory" (2 Cor. 3:18).

When you look at Jesus in the Bible, it is like looking in a mirror. You can see who is inside of you. *Therefore, we do not lose heart.* This is a military term used to describe a soldier in battle, in great danger of becoming fainthearted and cowardly. In the heat of the battle, she might turn and run, but she never does. Instead she stays. She stays with the same loyalty pledged by Ruth.

This description of Ruth's promise became Willie Pat's story. I pray it plays a significant role in your story as well. We do not lose hope. We do not act like cowards when the pressure rises and the world shouts for us to turn and run. Why? Because our hope is not based on what we can see or how we feel at that moment or by what others say or do. Our hope does not rise and fall with the stock market or the medical diagnoses.

God is at work in us and through us, so we do not lose hope and we do not fear death. If you intend to live with hope, you will have to learn to live without fear of dying. Death does not mean the end; it is only the end of this earthly container. "Because we believe Jesus was raised from the dead, we also believe that He will raise us up in glory" (2 Cor. 4:14). That is your hope. That is the horizon of the new creation. The reality of the resurrected life of Jesus is inside you no matter how many trips back to the hospital, no matter how many times they wheel you into the operating room, no matter how many tubes become attached to your body, no matter how many days you wait beside death's door.

Our bodies are decaying and dying, yet we are more alive and hopeful than ever. That condition is a paradox. A *paradox* is two or more true statements that sound opposite to one another. The two ideas seem contradictory, incompatible. Common sense would tell you they both cannot be true, yet they are. As we die, we live.

We see ourselves dying, but how is it that we are living? In God's terms, this is a "simultaneous" paradox. It is not die and then you live, but rather, as you die, you live. The life of Jesus is most clearly seen when you are weak and at the end of yourself. As you die, He lives in you. As you decrease, He increases. The sicker Gary became, the more we saw Jesus inside of him. The more helpless Willie Pat felt, the greater the indwelling Treasure appeared.

This is how God uses suffering in our lives—the decaying of our bodies, the external dying of ourselves—He uses those things to showcase the reality of His life in us. Sickness and suffering never prevent the purpose of God from being fulfilled in your life. In reality, they become part of God's process to produce that which He desires within you.

God has placed the treasure of Jesus's life and love inside this outer container, this delivery package called your body. God squeezes you to show others what is inside of you. Suffering and sickness and sorrow are things we all have in common. Your response to those trials should be different from those who do not know God. Unbelievers are not convinced of Jesus's love by theological or religious platitudes. They need to personally witness the reality of hope and steadfast love in the midst of life's struggles, so Jesus leads you into their lives as a living picture of His presence.

Jesus lives inside of Willie Pat. He lives inside of you. Now look at the Bible and see what Jesus does. He always gives His life away to help others, whether that is caring for a sick loved one or ministering to the hurting masses. Jesus always gives His life to you for you to give His love away to others with a steadfast loyal love that will never give up in the midst of the circumstances.

I believe this becomes one of the most difficult aspects of Christianity to really live out. Your life is not about you. It is not even about what you might do for God or your husband or your family or the whole world. Your life is all about what the Jesus inside you will do through you to love others.

In life, it really does not matter how great the pressure is, what really matters happens where the pressure lies. Does it come between you and God, or does the pressure push you closer to God's heart? If the sickness or suffering or sorrow presses you closer to God's heart, then you can keep on rejoicing, not with some outward fake smile but in the midst of tears. This world can take away your health or the well-being of your loved one, but it cannot rob you of hope in God. It did not rob Ruth; neither has it stolen hope from Willie Pat.

Sickness is real, painful, unfair, unwanted, and frustrating, but it has purpose. How will you face your sickness and suffering? Friends and family can help, but when the medical staff wheels you or your loved one into the operating room, you need a God who will go with you where others cannot. In Jesus, there is hope. Hope turns sickness and suffering into reasons for rejoicing. We rejoice, not in the pain but in the purpose.

John Paton was one of the early missionaries to the New Hebrides Islands. Living in Scotland, he needed to quit school at the age of twelve to help his father support eleven children. He became a follower of Jesus at the age of seventeen and spent over a decade as a city missionary working with poor children in the slums of Glasgow. As a young man, he followed God's call to a faraway island where the Gospel had never been preached, an island inhabited by cannibals. In March of that year, he married Mary Ann Robson. In April, they set sail for the South Pacific.

Together, they served and prayed and worked in hope that God would shine the light of His love into the darkened hearts around them. Near the end of their first year on the island, Mary gave birth to a little boy but contracted a fever. In just a few short days, she would die, and three weeks later, so would the baby boy. Shortly before her death, Mary conveyed that she had no complaints or bitterness against God for what had happened.

She did not resent her husband for bringing her to the island so far away from family and friends. Then she said these words, which I have repeated to myself so many times during times of sickness, suffering, stress, and sorrow: "I have no regrets. If I had it to do over, I would do it with more pleasure. Yes, I would do it with all my heart."

Someday, we will be ushered into glory. We will look back on the sicknesses and struggles in our lives, and every one of us will say, "I would do it again, and if I were given the opportunity to do it again, I would do it with more joy. I would do it with all my heart."

Do not urge me to leave you or to turn back from you. Where you go I will go, and where you stay I will stay. Your people will be my people and your God my God.

Ruth's story is connected by divine conjunctions to your story. What was true then remains true centuries later. Faith, hope, and love are never just about the promise. It is the practice. We do not lose heart and hope in adverse circumstances. We practice faith, hope, and love while God connects all the dots for our good to His glorious purpose.

Love does what it does not have to do. Do you still need proof? Listen to Jesus. *I gave my life for you. I have loved you with an everlasting love. I will never leave you or abandon you.*

Where there is despair, *hope*. Jesus always practices what He promised. Always. In sickness and…in sickness. No matter what.

The Right Application of Hope

The love of God is in the Lord Jesus Christ. Love Him. Follow Him. Practice what you promised. Stay with your commitment for the long haul. Do it with joy and put your hope into action. Do something good for someone that you do not have to do.

"As for me, I will always have *hope*; I will praise you more and more" (Ps. 71:14; emphasis added).

I am not skilled to understand
What God has willed what God Has planned
I only know at his right hand
Stands one who is my Savior

I take him at his word and deed
Christ died to save me this I read
And in my heart I find the need
Of him to be my Savior

Yes living, dying let me bring
My strength my Solace from the Spring
That he who lives to be my king
Once died to be my Savior
That he would leave his place on high
And come for sinful man to die
You called it strange so once did I
Before I knew my Savior

My Savior loves
My Savior lives
My Savior's always there for me
My God he was
My God he is
My God he's always gonna be

—"My Savior My God,"
Aaron Shust

18

A Rock, a Hard Place, and the Hope Between

Susie's Story
Application of *God's Love*
To Forgive or Not to Forgive

Our purpose in life is to live and love like Jesus. Following Jesus is not about perfection but direction in life. Since none of us is perfect, then we all need forgiveness, and we all need to give forgiveness. Every day and in almost every way. We all share in common the basic human necessity to give and receive forgiveness in order to abide in some form of harmony.

Then why is it so difficult to forgive others? Because it is hard. It is very possible you have someone in your life, as did Susie, whom you have placed outside the boundary lines of forgivable offenses. They are permanently on your "never forgive" list.

The need to forgive and be forgiven always begins in the halls of hurt. Most family conflicts begin there, whether by hurtful words thrown around like hand grenades or more serious issues such as child or domestic abuse, drug or alcohol addiction, or lifestyles consumed by gambling or pornography or unfaithfulness.

You may feel that your offender needs to know how badly he or she has hurt you. Hey! The whole world needs to know. That is usually why you carry around the burden of bitterness toward them as if it is chained to your soul. You might even carry around your own little black book of unforgiveable persons. (I met a man who actually did that. He called it his "get-even" book.) Perhaps you think your hurt from the other person's action or inaction deserves public acknowledgment. So you roll your eyes at the mention of their name, you turn and walk away, or maybe you spit on the ground and curse.

It is a staggering challenge just to cope much less forgive. You strive to protect yourself and your children physically, emotionally, and spiritually. The offender's embarrassment, rejection, insults, hatred, ridicule, mean-spirited criticism, and lack of love have inflicted deep wounds into the heart and fabric of the relationship. Now there is no relationship as far as you are concerned.

Forgiveness is not what comes to mind. You pray for help. You search for hope. Some days, you feel neither. Forgive them? Never! They do not deserve to be forgiven. It would be hard, no impossible, to forgive them unless you were God and even then it would be so stinkin' humbling. Kind of like the way Jesus forgave you of all your sins? Hard and humbling?

All forgiveness is hard and humbling. It cost Jesus His life to forgive you. He laid aside His crown in glory and took on the form of a humble servant to show His unending love for you. His relationship with you is important to Him, even when you do not care. Nothing, not even you at your worst, can ever separate His loving forgiveness from you.

So what should you do when you cannot and will not forgive someone? You have to examine and adjust your way of thinking. You cannot change the past, but you can make the future better. Take time to carefully consider the forgiving love of Jesus in Susie's story. It might give you a different understanding of forgiveness. You might even discover there is hope between the rock and the hard place in your broken relationships.

Susie's Story

> For if you forgive men when they sin against
> you, your Heavenly Father will also forgive
> you. But if you do not forgive men their sins,
> your Father will not forgive your sins.
>
> —Matthew 6:14.

I was the daughter of a confirmed alcoholic. My father was never physically abusive, but alcohol destroyed our family. Only people who have lived through this nightmare will understand the full implication of my experience. It was only through the wisdom and devotion of my mother that I survived those years. She was a strong Christian and kept us involved in a church where we heard God's Word.

My journey to forgiveness started with hurt and anger.

It started as a little girl who wore hand-me-down dresses and shoes provided by the local school board. I was a child of poverty who knew that something vital was missing from my life. When I was twelve years old, my parents divorced, and my father purposely disappeared from my life. This rejection planted the seeds of anger that grew with each year. The neglect I had suffered caused serious emotional pains; thus, I rejected him because I wanted no part of him. I saw very little of him from age twelve until age twenty. At that time, he came to see his first grandchild and then disappeared again. The anger continued to build.

My mother always encouraged me to make peace with my father. But I refused. "I don't need him. I don't want him to be a part of my life. He left me. I didn't leave him." These words echoed through my mind over and over. Anger and an unforgiving spirit festered in my heart. I held tightly to this sin; in refusing to forgive my father, I gave Satan a stronghold on my life. I did not know or feel the peace God promised.

Forgiveness is learned.

Mom also told me she knew how to contact him, and when I was ready, she would provide the information. I was emphatic when I told her, "I will never be ready!"

Years turned into decades. God's love for me was so great He would not leave me captive and enslaved to an unforgiving spirit. In the early spring, my pastor preached from Matthew 6:14. The Holy Spirit gave me no choice. God knew I was languishing in a desert wilderness. He knew He could pour out blessings of grace if I would reach out in love and forgive my father. I did not know how, but it was a clear message from God that I had to forgive and I had to do it right away. Then my Lord encouraged me through the words of the song we were singing, "*God will make a way where there seems to be no way,*" that He would open the door if I would only walk through it.

When I got home from church, I called my mom and asked for Dad's phone number. My stepmother answered the phone. I asked her if she knew who was calling, and she said, "Yes, this is Susie, and your dad and I have been waiting for this call for fourteen years."

When Dad came to the phone, I cried out to him and asked for forgiveness for being so angry and could he please forgive me. He said, "Yes, but you must also forgive me because I was not the father you needed. I let alcohol become more important than my family. I have been sober fourteen years waiting for your call." I asked him why he had not called and shared this information with me, and he said, "You were not ready."

And then you know what he said? "Now let's not worry about the past, but let's begin again and forget the past." Isn't that just what our Heavenly Father does for us?

Forgiveness is like starting all over again with a clean slate.

Finally, I was free of the anger and bitterness. I had the peace God promises us when we walk in obedience and not rebellion. I was free to love my father just as Jesus loved me and forgave me. We had five wonderful, rewarding years together before God took him to heaven. I thank my Heavenly Father for this restored relationship with my earthly father.

Desert of Despair

Have you been hurt, betrayed, offended, mistreated, or abandoned by someone close to you? Of course, you have. What happened cannot be undone and those feelings never disappear on their own accord. However, God did show us a way to help heal the hurts in life. His way does not come with some brief philosophical snippet or bright celebrity endorsement. It is not sold in stores and it does not grow on trees, thus the reason it is in such short supply.

The healing hint could come into your life through a chapter in a book like this that points you to the truth from the only book that matters—God's Book, which never discounts the hurt in a life's story; it just highlights the theme of forgiveness in every chapter. So I say with some confidence, reading this chapter might just lead to changing someone else's life for the better, but that all starts with the offended person setting aside the hurt for something better. Perhaps that person is you.

God's Word teaches us that when a tree falls, it cannot be undone (Eccles. 11:3). If it falls to the south, it fell to the south. If the tree falls to the north, it fell to the north. The Bible is not giving a lesson about falling trees or a lecture on forestry. This is an illustration about life. Once the tree falls, there is no profit in questioning what if it fell over there or what if the tree were still standing upright.

When something happens in your life outside of your control, there is no benefit to you or to anyone else to complain and moan and grieve over what might have been. There is no advantage to spending your thoughts on what if a certain thing had not happened the way it did. If the cut tree has fallen, it is down. It can never be put back in place the way it was or the way you would want it to be.

There are two options in your response to where the tree fell. Despair or hope. You can get angry and depressed about it, but it will never change what happened. Or you can forgive and figure out how to make the best of an undesired situation. How you react is now your choice but please take note of this: A response of unforgiveness can do more damage than where the "unforgiven tree" fell.

In the next section, we will review (1) the damage our refusal to forgive does to the encouragement we receive from our relationship with God—hiding hope because we are blinded by our own standard of justice, (2) the damage it does to us—robbing us of the enjoyment of living the abundant life with all its blessings, and (3) the damage it does to our showing and sharing Jesus to others—making it even harder for others to see Jesus in us because we prefer for them to notice we still carry the neon sign of our unforgiving spirit while dragging around the ball and chain of our hurt and bitterness.

"Get rid of all bitterness, rage and anger, brawling and slander, along with every form of malicious hatred." How? "Be kind and compassionate to one another, *forgiving each other, just as God forgave you for Christ's sake*" (Eph. 4:31–32; emphasis added).

Forgiveness willingly overlooks, looks past, or sets aside the hurts done to you by others. You voluntarily agree to give up the hurt, let it go, and take it away from the relationship without any resentment, revenge, or repayment in order to reestablish the relationship purely on the basis of your love for the other person. That truth is worth a second look and some serious contemplation.

Forgiveness *releases* the *right* to any *resentment*, *revenge*, or *repayment* in order to *restore* the *relationship* based solely on Christ's love through you for that person.

Wait a minute! That might be a valid description of forgiveness, but how do you forgive someone who has hurt you so badly and sometimes so often? Someone who does not deserve forgiveness? There is a way. Susie can loan you some spiritual binoculars that work even when standing between a rock and a very hard place for you to see how the undeserved restoration of a relationship will be better than continued resentment. They can enable you to see the springs of hope where "all things," including the suffering damages caused by others' wrongdoings, can be worked together for good.

Springs of Hope

> Who will bring any charge against
> those whom God has chosen?
>
> —Roman 8:33

Forgiveness is a divine act.

It is hard and humbling because forgiveness is always undeserved. Only God can forgive sins, because every sin, including the hurt inflicted onto your life, is ultimately against Him (Mark 2:7). Forgiveness is an act of God's mercy, grace, and love that has been designed to preserve the fellowship of our relationship with Him. Forgiveness clears the way of any obstacles so He can express His love to us. In other words, God forgives in order for you to feel the greatness of His love. That is why we are to forgive—for others to sense the greatness of God's love to them.

Before we can forgive each other, it is best to understand why and how God has forgiven us. All of us are sinners in need of God's forgiveness. We have all failed to carry out the greatest commandment, which is to love God with all of our heart, soul, mind, and strength (Mark 12:30). Sin becomes a love affair with anyone or anything at the expense of our first and foremost love for God. The companion to God's greatest commandment is to love others the way you love yourself. We have all fallen short of that in life as well. Our love of self has led us to hurt others in words and actions or simply by neglect. Do you understand the seriousness of our need for God's forgiveness? Every one of us has committed the greatest sin by failure to express the greatest commandments.

There are six New Testament words used to describe our failure to love God and others as we should.

1. *Transgression.* We have all stepped across the boundaries of right and wrong; we have all colored outside the lines of love (Col. 2:13).

2. *Lawlessness.* We have all been rebels who flagrantly and intentionally violated God's law to love others (1 John 3:4).

3. *Trespass.* We have all slipped and fallen, taken a false step, and lost control without any guarantee we could get back on track (Eph. 2:1).

4. *Sin.* We have all missed the mark of what God intended to be best for us by loving Him and others ahead of ourselves (Rom. 6:23).

5. *Debt.* We have all failed to give God what is rightfully His, our wholehearted devotion. We have all short-changed others in the love due them (Matt. 6:12).

6. *Iniquity.* We have all corrupted, twisted, and perverted God's love to fit our own desires and lifestyle choices (James 3:6).

We all need God's forgiveness. Has someone crossed the line with you? Did they intentionally hurt you or lose control in a way that was detrimental to your welfare? Did they miss the mark for what would have been best for your life? Did they fail to love you or perhaps even abuse or pervert that love? What someone else has done to you, you have done to God.

The hope of forgiveness is found in the divine conjunction under the wings of God's refuge for sinners. "*But God* demonstrated His own love for us in that while we were still sinners, Jesus Christ died for us" (Rom. 5:8). God has forgiven us through Christ's death *and for Christ's sake* (Eph. 4:32).

If we are to forgive for the same reason and in the same manner as Christ has forgiven us, then we need to know what *forgiveness* looks like. The Old Testament previewed God's forgiveness of us with five primary descriptive terms.

1. *Take away.* God lifts your sin off you and places it on Jesus to take it away forever (Isa. 53:6).

2. *Cover.* God covers your sin with the blood of Jesus (Ps. 85:2).

3. *Blot out.* God blots/wipes out your sin because of Jesus's righteousness on your behalf (Isa. 43:25).

4. *Scatter.* God scatters/disperses/sends away your sins as far as the east is from the west, never to return (Ps. 103:2).

5. *Bury.* God buries your sins in the depths of the sea where they sink like a heavy boulder, never to float to the top (Mic. 7:19).

God has forgiven you of all your sins through Christ and for Christ's sake. "The blood of Jesus Christ cleanses us [place your name in this verse] from all sin" (1 John 1:7). *All* sin. Whatever your sin. Wherever your sin. Whenever your sin. Past, present, and even future ones, since all your sins occurred after the death of Jesus on the cross.

God's forgiveness of you is unilateral, all-inclusive, and unconditional.

God has blessed you with forgiveness (Ps. 32:1) and placed you under the refuge of His wings where His loving-kindness surrounds you now and forever (Ps. 32:10–11). *Who can separate you from the love of Christ?* Absolutely no one can separate you from God's love and goodness. No one and nothing. Not anything you say or do not say; not anything you do or not do. Not anything in your past. Not anything in your present. Not anything in your future can ever separate you from God's forgiving love.

Have you forgiven all of your offenders in the same way God has forgiven you? Even that one you swore you would never forgive? Have you taken away, covered, blotted out, scattered, and buried all their selfish wrongdoings against you? Have you attempted to restore the relationship? Forgiveness is hard and humbling. It takes a divine act, both inside and through you to "forgive others just as Christ has forgiven you."

Unforgiveness always hurts you the most.

Life is not about what might have been. Life is about what is. There is no advantage to living your life depressed, angry, or bitter over the direction you wish your parent or spouse had taken. There are things in life you have no control over such as an alcoholic father who chose to abandon his family. It is like the fallen tree. It would be better to accept that reality and move on with your life. Anger, bitterness, and unforgiveness are roadblocks to joy. You will never recover from the hurt inflicted by someone else until you forgive them.

Maybe your father or whoever messed things up when they purposed for their life to go north, but it went south. God can handle south. God can cause south to work together for good even when you consider north to be the best option. Any argument with that is a problem with God, not the one who disappointed you.

If things in your family life have not turned out as you expected, you do not need to hang your head in shame or disgust. Anger, bitterness, and unforgiveness will only shrink your heart and chain your life to the past. There are still blessings to enjoy in the abundant life God has promised. Find them. God is in control even when the family tree falls. That fall might have come with pain and hurt, but your capacity to love has been enlarged, not hindered.

Susie had to learn that. She had been hurt by the alcoholic father who abandoned her. The whole matter left her angry and bitter. That is exactly where we find Naomi when she returned to Bethlehem, the home of her childhood, now bereaved over the death of her husband and two sons. She was hardly recognizable to those who had known her.

They asked, "Is that you, Naomi?" to which she replied, "Do not call me Naomi (sweetness); call me Mara (bitterness). I went away full, but God has brought me back empty."

Susie grew up in that emptiness. Like Naomi, she had a God watching over her, but often she felt as if much of His goodness had bypassed her. Instead, she felt the poverty, the loneliness, the feelings of abandonment followed by anger, bitterness, and the desire to hurt and reject her father to even the score.

It would take the kindness shown to Ruth by Boaz, the guardian-redeemer, to begin the healing for Naomi. This previewed the same kindness and undeserved favor bestowed upon Susie by her Guardian-Redeemer, Jesus Christ.

Let's look closely at where these two stories turned to hope—"under the wings of God" (Ruth 2:12). The imagery of finding refuge under the wings of God was used in the Song of Moses, which was composed to celebrate God's loving providence for undeserving people (Deut. 32:11). The song illustrates God's love as an eagle stirred from its lofty nest which swooped down, spread its wings to catch its faltering young, and then carried them on those wings of love back to the safety of the nest. God has sworn *to care* for us in loving forgiveness when we falter and *to carry* us in His loving favor at all times.

We all need God to care for us and carry us when we falter. Ruth and Naomi took refuge under the Lord's wings where they found the forgiveness and favor they needed. They sought and received His refuge of mercy. Susie's story also found herself under the wings of God's undeserved forgiveness and unending favor even as she struggled to forgive her father.

Now what does that have to do with you forgiving the hurtful offender in your life? Everything. You are now free to love and forgive others in just the *same way* God has lovingly forgiven you. And for the *same reason*.

You are empowered by God to forgive those who hurt you. Forgive them fully, freely, and forever for the sake of Christ. Forgiveness is not just setting aside the offense; it is clearing the way for you to do acts of love for the person who hurt you. In forgiveness, you release the right to any resentment, revenge, or repayment in order to restore the relationship based solely on Christ's love through you for that person.

It was not easy for Susie to forgive. C. S. Lewis says, "Everyone believes forgiveness is a good thing until they have someone to forgive." When Susie realized this forgiveness business was an issue of obedience to God, it was time to act. God had placed her alcoholic father in her life so Susie could forgive and love him the same way and for the same reason God has forgiven her.

It might be hard and humbling to forgive, but it is always right to forgive. *Always!* Forgiveness is precious and priceless. The people whom God places in your life are all precious. The relationships that require enduring loyalty and forgiveness from you are priceless.

Some people in your life will disappoint you. Some will hurt you. It is increasingly painful if you invested your life and love in them, but they did not stick around. The cry of their selfish heart and the allurement of the world enticed them to abandon those in need of their love. That is just the way people are, but for the grace of God, that would be how you treat others.

When it comes to those who have disappointed or hurt you, you have to decide whether that relationship God placed in your life is still valued as precious and priceless or wasteful and worthless? If you walk with God, you will forgive others, love those who hurt you, and pray for God to bless them (Luke 6:28). Are you going to become angry, bitter, critical, judgmental, and condemning of them, *or* do you realize that there have been times that you have disappointed God when He did not consider your relationship to be worthless but precious and priceless?

Forgiveness is always undeserved. So do not use that as an excuse. Forgiveness is unlimited so do not complain about how many times you must forgive (Matt. 18:21–22). There is never a place where God allows you to say, "This is as far as I will go." There is never a "last time" or "not again" occasion. No one has hurt you as badly or as many times as you have hurt God. "The one who has been forgiven much (you), loves much" (Luke 7:47).

Forgiveness is not a feeling; it is an action.

Forgiveness comes directly from the heart of God. Take that heart to the person in your life who needs your forgiveness. Forgiveness is not a forced activity, and it certainly is not a feeling. It is a willful act of love to give up your perceived rights in order to honor Jesus Christ. A great heart is a forgiving heart forged in the fires of sufferings.

Susie acted in love toward her father. Her forgiveness did not change what happened, but her act of love did change the relationship for the better. It certainly changed her! The family tree fell in an unwanted place, but Susie chose to share the mercy and love which she had received in God's forgiveness of her bitter, angry, unloving spirit. In a willful act of love, Susie took the heart of God to the one who chopped down the tree. That always honors Jesus.

Bitterness can be replaced by forgiveness. Anger can be supplanted by love. Suffering can be transformed into goodness. That needs to be your life story! Set aside your bitterness, anger, grievances, and grudges in order to seize every opportunity to express Christ's love. Be kind and tenderhearted. Treat others in the same manner God treats you, as if you had never sinned. Get started today. Do not wait.

The Bible illustrates the urgency of communicating forgiveness by referencing a person ready to sow the seed for the harvest, but they keep waiting for the perfect opportunity (Eccles. 11:6). In the morning, it looks as if it might rain, and in the evening, it feels as though the wind might be blowing. So they end up doing nothing. They always say, "Someday, when everything is right."

Many people live their lives that way, always waiting on the "someday" they might forgive. Now is the time to forgive. If you have the opportunity to restore a relationship, do it today. Do good to others now while there is still time.

God has given you the seeds of love to enjoy life. Sow them. Do not miss the joy of life by worrying or fretting over what might have happened or what did happen in your life. You are the steward of those seeds. Invest them wisely. Start now.

> People are often unreasonable, irrational, and self-centered. Forgive them anyway. If you are kind, people may accuse you of selfish, ulterior motives. Be kind anyway. If you are successful, you will win some unfaithful friends and some genuine enemies. Succeed anyway. If you are honest and sincere, people may deceive you. Be honest and sincere anyway. What you spend years creating, others could destroy overnight. Create anyway. If you find serenity and happiness, some may be jealous. Be happy anyway. The good you do today, will often be forgotten. Do good anyway. Give the best you have, and it will never be enough. Give your best anyway. In the final analysis, it is between you and God. It was never between you and them anyway.
>
> —Attributed to Mother Teresa

Forgiveness might not change the other person's behavior, but it will change you.

God always uses your opportunity to forgive to make you more like Christ. Forgiveness frees you once again to appreciate the preciousness of the relationship and to cherish God's loving forgiveness to you. It will keep you from a root of bitterness that will most surely blossom with the fruit of anger and anxiety. It is far better to carry around the sweet fragrance from the flower of forgiveness.

God will settle all the accounts. It is not for you to judge and condemn. You are to pray, forgive, love, and do all that is within your power to restore the relationship. There is a cost for enduring loyalty. Part of that cost is forgiveness of those who have hurt or disappointed you. You forgive others so that Jesus Christ might be lifted up in your life for others to see.

Forgiveness is not just a way of thinking or feeling something; it is an intentional act of Jesus's love for the other person. Your forgiveness is an act of obedience to God's Word. God's grace enables you to convert forgiveness into reality. You obey; love swoops in. Instead of your old ball and chain of despair, others see a window of hope, hope for you and hope for them.

You never show God's love more than when you forgive the one who hurt you the most.

Forgiveness is a process. You probably need to get started. It will be hard and humbling. It will not be easy, just worth it. Start with the Rock, the Lord Jesus. Go to a Hard Place, the person whom you have not forgiven. Share the Hope of God's forgiveness.

The Right Application of Hope

There is more than enough *hope* to cover the distance between the *rock* and the *hardest place* you will ever go to *forgive*. Forgive someone today. Start with the hardest one to forgive.

"Love keeps no record of wrongs...Love always trusts, always *hopes*, always perseveres. Love never fails" (1 Cor. 13:5–8; emphasis added).

My hope is built on nothing less
Than Jesus' blood and righteousness;
I dare not trust the sweetest frame,
But wholly lean on Jesus' name.
On Christ, the solid Rock, I stand;
All other ground is sinking sand,
All other ground is sinking sand.

—"My Hope Is Built on Nothing Less,"
Edward Mote

19

Never Good Enough on the Performance Treadmill

Lin's Story
Application of *God's Love Is More Than Good Enough*

Many women have been controlled all their lives by what other people think about them or what others expect from them or how others respond to them. They often sense the pressure to perform to some social standard or media ideal, seeing themselves as society-made puppets in the hands of string masters being compelled to perform to please different audiences. They fear their worth is attached to their "performance" measuring up to others' expectations. Do you feel that way? Do you struggle with feelings of inadequacy, insecurity, insignificance, and worthlessness?

The young and not so young fret over Facebook likes and social media comments. While many are posting their latest selfie, some feel left out, overlooked, and unwanted. They become plagued with stress and anxiety over what others might think about their child's birthday party or daughter's wedding, their size or hairstyle, their fashion choices or career decision regarding what is best for their family. What women really long for is to feel accepted, valued, and loved for who they are and not what they accomplish or do not accomplish.

It is easy to feel insecure living in a disposable world of paper plates, plastic bottles, fast-food utensils, disposable diapers, discarded marriages, and throwaway fetuses. The landscape is covered with things and people that are no longer wanted, just used and tossed aside, so someone can get something new.

Behind the pleasantries and canned answers at church or work lies the hidden pain of insecurity. Some laugh the loudest in a crowd and then go home and cry themselves to sleep. The self-doubting performer will smile the brightest in public and then race home to stare at the blank walls, gripped in a deadly silence of perceived disapproval. Or they just exist—part of the wounded society searching in self-help books to shake the self-appointed title of "total failure."

These women struggle to embrace God's unconditional acceptance, which is not based on their performance level. They become entangled in a vicious cycle, sometimes starting as a young girl, of trying to please others while feeling or being made to feel that they never match up. They often battle low self-esteem, insecurity, and even despair when God's Word promises freedom from trying to please others. You may be one of those burdened with feelings of guilt and inadequacy. You are probably very familiar with the drill.

There will always be someone close to you whose mission in life seems to be pointing out your flaws and faults. They might even start the conversation with praise; however, they just have to mention that one wrong note, that one missed spot, or that one better way to cook. They envision themselves as experts on everything regarding weight loss and flower beds and raising children. Ouch! They just have a way of calling attention to imperfections in your parenting skills or worse, in your children. Your heart races, your throat constricts, and your stomach churns. You want to strangle them or at least scream at them to get a life! (Ooops! This is a Christian book.) Instead, you go home and cry. Your tears run down your cheeks like unlovely rivers of imperfection. Some days it seems as if you cannot even do the mad or sad things right! Whatever they say or however they communicated their opinions, they only reminded you of what you already fear, not being good enough.

What should you do if you feel you are never good enough? Do you get back on that performance treadmill and turn up the speed or do you just discount its value in a garage sale and quit life altogether?

God says you do not have to be perfect to be loved. Lin needed to hear that over and over. It took time for her to believe it could be true for her. Perhaps, you or a loved one shares those same struggles and needs reassuring reminders of God's truth.

God loves and accepts you just as you are; He wants you to feel loved and accepted. God prefers you running into His arms of love, not plodding along on some performance treadmill. God is on your side; He assures you that *nothing can ever separate you from His love* (Rom. 8:35–39).

Does that sound strange to you? Unbelievable? Unconditional love and acceptance might go against the way you were raised. That concept certainly counters our cultural expectations. *But God* leaps to the limits of language to express His unlimited love for you even when you fall and fail. What pleases God? Faith in Him and His goodness (Heb. 11:6). When you do not feel good enough, trust God's love to be good enough for you.

Lin's Story

Never enough. Despite my best efforts, I was simply never enough. Never good enough, never smart enough, never pretty enough, never talented enough, and the list went on and on.

I struggled with feelings of worthlessness.

At an early age, I had this insatiable hunger to be loved, appreciated, or even acknowledged. I was incredibly small for my age and younger than all but one in my class. I was always less in some way than everyone I knew—never measuring up with classmates at school and certainly not at home. Both my sisters were popular, intelligent, athletic, talented, and beautiful. I never felt I was any of those things. My parents were both busy working and providing for us, and I sensed that I was insignificant to them. I struggled with feelings of worthlessness. My efforts were constantly aimed at convincing the world, and myself for that matter, that I was good enough to be worthy of friendship or love.

I have always loved to sing, and it came somewhat easily for me. When I was young, I loved to harmonize; I got bored with the melody quickly and often experimented with different parts, simply to keep it interesting. When I went to college, I majored in music where I naturally began to hone those skills. Marrying and moving out of state put an end to my college education; however, I continued to sing in the choir at church and in an ensemble. Despite my experience and God-given abilities, I never attempted a solo because of my insurmountable fear of rejection. Then we moved to a new city and a new church, and somehow, the minister of music found out I could sing and *told* me I was going to sing a solo on an upcoming Sunday. I couldn't say no to this imposing request, so I anxiously began preparing to sing. I did a decent job, not perfect, of course, but it seemed that I might be able to handle this type of thing, and I was soon singing solos often in our church. I was thrilled to be able to sing for the Lord.

There was a beautiful songbird with a haunting melody.

I continued to sing in church, even during a very dark time in my life. I had a wonderful life—a great husband, precious children, and a happy home, but somehow, I continued to be haunted by thoughts of unworthiness and inferiority. I was dominated with these thoughts throughout each day. I was frequently on the verge of buckling under the pressure of striving to measure up, despite being utterly convinced that I *never* would. I was inflicting mental anguish with all these self-loathing thoughts; they were about to take a devastating and destructive turn in my life.

I do not know if I can convey how grave my situation became. Anyone who has been there can certainly identify even if I cannot adequately express it. I had suicidal thoughts throughout each day. I had so much to be thankful for, but that only added to my despair. I struggled with guilt for feeling as though life were not worth living. How could a Christian think that her pit is so deep suicide is the only way out? I was afraid to share my desperation with my mom because I did not want to hurt her. My lonely anguish felt as though I were being stalked and haunted by something evil. I was literally in a fight for my life.

Give your thoughts to the Lord.

It was at this time that I began to learn that I could overcome this negative pattern through relinquishing control of my thoughts to the Lord. I began applying Ephesians 4:22–24: "You were taught, with regard to your former way of life, to put off your old self, which is being corrupted by its deceitful desires; to be made new in the attitude of your minds; and to put on the new self, created to be like God in true righteousness and holiness."

I practiced "putting off" the wrong thoughts and "putting on" the right thoughts. I began to see a glimmer of hope in this previously hopeless life. I learned that *as a man thinks in his heart, so is he* (Prov. 23:7). God began to change my mind-set as I began to "take captive every thought to make it obedient to Christ" (2 Cor. 10:5). Also, my thought pattern changed from negative, crippling thoughts to those taught in Philippians 4:8: "Finally, brothers, whatever is true, whatever is noble, whatever is right, whatever is pure, whatever is lovely, whatever is admirable—if anything is excellent or praiseworthy—think about such things."

The Lord began to do an extraordinary work! I was being transformed. I became increasingly secure and confident in Christ. I accepted that He loved and valued me, and this affirmation made an immense difference in my life. Even though I still had to deal with occasional feelings of inadequacy, both internally and from those that occurred from living in a fallen world, I didn't despair anymore. I knew how to keep myself out of that abysmal pit. I faithfully preached those scriptures to myself, and I continued to preach to myself whenever those treacherous feelings of unworthiness would arise. As my pastor taught me, "It's not perfection. It's direction!"

My God is infinitely good enough.

I progressively sought the Lord and His path for my life by applying His Word. God kept me stable and encouraged, qualities which have been my constant strength through the harrowing storms of life.

My depression had been incredibly oppressive. It had led me down a dark path that wound and twisted through the most desolate and dismal of places. Although at times I may have felt very isolated and alone, God never left me alone. He was my comfort and strength; He helped me out of my despondency. As I made the consistent effort to apply scripture to my weighty situations, He lifted me up and carried me out of despair. He strengthened me in His Word, and today He *is* my Strength. When difficulties arise, He *is* my Hope. I will be enough, because He is infinitely good enough.

Desert of Despair

Have you battled thoughts that everyone else would be better off without your being around? Do you hide and cry, fret and worry, stress and beat yourself up emotionally? Has your struggle led to despondency or contemplations of suicide? Do not give up. Do not give in to your feelings. Let Lin's story point you to help. Where there is despair, hope.

Perfection or comparison to others has never been the right standard. Just be the best version of yourself; even that will be a lifelong process. However, it can be a joy-filled process, not a hopeless one.

You were never supposed to be like everyone else. You are not a puppet on a string performing for the culture and times you live in. God made you unique. God designed you specifically to fit into your family and into the lives of those linked by the circumstances. You may not see that right now. You might not feel that way or think that or hear that from others, but it is true. You need to listen to the right voice, the only one whose opinion matters. You need to learn to ask the right questions. *Since God is for you, who can be against you? Who condemns you? Certainly not God. What can separate you from the love of Christ? Absolutely nothing.*

Too many women suffer on the performance treadmill trying to gain acceptance and love. I always marveled at Lin's inner struggle when her talents were off the charts. Others would have gladly traded places with her, but in reality, no one else knew what that other place felt like or what had to be overcome. Perhaps everyone else would be shocked to learn of your struggles with insecurity or your fight just to survive. Guilt, shame, embarrassment, and performance-driven stress can become a burden too heavy for any heart.

Not good enough. Where do thoughts like that come from? When do they begin? For Lin, they began early in life as comparisons and neglect led to feelings of insignificance and unworthiness of love. Did Ruth battle those feelings? She arrived in Bethlehem as a "nobody." She was from the wrong side of the tracks; she had nothing. She was unwanted and criticized. She worked hard and loved well, but did she still feel worthless?

How did Ruth find acceptance? In the first chapter of her story, she found herself alone and unloved, an unwelcomed partner on a bitter journey down a hopeless road. In the last chapters, she finds favor and acceptance and love. It was all orchestrated by the hidden hand of God's love as a preview of God's love for you.

When others walk away, love stays. When others quit, love goes on. When others complain, love accepts. When others come to the end of their giving, love has just begun. Love does what it does not have to do. Love fills up life with divine conjunctions and new horizons. "But God, being rich in mercy, because of the great love with which He has loved us...saved us" (Eph. 2:4). God brought us back from being dead in our sins and trespasses and made us alive in Jesus Christ. This gift was not deserved and certainly not earned by some performance treadmill test. It was solely the result of God's grace.

Ruth discovered the truth that conquered Lin's fears. That same love of unconditional acceptance is available to you as well. When the skies of your life darken and the mood ring dims, it is vital to remember the truth. Take refuge under the shelter of its wings. You will find no performance treadmill anywhere around. There are no measurements to match or tests to pass or comparisons to supersede. United to Jesus Christ, you are fully and forever accepted. Period. Done. Never to be changed. You will never need to ask, "How much is enough?" God's love for you will always be good enough.

Springs of Hope

> For I am convinced that neither death nor life, neither angels nor demons, neither the present nor the future, nor any powers, neither height nor depth, nor anything else in all creation, will be able to separate us from the love of God that is in Christ Jesus our Lord.
>
> —Romans 8:38–39

There is good news for all performance treadmill runners chasing love and acceptance. Actually, it is great news, life-changing news. It will greatly help if you learn to ask the right questions. Instead of asking what you have to do to be loved or how well you have to perform to be accepted, try these questions.

"Who will bring any charge against those whom God has chosen? Who is the one who condemns you?" (Rom. 8:33–34).

Not God. Jesus Christ died on the cross to demonstrate God's love for you and satisfy God's judgment for your lackluster performance. Because you are sinful and imperfect, you will always battle with guilt, but there is now no condemnation. For the rest of your life, Jesus continues to intercede for you in the courts of heaven. That is where guilt and insecurity and feelings of worthlessness lose their power to control your thoughts.

God loves you more than you have ever realized. "I have loved you with an everlasting love" (Jer. 31:3). Will God's everlasting love ever end or take a break? No. Never. What do you have to do to be loved that long? What does it cost? "I will love you freely" (Hosea 14:4). Freely. What do you have to do to get God to love you or to keep God loving you? God loves you freely. What if you are not "good enough"? "I will love you freely." God's love cannot be earned, deserved, purchased, negotiated, or won in some competition. And God's love can never be lost, stolen, or forfeited by a nonperformance clause. Wow!

Who can separate you from the love of Christ?

That is a question worthy of your contemplation. You are unconditionally accepted as God's child. Freely, fully, and forever loved and forgiven. God sees you as perfect in Christ. Embracing this truth can liberate you from the toxicity of cynicism and self-criticism which overwhelm the heart. No one has God's right to judge you, and nothing has the power to make God stop loving you. No one. Nothing. Not even you with all your self-doubts and low esteem. Place your hope in God, not in "doing your best" or "trying harder."

God has rescued many women exhausted from the never-ending exercise of trying to be good enough to please everyone. Cut the puppet strings. Trash the comparison checklists. Shake off the self-doubts. Get off the performance treadmill. Run on a different road controlled and compelled by the love of Christ (2 Cor. 5:14–15). When we get caught on the performance treadmill seeking to please ourselves or others, the love of Christ controls, compels, constrains, and "overmasters" us with the ambition to please Him. We please God by faith that acts in love, not performance tests or religious activities.

Put away the measuring tape for you and your children. Performance competition breeds envy, disappointment, and discontentment. Comparison shopping will rob you of joy in Christ. If necessary, stay away from social media and its thoughtless, insensitive comments. The things that worry and discourage you today will not matter in twenty years. Most will not matter tomorrow.

God's love for you is unconditional, unchanging, and unlimited.

God's love is designed to control and compel you to keep loving regardless of your performance ratings. If you mess up, you start again, every new day, every new breath; God's love for you is not based on your accomplishments. You no longer have to live worried about your performance being judged by other people. You no longer have to fear not measuring up to expectations or not being good enough. God's love does not change according to your proximity to perfection. If you do well, God does not love you more, and if you do poorly, God never loves you less.

God loves you based on who He is.

Have you been controlled all your life by what other people think about you or what they expect from you or how they respond to you? There is a solution to that. You can be controlled by the love of Someone who loves you unconditionally, with an unchanging, unlimited, long-suffering, long-lasting love regardless of your performance. God promised to love you forever even when He already knew the worst about you. Every woman needs to learn that. Preach to yourself. Sing it to your soul.

Nothing can separate you from that love. Nothing. That's it. That is all that needs to be said, all that needs to be known. This truth changes how you live and how you love. It changes how you look at other people and how you treat them.

The ugly accuser of God's children will seek to separate you from clinging to that hope. The opinions or comments of others might threaten to divide your thoughts and tear you away from the assurance of God's love. But God (with all His divine conjunctions) will lift your eyes to the horizon of Jesus Christ where love knows no bounds, no limits with no end. Lin learned to look there. She recommends the view.

"For I am convinced that neither death nor life, neither angels nor demons, neither the present nor the future, nor any powers, neither height nor depth, nor anything else in all creation, will be able to separate us from the love of God that is in Christ Jesus our Lord" (Rom. 8:38–39).

There is no better description of this beautiful breathtaking horizon than the all-encompassing, biggest, most powerful, and most feared "performance separators" in this list, all eclipsed and conquered by God's love for you.

1. *Death.* This is the big one. Death is final. It cuts you off from this earthly journey. However, the same ship responsible for the departure from all you have known carries you to the arrival dock where all your hopes become reality. Death can never separate you from God's love.

2. *Life.* There are many separators in life. Gender, race, religion, nationality, age, social status. Health and wealth or the lack thereof are bitter dividers. Critics and complainers can feel like monster scissors cutting you into tiny pieces. Conflict tears nations and families apart. But God never takes a break from your life's journey. He never glances away or forgets a need. There is nothing in life which can separate you from God's love.

3. *Angels and demons.* These are the most powerful "unseen" things operating in both the physical and spiritual realms. They are more powerful than you but not more powerful than God's love from which they can never separate you.

4. *Time.* Things present or future might fill your mind with fear, worry, and anxiety. Time will eventually unveil "seen" troubles and "unforeseen" problems. God's love for you is everlasting. It has no time constraints. Nothing from eternity past to eternity future can ever separate you from God's timeless love.

5. *Spiritual powers.* The enemy uses supernatural powers to execute his well-designed and effective plans to chain many to a lifelong journey on the performance treadmill. Those powers breed doubts and raise questions, but they are powerless against the almighty truths of God's Word. All the enemy can really do is to use those supernatural powers to get you to embrace the lie that "God is not good enough to you." That was the tactical lie presented to Adam and Eve. That was the issue in Job's story. That was Naomi's bitterness and Ruth's dilemma. That was Jeremiah's lament. But God is good enough. Infinitely, incomparably, incredibly, inconceivably good enough! Oh, what a God! God accepts you unconditionally and loves you endlessly. God wants you to know and live your life based on the truth that nothing, not even something supernatural can ever separate you from His steadfast love.

6. *Space.* Height and depth are effective separators. Some things can be placed too high out of your reach or buried so low you cannot dig them up, but they are not too high or too deep for God. God's love swallows up space faster than the speed of light. The highest heaven, the widest distance, and the lowest depth are not beyond the circumference of God's love. God's love for you is higher, wider, deeper, and bigger than anyplace you will be in life and eternity. There is no space empty of God's love for you.

7. *Anything else in all of creation.* Just in case someone thinks God might have forgotten something or somewhere or

sometime, God throws this into the mix. God is not ignorant or unacquainted with anything that exists. He created it all. If the astronomers discover another galaxy or gravitational waves rippling through the fabric of space-time or even another universe somewhere, God created it. God told us He created all of it for our good, so none of it will ever separate us from the goodness of God's love.

Oh yeah, what about yourself? What if you decide you want a separation? The last time I checked, you and I still fall under the category of created things and no created thing will ever separate us from the love of Christ. *That includes all the bad people and bad things. It encompasses all your decisions, both right and wrong.* Sometimes you might struggle with doubts. Doubting is not a sin; it's a place on the road of faith where you are faced with a decision whether to believe this world's lie about your circumstances and how you are not good enough or you embrace the truth of God's Word regarding God's unconditional love and acceptance that is always more than good enough.

It is essential that we learn to think right. The only way to think right is to saturate our minds with Scriptural truths. At the root of insecurity and feelings of worthlessness, we find Satan attempting to convince us that we are unworthy, our sins are too great, and others appear more righteous. And then the struggle begins. We spiral down mentally and emotionally. To salvage ourselves, *we begin to do better*. For a short time, we run the treadmill. There is a better way! Lin chose to go to God's Word and arm herself against the enemy tormenting her mind. I hope you will as well.

Reminders of God's love are on every page of God's Word. When our thoughts become saturated with truth, we are ready for a conversation with our accuser, "I once was unworthy. I was a sinner headed to hell. *But* God poured his grace all over me, and now I am His beloved child. Jesus Christ gave His body for me. His blood washed away my sins, and now I am clothed in righteous garments of His life and love. Now I am united with Christ and wear His garland of grace. I have been justified, I am blessed with every spiritual blessing, I am alive, I am not alone, I have access to the Father, I can approach Him with freedom and confidence, I have peace, I have not been given a spirit of fear but one of power and love, and because I am His workmanship, I am confident that He will perfect the work He has begun in me. *And* one day, I will sit at the marriage feast table with my Savior. Loved forever? Accepted? Good enough? Ask the One with the nail-pierced hands."

This kind of thinking is liberating. I am convinced of that. God proved and publicly demonstrated His own love toward us in that while we were still sinners, His Son Jesus Christ died for us—*for you.*

Oh, how can you not love Him? Your God watches over you as a caring Father for His little ones. He has numbered all the hairs on your head, charted all your paths, and ordered all your steps. He holds your hand in the dark, chases away every fear, and wipes off every tear. He hears every whisper and notices every sigh. Where there is despair, *hope.*

God alone determines your identity and value. Do not be enslaved to the whims of others' opinions. Your importance does not depend upon how many "likes" your Facebook picture attracts or how many follow or unfollow your tweets. Do not diminish the significance of God's love by climbing back on your performance treadmill or crawling back into your suffocating hole of solitary silence. Turn on some music and join Lin and the countless multitude of women singing love songs of perpetual praise to their God!

You are greatly and marvelously loved. Why? Because God's love is good enough.

Do not marginalize the perfection and sufficiency of God's love for you. You are fully and unconditionally loved and accepted because of one magnificent reason. God's love is good enough. I pray this glorious truth will rise up from the deepest part of your heart to fill your life with hope. When you are not good enough, God's love for you is still good enough.

There is no greater love! God loves you to the max. He will never love you less!

The Right Application of Hope

Stop. Rest today. Enjoy being loved by a love that cannot be separated by death, life, time, space, unseen things, spiritual powers, or any other created thing.

Spend some time in the arms of the One who loves you the most and will keep on loving you without judging your performance. Sing to the Lord. It does not have to sound perfect for it to be pleasing to Him.

"The Lord delights in those who put their *hope* in His unfailing love" (Ps. 147:11; emphasis added).

What if I climbed that mountain
What if I swam to that shore
What if every battle was victorious
Then would you love me more?
Would you love me more?

What if I were everybody's first choice
What if I went farther than before
What if I stood high above the rest
Then would you love me more?
Would you love me more?

You say I belong to You apart from the things I do
You say I belong to You, I'm in awe of why You do
Why You do, why You do
I'm in awe of You

What if I ignored the hand that fed me
What if I forgot to confess
What if I stumbled down that mountain
Then would you love me less?
Lord, would You love me less?

What if I were everyone's last choice
What if I mixed in with the rest
What if I failed what I passed before
Then would you love me less, Lord?
Would you love me less, oh no, oh no, oh no

What have I done to deserve Your son sent to die for me?
What can I give? I want to live; give me eyes to see
In a world that keeps changing, there's
one thing that I know is true
Your love is staying, there's nothing else I'll hold onto

The way You love me, the way You do
The way You do, the way You love me,
You love me! You love me!

—"What If," Jadon Lavik

20

The Childless Mother

Tweet's Story
Application of *God's Love for a Big Family*

Suffering runs like a common thread through us all. It comes in various forms, but it has its own universal language. Tears mean the same thing for every woman. Life hurts and dreams fade from the sting of heartache and heartbreak.

Have you questioned God's sovereignty and goodness at some point in your life? Maybe your life seemed ready to crumble. Perhaps unwanted circumstances fractured your dreams into countless pieces. In those moments of darkness, you cannot see or even imagine how a good God could possibly be in control of your situation. Your tears do not lie. Your heart is in pain. Real life hurts.

But God uses great suffering to make a great heart. Do you trust God to do that in your life? No matter what? A better understanding of God helps us see He can be trusted in every situation. God is always good, and God is forever faithful. God's love is never changed by time, distance, or circumstances. It never lessens. It never weakens. It never disappoints.

The Bible is filled with stories of women who chose to build their lives on the solid rock of God's faithfulness and not the shifting sands of culturally defined roles. Women named Sarah, Ruth, and Hannah were well acquainted with the heartache and heartbreak going on in Tweet's life from her childlessness. God had a specific plan for each of them and for you as well. There is a child for you to love. Your God-designed path to that child's heart might be through birth, adoption, foster parenting, or ministry. The journey might have different kinds of pain, but the agony never lessens the impact of your influence. You are God's picture of hope for some child.

Tweet's Story

I, Mary Alice, do take thee Billy, to be my lawfully wedded husband. Thus, began my marriage. Billy and I had all the same dreams as other young couples—a nice house, good jobs, and children. But we found as the years went by and I had to have a hysterectomy in my early thirties, these were not God's plans for our life together. There would be no children. We could have questioned God's plans, we could have become angry, we could have been jealous of all our sisters and brothers and friends who were having babies. Instead, we accepted God's will.

We trusted God to write the chapters of our life and what a surprise we found waiting for us in God's book. First, God wanted me to serve Him by being a fulltime caretaker for my mother who lived with us for seven years. Then I felt as though He rewarded my obedience by calling me to work with the children in our church. Every page of God's book had a different child's face on it. I was in charge of the Cradle Roll, so Billy and I met those precious children and their parents at the hospital. What a joy to share in that time of their life. I gave them their first New Testament; my prayer was that they might hide God's words in their hearts for the rest of their lives. I continued serving by working in the nursery every Sunday during Bible studies.

There was sorrow in the night but bright joy in the morning.

My Sunday mornings started with blessings from God as I looked forward to loving on every child who went through our church. We had snacks, we put puzzles together, we sang about how much Jesus loved the little children. (And yes, I changed diapers.) I encouraged young families to take part in Baby Dedication Sunday to openly ask for God's divine guidance as they raised their children and taught them to bring honor to their Heavenly Father.

They all called me Mrs. Tweet, an affectionate name my brothers and sisters had given me at birth. And you know God is so good. Those hundreds of children, whenever they return to church, come to find me and cover me up with hugs. God showered me and my husband with more love than we could ever have imagined.

We have been devoted to one another—each other's best friend for more than fifty years now. We have around sixty brothers, sisters, nieces, nephews, and great nieces and nephews we call our family. I cannot even count all the children in my church family. There may have been sorrow for a night, but God brought joy in the morning as He promises His children He will.

Desert of Despair

Tweet asked many questions as she sought to grasp the promised goodness of God in our lives that sometimes feels like anything but that. The news of no children was not as easy as transitioning from the first paragraph of her story to the next. There were real struggles to keep emotions controlled by faith and not feelings. She had memorized the promise "Trust in the Lord with all your heart and He will direct your paths. Do not lean on your own understanding, but in all your ways, acknowledge Him" (Prov. 3:5–6). This was her test, the hardest test for a woman who loves children.

The Old Testament book of 1 Samuel records Hannah's story as she grieved over her childless situation. She prayed for a baby, but her prayers seemed unanswered. She cried and lost her appetite. She even went to worship with bitterness in her soul. She was frustrated, confused, and hurt.

Some of you are praying the same prayer as Hannah. You carry the same pain and disappointment. Something you desperately want is being denied. It can even be difficult to come to church because there are so many children there. Inevitably you will hear of a new mother's announcement or be passed the picture of a joyful woman's granddaughter. Hopefully, you have the grace to smile, but inwardly, it is another painful puncture to your hurting heart.

God blessed Hannah with a baby boy she named Samuel. She understood he belonged to the Lord. God chose not to give Tweet her own child. She was not loved any less. God needed a special heart to care for all the children who belonged to Him. However, both ladies teach us a very important lesson.

God does not always answer our prayers the way we want, but His love will saturate whatever answer He gives, even if it is "No."

In those moments of crisis and lost dreams, your view of God will determine your response to God's plan for your life. For Hannah and Tweet, everything God does is always wise, right, and good. Hannah composed her own song of praise. "There is no one holy like the Lord; there is no one besides you; there is no Rock like our God" (1 Sam. 2:2). God never abandons His girls who stand on the Rock through the storms of life and He loves to tell their stories with surprise endings like those of Hannah, Tweet, and Ruth whose story has moved into its last chapter.

The book of Ruth is a love story orchestrated in God's providence, which leads to the marriage of Ruth and Boaz and then the birth of a baby boy. The romantic chapters weave a storyline which surpasses Cinderella and the prince for reality and significance. We have already alluded to the marvelous twist in the tale provided by the baby's genealogy, revealing his place in the lineage of King David and ultimately his connection to Jesus Christ. Ruth will become the great-grandmother of the greatest king in Israel's history and will be linked to the human genealogical records of Joseph and Mary, the parents of Jesus.

The heart of the story reveals the transformation of two women's journey from hopelessness to hope. Two women without children, one bereaved and one barren, lived their ordinary lives as best they could. Divine conjunctions of providence led to a child they both would love and nurture. The beautiful account of their journey of hope ends with the woman left without children now rocking a newborn baby in her arms, rejoicing at God's goodness to her.

"In all this you greatly rejoice, though now for a little while you may have had to suffer grief in all kinds of trials. These have come so that the proven genuineness of your faith, of greater worth than gold, may result in praise, glory and honor when Jesus Christ is revealed" (1 Pet. 1:6–7).

God loves to show you and others what He already knows, the genuineness of your faith. Nowhere is that faith, hope, and joy more on display than in the midst of suffering and trials. Hurts expose your heart in ways nothing else can, but they always serve a purpose in God's promise to do you good. Naomi's heart was placed on full display, and God knew what the world would see because He had already written the last chapter. Even when her heart felt "empty," it was not void of hope that would someday rejoice in God's goodness.

The message of the book of Ruth is that no matter what we go through, there is hope. It illustrates the truth of the promise found in Romans 8:28. The road of life is often long and winding and difficult. The signs along the way remind you to notice the divine conjunctions. This is not a dead-end journey. This is not a wasted trip. Keep your eyes of hope on the horizon.

Springs of Hope

> For I am convinced that neither death nor life, neither angels nor demons, neither the present nor the future, nor any powers, neither height nor depth, nor anything else in all creation, will be able to separate us from the love of God that is in Christ Jesus our Lord.
>
> —Roman 8:38–39

There is hope for the hurting. Our hope is a Person, not our circumstances. Hope is not the absence of trials and heartaches but the joy of overcoming them. Naomi and Ruth and Hannah and Tweet saw the reality of God at work in their lives. None of them could have imagined the greatness of God's goodness in their future. None of them could have dreamed of the great heart God would create inside them through their trials of adversity. Everyone who builds a life on the Rock will survive the storms and enjoy the goodness of God. You will too.

God is the ultimate giver of all good things. He promised to cause all things to work together for our supreme good and His ultimate purpose. God gave a baby to Ruth, Boaz, Naomi, and the people of Bethlehem. God gave a baby to Hannah; He gave Mrs. Tweet to babies. Children are a gift from God, but they are not privately owned. They are a stewardship from God. In the birth of Ruth and Boaz's baby, the women of Bethlehem sang a song to Naomi, "Blessed be the Lord!" They saw the newborn boy as the restorer of life to Naomi.

Mrs. Tweet learned to see every newborn in her church in that same way. Her love for the children honored God and restored new life to her. She rejoiced in every visit to the maternity wing of the hospital. Tweet never missed a birth. Never. For over forty years, not one child born to members of our church family missed out on Tweet's joyful welcome. She considered it important to embrace each baby into the larger family of God's community and to present them their first pink or blue bible. "Her children" grew up thankful for her love. Their hugs continued long after childhood. Mrs. Tweet rocked babies and played with little children every week of every year until the day she beheld Jesus, the glory of her story and song, "Blessed be the Lord!"

One chapter in life never tells the whole story. Our lineage, heritage, and significance are all linked to the story of Jesus. There are divine conjunctions, magnificent promises, and guiding principles, all pointing to a new horizon of God's goodness beyond our imagination. Hope is forged and shaped by heavenly assurances of no condemnation for sinfulness and no separation from Christ's love with all things working together in God's purpose for our ultimate good.

God may have given you a child through birth or adoption or foster care. If not, God may still enable you to conceive or have you invest your love in many children not birthed by you. But ultimately, each child belongs to God. Their journey through life will be surrounded by His love and filled with divine conjunctions connecting them to hope. That hope might come through you.

There is a divine purpose for each child and a Guardian-Redeemer to give them love. Ultimately every story is connected to the story of the greater Son of David born in Bethlehem who now sits enthroned above, interceding for us, the children of God. This Jesus is the greater purpose of life, the reason and pattern for how each one of us should live and love.

Every baby, like the ones in Ruth's and Hannah's stories and the hundreds in Tweet's life, has a purpose and significance far beyond what any onlooker can imagine. All children's stories begin with the God who gave them life and their journey will return them to His loving arms. In between, their circumstances will fluctuate with joys and sorrows, health and sickness, blessings and sufferings. But there will always be hope.

What shall we say to all this? Maybe we should join in the one song we know for certain will be sung in heaven throughout the ages. It might not be sung exclusively, but the Word of God assures us it has a definite and prominent and everlasting place in the heavenly sounds. The song unfolds in a double (maybe infinite) crescendo of thunderous praise!

> They sang a new song, saying: "You are worthy to take the scroll and to open its seals, because you were slain, and with your blood you purchased for God persons from every tribe and language and people and nation. You have made them to be a kingdom and priests to serve our God, and they will reign on the earth."
>
> Then I looked and heard the voice of many angels, numbering thousands upon thousands, and ten thousand times ten thousand. They encircled the throne and the living creatures and the elders. In a loud voice they were saying: "Worthy is the Lamb, who was slain, to receive power and wealth and wisdom and strength and honor and glory and praise!"
>
> Then I heard every creature in heaven and on earth and under the earth and on the sea, and all that is in them, saying: "To him who sits on the throne and to the Lamb be praise and honor and glory and power, for ever and ever!" (Rev. 5:9–13)

The ultimate purpose of everything and everyone in this universe is to glorify Jesus for what He did on the cross to demonstrate the love of God to us. "Worthy is the Lamb who was slain" (Rev. 5:12). Every chapter of every life is linked by divine conjunctions to that purpose. Every story of God's goodness in the midst of life's tragedies and triumphs connects to that purpose. All of heaven will be full of endless praises to Jesus for that purpose.

You and this chapter in *your* life are divinely included in God's story. Hidden from view but not from impact, God is at work through His providence and grace to do you the greatest good and to use your life for the greatest purpose. "To Him be the glory both now and forever" (2 Pet. 3:18).

The Lord has led you beside green pastures and still waters. He has led you down the paths of righteousness and restored your soul. The Lord has walked with you through the valley of the shadow of death. Now get on with your life! Your cup overflows! God's rod and staff comfort you. His goodness and mercy pursue you every day of your life.

Every day of your life is a blessing. Some days just get mistaken for something else because of the foggy mornings, cloudy skies, and dark nights. When your life, like that of Ruth and Naomi and Tweet, looks and feels like *nothing* is going right in the worst of times and *nothing* good could ever possibly come during the darkest of nights, hope in God. The last chapter of your earthly life has not been completed, but it has been finished in the heart of God since before the foundation of the world and written by His invisible hand as part of the greatest story ever told.

God not only writes, but He also paints stories of hope for the hurting. He uses many colors. Perhaps, right now all you can see are the darker shades, but the skilled artist uses them only for contrast to be dominated by the brighter colors. Your portrait is not completely finished. The end result will be praise, glory, and honor for the God who caused all things to work together for your good. All things.

A life portrait is never just about the colors and shading, and a life story is not just facts and historical events. Together, their exposure of the pains and joys of the heart allows other women sojourners to identify with the hurt and the happiness. They serve as a map to guide others traveling down that same road in life. Most importantly, they become windows of hope and spiritual binoculars for other women in their darkest days of despair.

Some Suggestions for Struggling Sisters

1. *Recommit your life to its divinely designed purpose.* "To Him be the glory both now and forever" (2 Pet. 3:18). Give your heart to greatness. In suffering, glorify Jesus by faith, hope, and love. Use whatever talents you have been given and redeem whatever time you have remaining for His glory.

2. *Live your ordinary life on the solid rock of God's faithfulness.* Where there is despair, *hope*. When the storms of life hit with hurricane force winds, you will not fall apart and crumble. You will stand strong and still see all the future goodness God has promised.

> The LORD is my light and my salvation—whom shall I fear? The Lord is the stronghold of my life—of whom shall I be afraid?
> One thing I ask from the Lord, this is the only thing I desire, that I may dwell in the house of the Lord all the days of my life, to gaze on the beauty of the Lord and to seek Him in His temple. For in the day of trouble He will keep me safe in His dwelling; He will hide me in the shelter of His sacred tent and set me high upon a rock.
> I am confident of this: I will still see the goodness of the Lord in the land of the living. Wait and hope in the Lord; be strong and take heart and hope in the Lord. (Ps. 27:1–14)

3. *Tell your story with all its sorrows and joys in a way that honors Jesus.* Write a short version of a chapter in your life or one of a woman you greatly admire. Add it to the back of this book and pray it becomes a window of hope for someone else. Share it with family, friends, and fellow sojourners who walked through the valley of darkness ahead of you and those still there behind you. "The Lord is good to those who hope in Him" (Lam. 3:25).

4. *Join in the song* of Hannah, Ruth, Naomi, the women of Bethlehem, the "ordinary women" of this book, and the multitude of the redeemed from every tribe and language and people and nation uniting their voices with the many angels, numbering thousands upon thousands, and ten thousand times ten thousand encircled around the throne singing, as every creature in heaven and on earth and under the earth and on the sea, and all that is in them harmonize with you in wonder, awe, and love:

"To Him who sits on the throne and to the Lamb be praise and honor and glory and power, for ever and ever!" (Rev. 5:13).

The Right Application of Hope

Show hope in every situation and share hope with someone else. Difficult people and difficult things are not going to hinder you from experiencing and enjoying all the good God has promised you.

"That is why we labor and strive, because we have put our *hope* in the living God, who is the Savior of all people" (1 Tim. 4:10; emphasis added).

Before the kingdom, You were King
And when there was nothing
You were everything
Before foundations stood
Before evil, before good
You were forever
Before the night, before the day
Before the man was formed from clay
Before life, before death
Before the first breath
You were forever
After the stars desert the sky
And after the rivers all run dry
When the earth is no more
And the heavens roar
You'll be forever
Then we'll gather 'round Your throne
Of every nation all Your own
And in one accord
Oh, we'll praise You, Lord
You are forever

Forever King, You're everything,
My heart has need to know
My first, my last, my future, my past
The strength of all my hopes
You're the Rock of all the ages
Eternal timeless Savior
Forever King, You're everything, forever

—"Forever King," NewSong

Application Review: *Hope*

1. What is hope?

   Hope: the confident expectation of experiencing all the future goodness God has promised you…somehow…someway…sometime.

2. How do you get hope?

   Get to know God better through the Word of God. All the scriptures have one goal: to sustain our hope. "For everything that was written in the past was written to teach us, so that through the endurance taught in the Scriptures and the encouragement they provide we might have *hope*" (Rom. 15:4; emphasis added). Saturate your mind with Scripture; then preach to yourself about the character and promises of God, knowing that hope is the byproduct of endurance in suffering.

3. What does hope do?

   Hope becomes your spiritual binoculars to see into the skies of suffering and the clouds of adversity. Hope sees God in control of everything for your good. Hope changes how you view yourself and your circumstances. It changes what you value. Hope changes what you do with your life—with your time, your talents, your treasure.

Hope overflows in abundance. "Now may *the God of hope* fill you with all joy and peace in believing, that you may *abound in hope* by the power of the Holy Spirit" (Rom. 15:13; emphasis added). You have become a container of hope. *Hope* "abounds" in you in the same way ocean waves arrive at the beach, one after another in endless relentlessness. It super-abounds! The God of hope fills your present chapter of suffering and despair with joy and peace and a sufficient surplus of hope to share with others living in dread of their clouds of adversity.

4. How do you hope?

Express hope through actions of faith and love. "We have heard of your faith in Christ Jesus and of the love you have for all God's people— the faith and love *that spring from the hope* stored up for you in heaven and about which you have already heard in the true message of the gospel" (Col. 1:4-5; emphasis added). The biblical directions for those who hope in God are not difficult to comprehend.

Love God with all your heart, and with all your soul, and with all your mind, and with all your strength. Then love others as yourself.

Everything else hangs on those pillars of purpose calling us to use whatever platform of influence we might have in life to give help and hope to others.

Hope always takes love for God and for others to a higher level.

5. Why do you hope?

The ultimate purpose of hope is to glorify God. "(So that) we might have *hope*. May the God who gives endurance and encouragement give you the same attitude of mind toward each other that Christ Jesus had, so that with one mind and one voice you may *glorify* the God and Father of our Lord Jesus Christ" (Rom.15:4-6; emphasis added).

God's Word does much more than just give you endurance to persevere in suffering and encouragement to strengthen hope in despair. The hope on the horizon is the glory of God in Christ Jesus. As John Piper says,

> The ultimate aim of Christ and his apostle is to display the glory of God—the beauty of God, the greatness of God, the many-sided perfections of God. All of creation, all of redemption, all of church, all of society and culture exist to display God. Nothing and no one is an end itself, but only God. All things are "from him and through him and to him" (Romans 11:36).

God works all things together for our good so that He might be magnified. Suffering and despair become great vehicles in life to value seeing God at the center of everything, even the clouds of adversity.

The ultimate purpose of hope is to make much of the greatness and goodness of God.

Could we with ink the ocean fill,
And were the skies of parchment made,
Were every stalk on earth a quill,
And every man a scribe by trade;
To write the love of God above
Would drain the ocean dry;
Nor could the scroll contain the whole,
Though stretched from sky to sky
Oh, love of God, how rich and pure!
How measureless and strong!
It shall forevermore endure—
The saints' and angels' song.

—"The Love of God,"
Frederick M. Lehman

Conclusion

Convinced? Convinced!

What shall we say in response to these things? I would be most interested to hear what you will say after reading this book in light of your life's story. As for me, I join with the apostle Paul in exclaiming, "For I am convinced that nothing can separate us (you and me) from the love of God. Absolutely nothing."

For I am convinced and absolutely persuaded not by arguments or explanations or calculations or education or indoctrination but convinced by God, by who God is, by what God says, by what God has done, by what God has promised.

I can declare with the utmost confidence and unclouded hope, "It sure looks like Jesus is up to something!" I see it with the binoculars of faith. I observe it on the horizon. I study it in the clouds of witnesses. I shout it like a four-year-old full of hope and confident expectation of future good.

I am convinced because I *know God* better than ever before. I know God is supreme and sovereign. I know God's sovereignty is forever and always connected to His goodness. I know God is first and foremost in all my circumstances, the ultimate reality and unsurpassed value of all things earthly and eternal, before all things and above all things that threaten to disrupt and destroy my life. God is forever faithful and trustworthy.

I am convinced in *God* and by God as I see how He *works things together* in my life *for good*. God did not leave me alone in my journey. He never abandoned me or left me without help and hope. I have sensed my fellow worker and His divine synergy at work for both my earthly and eternal benefit. I am absolutely persuaded God will get me safely home.

> As I look back on the road I've traveled,
> I see so many times He carried me through;
> And if there's one thing that I've learned in my life,
> My Redeemer is faithful and true.
>
> My Redeemer is faithful and true.
> Everything He has said He will do,
> And every morning His mercies are new.
> My Redeemer is faithful and true.
>
> —"My Redeemer Is Faithful and True,"
> Stephen Curtis Chapman

I have experienced the *good*. I have tasted God's kindness. I have been satisfied in desert places while drinking freely and fully from His springs of hope. Therefore, I embrace *all things* in my life from adversity to prosperity because I better understand *God's purpose* to use all those things to work together to make me *live and love like Jesus*, imperfectly now with the hope of becoming the exact representation in the future.

I am convinced that *God is for me*. In His Son Jesus, He has given me all He is and all He has so I can be presently assured He *will supply all my needs according to His riches in glory*. Jesus stepped in as my substitute on the cross to be treated as if He had lived my sinful, self-centered life so I might never be condemned. Others may try to judge me, but there is no condemnation from my God. His Word convinces me of that glorious thought. No condemnation!

I want to cry! I want to shout! I want to join hands with you and dance! No condemnation!

I am convinced of my adoption and acceptance by God in which I am fully and forever treated as if I had lived and loved like His perfect Son Jesus. My acceptance is undeserved and unearned, but by grace, it is unconditional and unending. I do not have to tirelessly and fearfully and despairingly keep running on that horrible joy-reducing performance treadmill. Why? God considers me His child. Loved, instructed, disciplined, trained, assigned a place in His work, and promised a home and all the inheritance.

Do you think I am convinced of God's love when I know that nothing can ever separate me from Him? I am convinced that nothing can tear me away from God's embrace. Not life or death. Not space or time. Not anyone or anything. Not the supernatural, not even my own wrong decisions and actions. No separation from God's love! How can I keep from singing!

> O how marvelous!
> O how wonderful!
> And my song shall ever be:
> O how marvelous!
> O how wonderful!
> Is my Savior's love for me!
> When with the ransomed in glory
> His face I at last shall see
> It will be my joy through the ages
> To sing of His love for me
>
> —"I Stand Amazed in the Presence,"
> Charles H. Gabriel

For I am convinced that nothing can separate me from God's love; therefore, I have hope. I am absolutely convinced I will experience all the goodness God has promised me in this life and the endless ages to come. I will live and love in that hope, suffer in that hope, and die in that hope. And when I awake in the eternal reality of that hope, I will shout with joy and be lost in wonder at the wisdom of love as I run into the arms of the God who caused all things to work together for my good.

Ironically, I am writing this chapter in one of the toughest seasons of my life. Isn't that when a person is most in need of hope? From the darkness surrounding my soul, I look to the horizon and see hope…even here…even now…even this.

God is for me. My God is here with me and nothing can ever separate me from His love. I continue to preach to myself, "Where there is despair, *hope*. Though God slays me, yet I will *hope* in Him."

I am absolutely convinced that I will still experience all the future goodness God has promised me…somehow…someway…sometime.

"And we know God causes all things to work together for good to those who love God, to those called according to His purpose" (Rom. 8:28).

I am convinced. Are you?

Incomparable kindness to less than the least
To the broken, the battered, and weak
To all who are hungry there comes a call
To be filled with the fullness of God
It's beyond all you can see
Farther than you'd believe
It's a mystery
My prayer for you is that you would know

How wide, and how long, and how
high, how deep is the love
How deep is the love of Christ

The width of two arms outstretched on a tree
The length of the road to Calvary
The height of the crown on a cruel cross
The depth of the pain is the cost
All for you, all for me
All for love did He bleed
All to set us free
My prayer for you is that you would know

How wide, and how long, and how
high, how deep is the love
How deep is the love of Christ

—"The Love of Christ,"
Wes King, Michael W. Smith,
and Michael Card

Epilogue

My mom was a teacher and writer. She was not a writer in the normal sense of the word. She never wrote a novel or short story, just a couple of magazine articles. Her main work was written on my heart and the hearts of my brothers, her grandchildren, and her students. The impression has been lasting.

You do not have to write a book to have an impact in this life. You may never write a book or have a book written about you, but if the story of your faith in the faithful God gets written on somebody's heart, you are a writer too. For all of us, the full story has yet to be published, but it will be someday.

I hope you might write about a chapter in your life story and place it in the back of this book to be shared with someone you love. Maybe you will want to write your observations of a chapter in the life of some woman you greatly admire. It might be your mother, or sister, or mentor, or friend. She might be a survivor of suffering or a lighthouse of hope. Tell her story and tell her of the love and hope she has written on your heart.

I think each of us dreams of better chapters to come and yet, not one of us can truly know what those chapters will entail or how long they might be. However, there is one constant in life for those whose faith and hope is in God. The Eternal Coauthor always writes the last chapter, and it will be beautiful beyond imagination.

But God, being rich in mercy, because of the great love with which he loved us, even when we were dead in our trespasses, made us alive together with Christ—by grace you have been saved—and raised us up with him and seated us with him in the heavenly places in Christ Jesus, so that in the coming ages he might show the immeasurable riches of his grace in kindness toward us in Christ Jesus. (Eph. 2:4–7)

Where there is despair, hope.

Write Your Life Story or the Story of a Woman You Admire

Where There is Despair, HOPE